H Blocks

H Blocks

An architecture of the conflict in and about Northern Ireland

LOUISE PURBRICK

BLOOMSBURY VISUAL ARTS
LONDON · NEW YORK · OXFORD · NEW DELHI · SYDNEY

BLOOMSBURY VISUAL ARTS
Bloomsbury Publishing Plc
50 Bedford Square, London, WC1B 3DP, UK
1385 Broadway, New York, NY 10018, USA
29 Earlsfort Terrace, Dublin 2, Ireland

BLOOMSBURY, BLOOMSBURY VISUAL ARTS and the Diana logo are trademarks of
Bloomsbury Publishing Plc

First published in Great Britain 2023

Cover design: Eleanor Rose
Cover image: Plan of Long Kesh/Maze found in the
administration building, 2003 © Louise Purbrick

A catalogue record for this book is available from the British Library.

Library of Congress Cataloging-in-Publication Data
Names: Purbrick, Louise, author.
Title: H Blocks : an architecture of the conflict in and about Northern Ireland / Louise Purbrick.
Identifiers: LCCN 2022035511 (print) | LCCN 2022035512 (ebook) |
ISBN 9781350240025 (hardback) | ISBN 9781350240063 (paperback) |
ISBN 9781350240032 (pdf) | ISBN 9781350240049 (epub) | ISBN 9781350240056 (XML)
Subjects: LCSH: Maze Prison (Lisburn, Northern Ireland). | Prisons–Political aspects–
Northern Ireland. | Political prisoners–Northern Ireland. |
Collective memory–Northern Ireland.
Classification: LCC HV9650.L57 M356 2023 (print) | LCC HV9650.L57 (ebook) |
DDC 365/.9415—dc23/eng/20221021
LC record available at https://lccn.loc.gov/2022035511
LC ebook record available at https://lccn.loc.gov/2022035512

ISBN: HB: 978-1-3502-4002-5
       ePDF: 978-1-3502-4003-2
       eBook: 978-1-3502-4004-9

Typeset by RefineCatch Limited, Bungay, Suffolk
Printed and bound in Great Britain

To find out more about our authors and books visit www.bloomsbury.com
and sign up for our newsletters.

Ni un día más en la cárcel

This book was completed in a high-rise flat over-looking Plaza Dignidad, Santiago. It is dedicated to all the political prisoners of Chile's 2019 social revolution and also to Liam Heffernan, whose story will not be found in these pages.

Contents

Illustrations

Cover image: H Block plan, Long Kesh/Maze administration buildings (2002). Photograph: Louise Purbrick.

Acknowledgements

This book began more than twenty years ago. Over this time, I have worked with, and talked to, a great many people: former prisoners, community workers, activists, academics, archaeologists, curators, heritage practitioners, photographers, filmmakers. All have helped me slowly interpret the H Blocks. I have written a monograph that reflects my encounters and confrontations with the spaces of the Long Kesh/Maze prison and the forms of its material culture, but any understanding I have achieved has been shaped by that of others who have shared their thoughts about different sites of conflict with me. I would like to thank: Jim Aulich, Elizabeth Crooke, Graham Dawson, Simon Faulkner, Martin Hurcombe, Gabriel Moshenska, Kate Page, James Ryan, John Schofield, Deborah Sugg-Ryan, Liz Ševčenco, and Donovan Wylie.

My greatest debt is to Healing Through Remembering. It was in their Ormeau Avenue office at the monthly meetings of the Living Memorial Museum project that Long Kesh/Maze was included in a wider discussion of legacies of the conflict in and about Northern Ireland and its important place in processes of conflict resolution was openly debated. Many aspects of Healing Through Remembering's methodology, particularly the serious attention to process and participation, has informed all my subsequent work, not just that on the H Blocks. My thanks to Kate Turner for her patient intelligence as she guided our group, and to Kris Brown, Dom Bryan, Brandon Hamber, Alan McBrideabd, Alice McCartney, whose arguments, and sometimes exact words, I often recall. I, and this book, are especially indebted to the friendship, experience and knowledge of Laurence McKeown, whom I met before I turned up in the Ormeau Avenue office through his role with Coiste na nlarchimí. My very first piece of writing on the H Blocks, a short article for *Museums Journal* published in 2001, was based on an interview with him. A 2003 Coiste conference in Lisburn, organized by Mike Ritchie, was an important turning point in my thinking about the prison as a site of conflict and a contested space. Although I did not work directly with Claire Hackett in Healing Through Remembering until recently, her advocacy and analysis of community archives has always been inspiring.

Lyn Brandon provided a home for me in Belfast when I made my early visits to the H Blocks and, actually, my entire project starts with her. She thought I would be interested in the Long Kesh/Maze remove or remain, preserve or demolish debate because, as she said, 'You work on these kinds of things, don't you?' Her suggestion has shaped my academic and activist life. Debbie Lisle also had a Belfast bed for me when I needed it and always shared her astute insights into the politics of remembering conflict. Cahal McLaughlin, a critical friend throughout my H Blocks research, helped enormously with Prisons Memory Archive access. A University of Brighton sabbatical in 2020 did much to finally realize this slow-burning book but the constant encouragement of my colleagues in the History of Art and Design programme has been more important to me. It, and I, have benefitted enormously from the thoughtful, kind support of Yunah Lee, Zeina Maasri, Charlotte Nicklas, Ceren Ozpinar, Lara Perry, Bella Pollen, Megha Rajguru, Jill Seddon, Lou Taylor and Claire Wintle. Lucy Robinson's friendship has shaped this book; I want to thank her for all those conversations in her sitting room. I have written parts of this book alongside Sarah Cheang in her mother's quiet house and seated next to Polly Ruiz in St Peter's House Library. Their concentration on their own writing projects helped me as mine flagged. I finally completed writing *H Blocks* in Santiago, Chile, researching with Ignacio Acosta and Xavier Ribas on another project: *muchas gracias por permitirme espacio y tiempo para escribir*. Space and time to write has always been Ian Sewell's concern for me; I do not think I spoke my gratitude often enough, so I do so now. I am always grateful to my family, Seanin, Nik and Cate-May Hann, for being by my side and on my side. Cate-May arrived back home to live with my book as well as me, helping me through the slow days and celebrating the good ones. I do not have enough words with which to thank her.

Introduction

In *Long Meadow* (1982), the geometric forms of the letter H overlay a misty map (Figure 0.1). Rita Donagh's painting is one of a series that interprets the conflict 'in and about'[1] Northern Ireland through the repeating symmetrical stems and crossbars of an H. The H is the footprint of individual cell units built on the prison site renamed 'The Maze' after the Northern Ireland (Temporary Provisions) Act 1972 was passed. The Act suspended the Stormont Parliament and introduced Direct Rule from Westminster. But prisoners continued to call the place, in which they were detained and to which they were sentenced, Long Kesh. This was the name given to the internment camp hastily opened a year earlier next to a British military base on a disused Second World War airfield. Rita Donagh's *Long Meadow* draws attention down to the land below the runways and the hard lines of architecture above. The oil on canvas work comprises two aerial views but four visual planes: a landscape from above is evoked by faint lines indicating boundaries or contours of a mapped terrain that are obscured by the painting's next level, a foggy atmosphere created by grey brushstrokes. Above and intersecting the clouds is a horizontal plane of outlines of H letterforms in the repeating rows and columns of a typographical copybook. All is overlaid by the final dominating visual plane, a diagonal and dynamic perspective of eight H Blocks that reworks the angled aerial view of photographs of Long Kesh/Maze taken from a side window of an aeroplane.

This book is about the power of the H Blocks as architecture and as image. It examines the spaces of these prison cells and how they were inhabited. *H Blocks* is an exploration of the material relationships of political imprisonment in a British jail in Ireland. All prison architecture has a material force, a brutal effect over the bodies within its walls: the restriction of the space of existence. The H Blocks also had, and still have, a powerful material presence beyond their walls. They have been repeatedly represented, their outlines have been hand drawn onto placards then carried on demonstrations, stencilled for a run of leaflets that were pushed through letterboxes and given out on street corners, screen printed onto fabric, brushed onto walls, photographed for newspapers or art galleries, digitized for computer screens, filmed for

FIGURE 0.1 *Rita Donagh*, Long Meadow *(1982). © Rita Donagh. Photo: Tate.*

television and cinema audiences. The H Blocks have been painted in oils. When Rita Donagh visited Belfast to work as a Lecturer in Art, she witnessed the presence of imprisonment in Long Kesh/Maze on the streets of the city;[2] the shape of its cell units appeared in murals and was widely reproduced in the print culture of protest against the criminalization of republican prisoners (Figure 0.2). In *Long Meadow*, the repeating outline of the H, blocked in twice, is an imposition of architectural construction upon an Irish landscape; an occupation of the picture plane and of the land represented below. The solidity of architecture, the luminosity of oil paint, the convincing accuracy of photography, the urgency of the hand-drawn placard. The material forms of architecture and imagery carry a symbolic load. Architecture is not necessarily more material and less symbolic than its image. In the history of the H Blocks, both are caught up in a struggle over the meanings of imprisonment and

FIGURE 0.2 *'H Block in Protest', People's Democracy,* H Block/Armagh: Prisoners of Partition *(1980). Source: CAIN (ulster.ac.uk/cain).*

occupation, conflict and colonialism, resistance and political rights. From the construction of the eight flat-roofed single-storey structures in 1976 to the demolition of all but one in 2006, their site has been a contested space, physically and politically. This book tries to hold together the intimate oppression of imprisonment within the architecture of Long Kesh/Maze and the circulation of imagery about that imprisonment far across the globe. This is a hard task for an art historian. Forgive me when I fail.

Prisoners, prison officers and journalists have all produced books about Long Kesh/Maze prison.[3] My study of its cell units, the H Blocks, is not an attempt to write another official or unofficial history but to understand the spatial relationships of conflict and imprisonment. My sources are the site itself, the voices of prisoners and prison visitors recorded by themselves within the prison or at the prison site by researchers alongside an array of images and objects that comprise the material culture of Long Kesh/Maze. The archive of the H Blocks on which this book is based is highly dispersed; it remains at the 347-acre site near Lisburn, twelve miles south of Belfast, now managed by the Maze Long Kesh Development Corporation; it is held in documents, newspapers, books in holdings of libraries and institutions, many of which are also online; it is preserved as a work of art in public and private collections and sold as a second-hand commodity over the internet; it exists in the analogue, digital and digitized records of photography, film and television. Fragments from this archive, some carefully preserved, others quietly disappeared, are analysed in each of the chapters of this book that explore the design of the H Blocks, the resistance from its cells, the global witnesses to the oppression of imprisonment, the female visitors and war of waiting, the murals of a liberated zone and the sale of material culture of Long Kesh/Maze.

Different routes through the *H Blocks*: the architecture and this book

H Blocks is not the first book about the Long Kesh/Maze prison, nor the only one to consider its material culture. Laura McAtackney's, *The Archaeology of the Troubles*, based on her doctoral study, was published in 2014. An account of the heritage of the whole site, of all 'standing buildings', it also moves beyond the site.[4] The scope of contemporary archaeology is expanded through this exploration of Long Kesh/Maze to encompass its distributed effects as much as its in-situ artefacts. McAtackney's adaptation of a 'multi-scalar'[5] method blurs the boundaries between historical and archaeological to offer a survey of types of sources, from documents to dark heritage practices, that record the different scales of experience of the jail. Many of the types of things that comprise the distributed material culture of Long Kesh/Maze can be found in the pages of this book, but it circles more closely around the architectural form of the H Blocks, searching for small details that reveal large structures of power. I learnt this practice of looking at material forms from Marcia Pointon's strategy of reading visual ones, particularly portraits rendered in oil on canvas where there is concentration of effort to secure the authority of the sitter: a person's position in a social formation may be held in the tiny sparkle of painted light from a stone set in a ring placed over the carefully laid flesh tones of a little finger.[6] The H Blocks may not look like a work of art, but they can be read as one with the same attention to detail and showing how detail holds power. Within the confines of a prison and its restricted spaces, detail enlarges in significance. Everyday life is a series of brushstrokes with authority that establish or undermine it. I learnt this from talking to a former Guantánamo Bay detainee who described the fine lines of interpretation of the rules of a US military prison that occurred either side of the metal hatch of each cell door. Every day. Detainees argued with guards over the meaning of four. They pushed clasped hands through the hatch to demand a length of toilet roll wound four times around them refusing to let go of their fingers to receive just four pieces of paper. The more generous interpretation of four, four circles of toilet paper not four squares, enabled greater bodily cleanliness, personal respect and political dignity.[7] In prison, resistance to power is a struggle about detail.

'Prison is messy', writes ASBO, the name her prison 'mates' gave to the author of *Bang Up and Smash* (2017), a contemporary intersectional anarchist analysis of women's prisons. Prison is also 'relentless' and, 'like critique and analysis, it is on-going'.[8] My work on the H Blocks is on the messy side of things. I cannot remember when I first heard Lucy Robinson use the term 'messy' to describe her kind of historical practice, probably because memory is even more messy than history.[9] Messy history refuses to tidy up the complexities of experience into a pristine political structure of straight and straightforward oppositions. It is 'multi-layered'[10] with 'many loose ends'[11] and is the unfinished process of critique that ASBO describes as 'on-going'. Collecting a few fragments that have fallen through the cracks after histories of Long Kesh/Maze have been told, not only in commercial print publications but on cinema screens,[12] has helped me slowly reflect upon the sectarian separations of an architecture of conflict rather than all too quickly reproduce them. I hope.

The chapters of *H Blocks* do follow the broad chronology of putting them up and pulling them down, construction to destruction. Chapter 1 opens with the prison as a plan and Chapter 6 with the dispersal of its contents. In the chapters in between, chronological order matters less than the journey through its architecture. The cells of the H Blocks are the dwellings of Blanket Men in Chapter 2 and their outline, the H, is recognized as the shape of British colonial rule by the global witnesses of Chapter 3. Women occupy the waiting rooms around the H Blocks in Chapter 4 and loyalists parade along their wings in Chapter 5. Each chapter is an encounter with a different space in or around the H Blocks and offers a different critical lens through which to interpret their fragments and understand their details. Each chapter is also a critical encounter with – in the following order – panopticism, dwelling perspectives, necropolitics and the rights-bearing body, a feminist spatial theory and a feminist practice of writing, performativity, the appropriations of commodity culture and the agency of objects.

My writing about the H Blocks, a very slow process that began over twenty years ago with just a two-page spread in the *Museums Journal*,[13] has been guided by a series of anthropological, philosophical and political writings that have shaped my thinking about incarceration, the incarcerated body and colonialism, performance and protest, and the bonds of materiality. I have called upon these writings and their writers, including Michel Foucault, Tim Ingold, Paul Gilroy, Achille Mbembe, Sara Ahmed, Judith Butler, Alfred Gell and Bruno Latour, to help my interpretation of the H Blocks but I hope that neither they nor I dominate over the details of the spaces of the people who inhabited them. As they echo down the wings of the H Blocks or rebound off its walls, these critical voices clash with each other rather than harmonize into a smooth synthesis. Each chapter, as critical encounter, repositions the H Blocks beyond its settled place as a difficult site and subject of conflict, enabling the building to make its own theoretical intervention. In Chapter 1, for example, the H Blocks plans reveal the material foundations of visual control and revise the autonomy of the vision in understanding of prisons and power. In Chapter 4, Long Kesh/Maze as a male prison poses questions of history, theory and writing: how can the spaces from which women are excluded be understood through their experiences and words? Neither of these chapters, nor any of the others, need to be read in their numerical sequence; they can be considered as separate pieces of writing or one collective effort. In practice, most people read academic books against the grain and in a rather messy way.

Architecture in absence

How can an absent architecture hold such lasting power? Long Kesh/Maze may be 'one of the key heritage sites of the conflict',[14] but most of its once solid structures have been brought down, broken up and recycled as building materials or exported as waste. One of the eight H Blocks remains among a few listed structures, including: a watchtower and section of the perimeter wall; four Nissen huts, part of the compound system where internees were held; the administration centre, staffed by the prison service hierarchy that oversaw the operation of the jail; the hospital, the place where ten Hunger Strikers died in the summer of 1981; and the chapel. Long Kesh/Maze has been reduced to a representative example of historically significant building types, releasing most of the former prison estate for 'social and economic regeneration'.[15] Demolition was supposed to prepare the way for global tourism with the construction of an international sports stadium and an international centre of conflict transformation. Plans for both were abandoned, despite wide public consultations, complex masterplans, detailed planning permissions, a Daniel Libeskind architectural design and large allocations of funding syphoned through the Northern Ireland Executive from the British government and the European Union. All wasted. The expectation that the 'future' of Long Kesh/Maze could be built upon its past and, as other sites of conflict across the world, become a heritage destination, came to nothing. Worse, since its closure, its past has become a source of political stalemate, if not conflict, in the consociational arrangements of the Northern Ireland Executive. Representatives of the CNR (Catholic Nationalist Republican) have held out for a recognition of the pivotal role of H Block prisoners in the peace process whule those of the PUL (Protestant Unionist Loyalist) have opposed any memorialization of prisoners sentenced for 'conflict-related offences' especially republican prisoners. Indeed, discussion of development at Long Kesh/Maze has been frequently ruled out in the plush Stormont committee rooms on the other side of Belfast from the former prison, because it is assumed that agreement cannot be reached: the H Blocks are 'off the table'. Talking about policing, always contentious, was easier. The site of the H Blocks is a contested space; it has remained a site of conflict occupied with meanings, filled with attachments, weighted with an importance that cannot be easily managed into an official heritage destination or assimilated into authorized heritage discourse.[16]

All the key protagonists to the conflict in and about Northern Ireland held spaces in Long Kesh/Maze; they had a place within, and a relationship to, its architecture. The H Blocks were built on the orders of the British government and its perimeter patrolled by battalions of the British Army; prison officers, usually locally recruited, were aligned to Northern Ireland's Unionist security forces, the Ulster Defence Regiment (UDR), in particular; republicans affiliated to the Provisional Irish Republican Army (IRA) or the Irish National Liberation Army (INLA) or loyalists who belonged to the Ulster Volunteer Force (UVF), the Ulster Defence Association (UDA), the Ulster Freedom Fighters (UFF) or the Loyalist Volunteer Force (LVF), were its prisoners. Spatial divisions install material relationships of confrontation and political perspectives grounded in opposition that cannot be simply dispelled. Architecture is an acknowledgement of spatial separations and political oppositions; its material forms are lines of power. The past of repression and resistance within the walls of Long Kesh/ Maze is still present at its site despite the destruction of most of its buildings. Their vertical and horizontal structures are one of the site's surfaces and, like the visual planes in Rita Donagh's *Long Meadow*, are layers of its materiality and meaning that fall into and rise up from the once-occupied land.

The H Blocks have a secure place in a republican narrative of freedom: the collective campaign for political recognition, the Hunger Strikes, the commitment to education that took place in their cells and along their wings transformed the armed struggle into a peace process. But in the single identity, community practices of remembering according to the alternative republican and loyalist calendars of commemoration that have proliferated with the peace process,[17] imprisonment at Long Kesh/Maze has different meanings. Indeed, it often appears that there were separate conflicts unfolding in and about Northern Ireland, rather than division and sectarianism as the characteristics of those conflicts. The complex history of imprisonment at the site, the structures and spaces of the H Blocks, are not easily contained in a single narrative nor can the conflict be reduced to a simple dualism of opposition between republicans and loyalists. Here, the foundations of this binary reside in an architecture of imprisonment built on British instructions. British agency in the conflict is often overlooked, forgotten and denied despite the obvious material interventions and spatial occupations: borders, barracks, walls, watchtowers and prisons. The H Blocks are an architecture of conflict in which its British origins are all too evident. Their occupying force is still tangible, is still felt. The brutal obtrusiveness of their concrete cell units does not rest in the past but intrudes upon the planning and replanning of the future development of the former prison site.

The site of Long Kesh/Maze is not entirely derelict. The Ulster Aviation Society and the Royal Ulster Agricultural Society, organizations of Anglo-Irish and Northern Irish ancestry devoted to flying and farming respectively, host events that attract many visitors and are lauded as highly successful. The Balmoral Show, 'Northern Ireland's largest agri-food event', has been held on the former prison site since 2013 on an oval park that partially covers the gravelly oblong prison sports field; it draws very large numbers for 'a fun-filled day out for all the family'.[18] But the crowds have not reached the remaining H Block buildings. The new landscaping does not lead them to this part of the site where public access is prohibited, subject to application to the Northern Ireland Executive and rarely approved. A farming focus for the cleared spaces of the former prison is proposed in the West Lisburn Development Framework. 'The Maze Long Kesh site provides an opportunity to develop post incubation property supports for the agri-food sector and designation of at least part of the site as an Enterprise Zone could be the suitable vehicle to deliver such a use.'[19] Meanwhile, avoidance and neglect of the part of the site on which the listed buildings remain has created its own process of gradual change. Weeds break up the grey of the concrete footings of the H Blocks, grass grows tall against the wire mesh fences, bushes spread out along the walls, while the contested meaning of the sites continues to spin out into political forums, media narratives, commercial markets and everyday life.

Conflict in conflict histories

Imprisonment is a strategy of war. It was used in the conflict in and about Northern Ireland as in those all over the world. However, conflicts fought in contemporary democracies tend to adapt and subvert existing judicial and penal systems to criminalize types of organization, forms of expression, or acts of violence that might, in a conventional battlefield, earn the captured fighters the status of a prisoner of war. To make war a problem of law and order and to claim violence is always pathological rather than political is often politically expedient.[20] For example, the Northern Ireland (Emergency Provisions) Act 1973 contained a schedule that codified conflict-related offences, listed a schedule of actions of war that included producing explosives, using firearms, holding weapons, making petrol bombs and throwing them.[21] Trials for such scheduled offences took place in courts with low standards of evidence and without juries, these courts being named after Lord Diplock who chaired the commission that recommended them.

Long Kesh/Maze was a site of imprisonment for thirty years, first for internees, then for sentenced prisoners, and both were held together for a time. The use of the land of the wide Lagan valley for incarceration from 1971 to 2000, from the opening of the Long Kesh internment centre to the decommissioning of HMP Maze, corresponds to the period of conflict in Northern Ireland that is often euphemistically called 'The Troubles'. The conflict is usually dated from August 1969, when the British Army was sent to Northern Ireland and began its long-term, large-scale deployment, to the signing of the Good Friday Agreement in April 1998. The same thirty years, more or less. The site of the H Blocks is a site of the conflict. It is one of its most significant spaces that is now bound up a battle over its interpretation: 'a conflict about what the conflict is about'.[22]

No-one needs me to tell the history of the conflict itself. That work has been done. Northern Ireland, as John McGarry and Brendan O'Leary patiently point out, is an 'extensively interpreted region'. The amount of scholarship devoted to the conflict in Northern Ireland has produced, they observe, 'multiple disagreements' and a 'meta-conflict'.[23] Ethno-nationalism, the term widely deployed in the discipline of International Relations to explain conflicts across the globe in the post-Cold War period, is the most familiar explanation for it and underpinned the media narrative of 'The Troubles' for most of its thirty years. Two communities appear as ethnicities in a symmetrical opposition, a binary. On one side, PUL communities identify as Northern Irish or British and defend the particular place of Northern Ireland in Britain as long standing: confirmed rather than created by the partition of Ireland in 1920. On the other, CNRs seek recognition as an Irish people that the arbitrary border of an artificially constituted British state has long denied. Ethno-nationalist interpretations of the conflict,[24] in slightly varying formulations, have acquired greater authority post-conflict as the opposition between the two communities has been cemented through the attempt by the peace process to balance the different demands and desires associated with their traditions. Power-sharing institutionalized the binary in the consociational arrangements[25] of the Northern Ireland government, its Assembly and its Executive.

The architectural record of the conflict does not entirely uphold the binary of an ethno-nationalist account.[26] Another explanation is found in the fragments of the H Blocks left at the site of Long Kesh/Maze or in the images of other large structures of conflict, erected at its opening and removed as it was brought to its long close, such as the watchtowers of South Armagh, dismantled by the British Army and returned with them to Afghanistan.[27] These are material forms of an occupying force and a colonial conflict. With the structures of spatial control removed it may be easier to interpret a war over territory and identity as a conflict of identity alone. But as an academic and activist based in a British university, it is my responsibility, I feel, to recognize the colonial project of a place where I reside and ensure that it is subject to some scrutiny. The decolonializing imperative of academic life requires the recognition of how colonial conditions shape every field of study, especially those where power relationships are the product of physical and political borders. My own part in the activism against the colonial interventions and imperial alliances of the British state makes a similar call. But the most compelling demand arises from the materiality of conflict itself. In the material forms of conflict, designed and constructed, altered and appropriated, created and copied, such as the architecture of the H Blocks and the material culture that belongs to them, is a history that cannot hide those who constructed and controlled them. This book opens by reinscribing the absent overseer of the conflict found in the modern prison of colonial rule, of which the H Blocks is an important example.

1

Building the Blocks

When Joe Strummer walked onto a London stage in 1978 wearing an H Block T-shirt, he would have understood that it was an act of iconoclasm.[1] He was a punk, an image-breaker. The punk assault on power was through its imagery. The rhythm guitarist of The Clash recognized the political significance of a prison architecture only recently completed on a low-lying boggy site twelve miles southwest of Belfast, adjacent to Long Kesh internment camp. He recreated its image on a piece of clothing and wore an icon. An icon is a particularly powerful image. It is significant, still sacred in a secular world, because it cannot be completely separated from its subject. The outline of H Blocks printed on soft cotton fabric hanging from the shoulders of Joe Strummer embodied a challenge to state power. The cell units of a British jail in Ireland were an icon of repression and their appropriation a sign of resistance.

It was some three decades later that professional opinion fell in behind the punks. In a 2005 news item in the *Architects' Journal*, the site of the H Blocks, the prison known as Long Kesh and officially titled the Maze, was referred to as 'an icon of the thirty-year Troubles in the province'.[2] The global network of historic sites, museums and memory initiatives, Sites of Conscience, used the shorter phrase 'icon of The Troubles' to describe the former jail in a 2009 newsletter.[3] It has also been called a 'microcosm of Northern conflict' and a 'potent symbol' with 'talismanic status' as well as 'one of the most remarkable buildings in Britain'.[4] Headline writers have searched beyond their usual lexicon to find words to summarize how a structure can mean so much. For the H Blocks tell the story of 'The Troubles'. A history of the conflict in and about Northern Ireland, from the arrival of the British Army on the streets of Belfast and Derry in 1969 to the signing of the Good Friday Agreement in 1998, unfolds from the prison that opened and closed around the same time. Its concrete and wire were material forms of the conflict and are its actual history. The H Block struggle took place inside cells of the prison as their shape was distributed on leaflets, posters, placards and T shirts, like that worn by Joe Strummer, to the world outside. Simultaneously a site and a symbol of conflict, both real and representative, this particular prison is a powerful thing.

Panopticons: visual and material

A prison is pure power. Pure power is an unlikely thing, an exceptional state of affairs. Having power, holding authority, imposing order is tenuous; it has to be constantly sustained; it is never settled once and for all. The prison cells at the centre of this book, the H Blocks, built in 1976 and demolished twenty years later in 2006, were the site of the Hunger Strikes of 1981, which have come to epitomize resistance to the injustice of imprisonment. The H Blocks contain a history of the refusal to accept the rules of a prison and, fundamentally, a rejection of the power to rule. Nevertheless, prisons always represent an attempt to impose order, at least for the length of a prisoner's sentence or the lifetime of the prison building. Prisons represent the establishment of authority. However unlikely and exceptional, they are the materialization of pure power.

The power of the prison lies in its form. It is expressed in its plan; the design of a prison is an outline of how its regime should always operate, how its rules will reside in an arrangement of structures and spaces. Prison design is the prison in its ideal form: architectural drawings or architectural models of prisons are abstract forms wherein expected rather than actual prisoners cannot challenge its control. Their construction is a materialization of their ideal form, and the materials used are intended to maintain its order, that is, uphold its authority. Power is cast in solid form. The Smash H Blocks slogan, adopted by prisoner support groups, printed across T-shirts or on placards, worn or held to symbolize both repression and resistance at Long Kesh/Maze is some recognition of the power of material forms. The examination of the materiality of the H Blocks that takes up the pages of this book is offered as a way of understanding imprisonment during the late-twentieth-century conflict in and about Northern Ireland and, maybe, imprisonment in other conflicts beyond this contested space.

Michel Foucault, theorist of power par excellence, attended to prison design. Indeed, the plan of one prison, the Panopticon, described by Jeremy Bentham in the late eighteenth century is, for Foucault, a model of how all power works in the modern world. The Panopticon, comprising outer and inner circular structures, wide and narrow, is described by Foucault in this way:

> at the periphery, an annular building; at the centre, a tower; this tower is pierced with wide windows that open onto the inner side of the ring; the peripheric building is divided into cells, each of which extends the whole width of the building; they have two windows, one on the inside corresponding to the windows of the tower; the other on the outside, allows light to cross the cell from one end to the other. All that is needed, then, is to place a supervisor in a central tower and to shut up a madman,

a patient, a condemned man, a worker or a schoolboy. By the effect of backlighting, one can observe from the tower, standing out precisely against the light, the small captive shadows in the cells of the periphery.[5]

The view from the centre to the periphery, the observation from the tower to the cell, creates constant power premised upon two principles: 'power should be visible and unverifiable'. The structure of observation is ever present but not the actual observer. As Foucault put it, 'the inmate will constantly have before his eyes the outline of the central tower from which he is spied upon' but 'the inmate must never know whether he is being looked at in any one moment; but he must be sure that he may also be so'. The 'major effect' is 'permanent visibility'.[6] Perhaps it is not all prisons but only the Panopticon in which pure power is made permanent. Inside this structure, the watched watch over themselves. Those observed assume the duty of their own observation. Observation cultivates conformity. Appearing submissive attracts no extra attention; it brings some safety within the field of vision. Physical submission is all that is required of any regime. If resistance cannot be demonstrated by the body of the observed, no one can act upon any idea of opposition. We may survey ourselves for our safety but to guard ourselves from power only ensures its effectiveness. 'Visibility is a trap', states Foucault.[7]

The Panopticon's principles of visible and unverified power are reproducible. They are not fixed in the Panopticon; it is simply their most clear illustration. In this prison and, particularly, through its plan, power is stripped down to the framework that underpins its perpetual operation. The supervisor in the tower and the condemned in the cell reveal the purest form of power's principles but their arrangement, an asymmetry, a hierarchy, an inequality of vision is everywhere. The Panopticon demonstrates how all institutions can assume positions of control, how authority comes to be just that, how people are ruled, their bodies ordered into a system. The prisoner may look to the centre but cannot see while the supervisor examines, collects information, accumulates knowledge about a person who has been isolated from everything except his gaze. For the Panopticon's proponent, Jeremy Bentham, it promised a healthy and moral, a schooled and hard-working, populace that are obedient subjects: the disciplined and docile bodies of Foucault's analysis. Thus, the latter argues that the Panopticon must be understood as 'a generalizable model of functioning, a way of defining power relations in terms of the everyday life of men'.[8] We are all in prison. The shadows of visible but unverifiable power are cast in every institutional relationship, a hierarchy of sight embedded in schools and factories as well as prisons and hospitals. The prison is everywhere. An inequality of vision has shaped the globe as lands and peoples are surveyed from elevated positions; the Panopticon principle of power has spread out into a geography of colonial rule. From nineteenth-century travelling photographers to twenty-first-century spy drones, colonizing power is premised upon visual superiority of so many types of towers.

In Foucault's account of the Panopticon, power is exerted through vision. Indeed, power is vision. Its invasion, sweeping and insidious, everywhere into the 'everyday life of men' rests upon angles of light and lines of sight. He summarizes: '[p]ower has its principle not so much in a person as in a certain distribution of bodies, surfaces, lights, gazes; in an arrangement whose internal mechanisms produce the relation in which individuals are caught up'.[9] Foucault's Panopticon, his interpretation of Jeremy Bentham's plans for an eighteenth-century jail as the archetype of power through vision, has acquired such authority that it is regarded as a truth; it has generated a vast body of criticism that has deconstructed not only prisons but also museums, sites of pleasure as well as places of incarceration and, most radically, understood individual subjectivity as a condition of constant surveillance. If critical theory could achieve the status of meta-narrative then power as vision would be one. Most certainly, Foucault, critically but masterfully, has established a discourse of the analysis of power. Stanley Cohen remarked 'to write today about punishment and classification without Foucault, is like talking about the unconscious without Freud'.[10] A generation of Foucauldian thinkers have elaborated upon the 'swarming of disciplinary mechanisms',[11] have attended to the multiplication of visual relations that reproduce discipline and docility, have recognized myriad formations of power that persist through 'certain distribution of bodies, surfaces, lights, gazes' and thus attested to the power of vision that is both extensive and pervasive, if not omnipresent. Foucault emphasizes the 'imaginary intensity' of the Panopticon but insists that it

> must not be understood as a dream building; it is the diagram of a mechanism of power reduced to its ideal form; its functioning, abstracted from any obstacle, resistance or friction, must be represented as a pure architectural and optical system; it is in fact a figure of political technology that may and must be detached from any specific use.[12]

The Panopticon was no dream except insofar as all architectural plans are projections. Jeremy Bentham's Panopticon plan derived from a real building, designed by Samuel Bentham, his brother. Samuel Bentham, appointed to 'manage and modernize' the estates of Prince Potemkin in 'White Russia',[13] erected a school named an Inspection House or the Elaboratory, which was underway when his sibling visited. Rather proud of 'my brother's plan', Jeremy Bentham most admired how it instituted a state of almost constant inspection; it 'most completely secured' such a situation and this single structure was 'applicable' to all forms of incarceration: for punishment and asylum, for education and employment. He became its advocate, describing it under a now well-known name in a series of letters written from 'Chercheff' now anglicized as Krichev, Belarus. The first, written in 1787, presented the 'Panopticon; or the Inspection-House; containing the idea of a new principle of construction applicable to any sort of establishment, in which persons of any description are to be kept under inspection; and in particular to penitentiary-houses.'[14] Brother Jeremy extracted a general design from Samuel's specific building; one sibling projected that the architecture of another could be widely, even universally, applied, to become something like Foucault's 'generalizable model of functioning' (Figure 1.1). Although Bentham abstracted principles from actual architecture, the purpose of his letters was to erect another real building. He sought to influence the construction of a new prison in London and a series in Ireland. He sent the designs with the following explanation:

> I observed t'other day in one of your English papers, an advertisement relative to a House of Correction therein spoken of, as intended for * * * * * * *. It occurred to me, that the plan of a building, lately contrived by my brother, for purposes in some respects similar, and which, under the name of the *Inspection House*, or the *Elaboratory*, he is about erecting here, might afford some hints for the above establishment. I have accordingly obtained some drawings relative to it, which I here inclose. Indeed I look

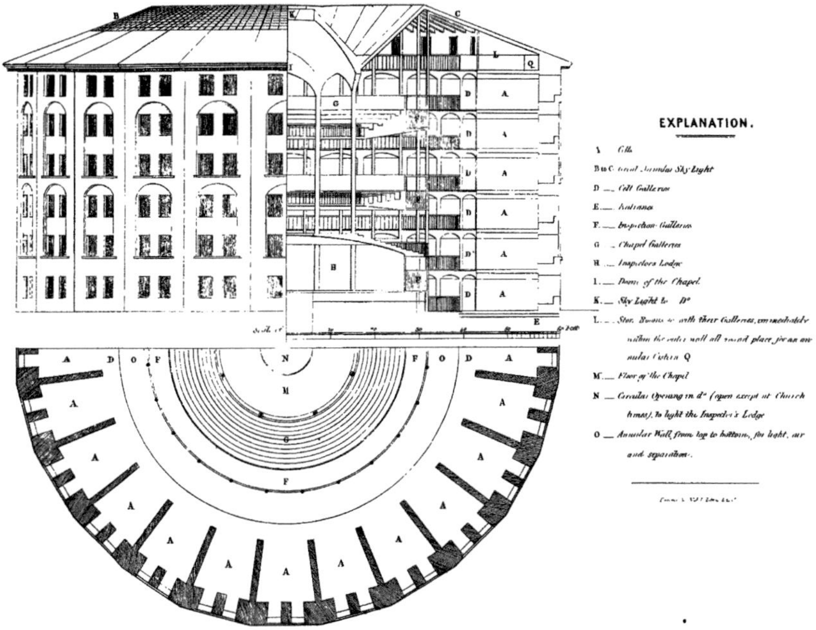

FIGURE 1.1 *'Foucault's Panopticon'*, *Jeremy Bentham*, A General Idea of a Petitionary Panopticon *[1787]*.

upon it as capable of applications of the most extensive nature; and that for reasons which you will soon perceive.[15]

His belief in the 'applications most extensive' was because it was exactly, or almost exactly, what was needed. It was fit for purpose in the contemporary jargon of administration. For Bentham, the founder of Utilitarianism, a liberal reformer interested in efficient government, it was an instrument of rule as perfect as it was possible to be:

> the more constantly the persons to be inspected are under the eyes of the persons who should inspect them, the more perfectly will the purpose of the establishment have been attained. Ideal perfection, if that were the object, would require that each person should actually be in that predicament, during every instant of time. This being impossible, the next thing to be wished for is, that, at every instant, seeing reason to believe as much, and not being able to satisfy himself to the contrary, he should *conceive* himself to be so.[16]

Foucault's principle of unverifiable visibility was Bentham's compromise. Such a slight difference is of little matter, for both the liberal and the liberal's critic see the same powerful effect of the Panopticon: subjection to the idea of 'constant inspection' or 'permanent visibility'. The material difference between these utopian and dystopian accounts of seeing and being seen is that the eighteenth-century original is devoted to providing details of the actual structures upon which the visual power of the Panopticon rests. This is Bentham's description of the building of the Panopticon (see Figures 1.2 and 1.3):

> The building is circular.
>   The apartments of the prisoners occupy the circumference. You may call them, if you please, the *cells*.
>   These *cells* are divided from one another, and the prisoners by that means secluded from all communication with each other, by *partitions* in the form of *radii* issuing from the circumference towards the centre, and extending as many feet as shall be thought necessary to form the largest dimension of the cell.
>   The apartment of the inspector occupies the centre; you may call it if you please the *inspector's lodge.*
>   It will be convenient in most, if not in all cases, to have a vacant space or *area* all round, between such centre and such circumference. You may call it if you please the *intermediate* or *annular* area.
>   About the width of a cell may be sufficient for a *passage* from the outside of the building to the lodge.

Fig. I.—Elevation.

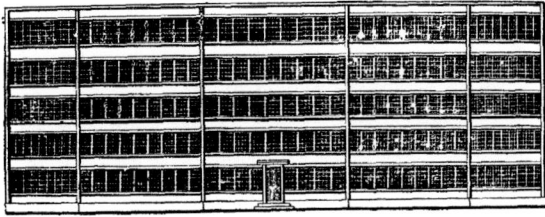

Fig. III.—Ground Plan.

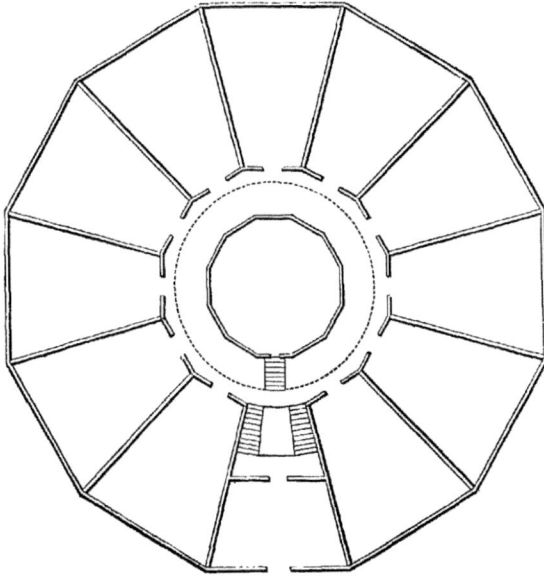

FIGURE 1.2 *Jeremy Bentham, 'Elevation and Ground Plan'*, A General, Idea of a Petitionary Panopticon *[1787]*.

Each cell has in the outward circumference, a *window*, large enough, not only to light the cell, but, through the cell, to afford light enough to the correspondent part of the lodge.

The inner circumference of the cell is formed by an iron *grating*, so light as not to screen any part of the cell from the inspector's view.

Of this grating, a part sufficiently large opens, in form of a *door*, to admit the prisoner at his first entrance; and to give admission at any time to the inspector or any of his attendants.[17]

The effect of constant inspection was beneficial, Bentham believed, upon those he called the 'incorrigible', the 'suspected', the 'insane', the 'vicious', the 'idle', the 'helpless', the 'sick' as well as the 'willing'. And it was achieved

FIG. II.—SECTION.

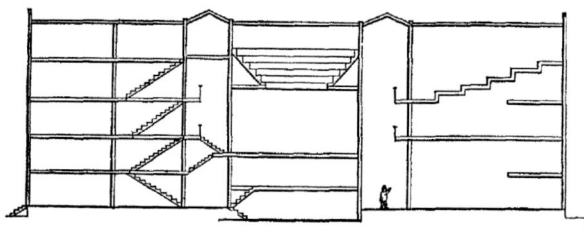

FIGURE 1.3 *Jeremy Bentham, 'Section', A General Idea of a Petitionary Panopticon [1787].*

by this: '*a simple idea in Architecture!*'[18] The Panopticon principle was a 'new' one of 'construction', as Bentham indicated in the title of his letters. It was a type of building. Certainly, Foucault does recognize Bentham's 'principle of construction' identified in the Panopticon and how its architecture contained an idea; he calls it an 'architectural figure'[19] in which permanent visibility is represented through a building. If the Panopticon is a figure, points of geometry in abstract space, one narrow cylinder that is the tower enclosed by another wider cylinder that is the cells, it is only a representation. The material form of an actual eighteenth-century Panopticon does not distract Foucault from all the possible prisons that its design represents. Regarding the Panopticon as the idealization of visual power meant that Michel Foucault overlooked its material force. Compare his to Bentham's description of its architecture. Foucault states that the cells of the 'peripheric building' have 'two windows' allowing light to cross the length of the cell, capturing its occupant. The building described by Bentham, however, has an 'iron grating' not a window on the cell's internal side, on its 'inner circumference'. This may seem such a small detail but it is of material significance. An 'annular building' spilt into cells with two windows, front and back, is a dream of a prison; cells idealized into see-through structures. There is the matter of how any of the windows might be made of a material transparent enough to allow light and strong enough to restrain those held within them. But before any consideration of a prisoner getting out, that person must be able to get in. Most importantly and most practically, a cell must have a threshold through which the condemned is sent. Within Bentham's iron grating was the door, 'a part sufficiently large opens', he states, 'to admit the prisoner at his first entrance'. The precise physical properties of materials necessary for the actual operation of the Panopticon was addressed by Bentham. For example, he was concerned that this internal grating was sufficiently 'light as not to screen any part of the cell'.[20]

He also wrote at great length about the dimensions of the Panopticon, all determined by the diameter. If the prison was too large in diameter, the light of the day would fade before reaching the inspector's lodge and that of the night, provided by 'small lamps' attached to his lodge and 'backed by a reflector', would not reach into the cell.[21] But if the diameter was too small, the prison would contain too few cells. That of Samuel Bentham's *Elaboratory*, a hundred feet, was used as the best working measurement for a Panopticon with two storeys, each with forty-eight cells, proposed by his brother for England. One hundred feet would allow for outside walls of six feet, ground floor cells of thirteen feet in depth 'from the window to the grating', inside walls of two-and-a-half feet and 'protracted partitions' of three feet to prevent prisoners from seeing each other. The cell to the inspector's lodge, a space called the 'intermediate area', was fourteen feet in length and with a diameter of thirty-five feet. The crucial distance over which light had to travel from the cells' windows to those of the lodge was measured by Bentham as thirty-two-and-a-half feet, calculated by subtracting the radius of the lodge, seventeen-and-a-half, from the fifty-foot radius of the Panopticon. To ensure that the distance was not increased over the upper storey, which required a gallery for access into the cells, their depth was reduced to nine feet.[22]

Bentham's details, the internal iron grating with its door opening, the calculations of the diameters, the cell depths and the distances that ensured sufficient daylight or lamplight for observation, projects a Panopticon of such greater material presence that it almost appears as an historical reality. This is the condition of Bentham's Panopticon. Almost. He lobbied for many years to build his version of his brothers' 'Inspection House' in London and sought to be appointed its first supervisor; the Panopticon would be placed under his 'personal direction'.[23] He curried favour with government ministers through a campaign of letter writing and cultivated public opinion with the exhibition of a model Panopticon on the 'dining table' of his town house.[24] A 1794 Act of Parliament granted permission for the purchase of land for a Panopticon penitentiary on the eastern side of the Thames but Earl Grosvenor objected to a prison so near his property. Bentham eventually abandoned his plan and in 1813 accepted £23,000 compensation for his trouble.[25] The abandoned Panopticon site later became the grounds of a national art gallery, now Tate Britain. Other attempts to realize the Panopticon were made as the London plan floundered. Bentham 'transmitted it to Ireland'. He corresponded with the Chancellor of the Exchequer Sir John Parnell and met with the Lord-Lieutenant Lord Westmoreland.[26] The first revolutionary government of France, the National Assembly, agreed to proposals presented Bentham but the Panopticon's aristocratic advocate, Louis-Alexandre de La Rochefoucauld, was killed in the September 1792 massacres. Only a few have ever been built. One, the Cuba Penitentiary on Isla da Pinos, opened in 1932 and 'consists of circular cell house, each with galleries of doorless cells which are watched from a central guardhouse'.[27] From a proposal accepted by Parliament to an actual structure, the Panopticon was always intended to be a building. Its principle of constant inspection or unverifiable visibility, in other words, its penal system, operates in and through a specific structure, a particular and actual architecture. Vision and power, to follow Foucault only part of the way, actually rest upon materiality.

Two points should be made here, in the wrong chronological order for ease of argument. First, Michel Foucault and his many followers have disregarded the materiality of the Panopticon, replacing it with mobility. While the prison is recognized as architecture, it is architecture with a light touch. The Panopticon works so very well, Foucault claims, because 'without any physical instrument other than architecture and geometry, it acts directly on individuals'.[28] It affects a body, makes a prisoner move into line, metaphorically or literally, without the obviously intrusive force of the chain or whip. Bentham had made a similar assertion but he regarded the bodily effect of surveillance as beneficial in more than its utilitarian sense; it was humane.[29] A system of constant inspection would eradicate the maltreatment of prisoners by prison guards. Certainly, the architecture of the Panopticon projects a geometrical order that has no other enforcement; lines of sight that appear as lines drawn on the paper of a prison design do seem cleverly banal rather than brutally violent. Yet, I would suggest, some attention should be paid to the physicality of this 'physical instrument'. What is the effect of these lines when they are built as walls? The important matter of prison walls is the second point. Some of the public figures and government ministers that Bentham sought to convince of the utility of the Panopticon decried it as entirely impractical because its structures were not sufficient to keep prisoners incarcerated. 'They will all get out', stated Lord Westmoreland.[30] His dismissal was deemed unworthy of debate by Bentham since the Panopticon, like any ordinary dungeons, would be built behind a wall. He wrote: '[f]or of those safeguards, which are common to all prisons, no graphical representation was, I believe contained, nor even for want of room, the plan of external fortification and circumvallation'.[31] Whilst Foucault neglected the materiality of the Panopticon design, Bentham himself acknowledged an important material absence, an oversight in the paperwork: no drawings of walls.

What forms of power are projected by, and embedded in, prisons walls? The higher and thicker the wall the more absolute, more oppressive, more pure is the power. It is not the invisible geometry of the architectural system but the brute force of a barrier, a border, that can so completely dominate: to detain and to deny freedom. Hard, unwavering, walls control the movement of bodies and form physical resistance. Seeing or feeling the power of a wall is not a particularly sophisticated reading of the material culture of imprisonment as a border but it should be borne in mind. There is room for more precision and consideration of the relationship between design and building.

Power in its idealized form is expressed prison design; architectural drawings demonstrate the perfect operation of a penal regime; they delineate the spaces of incarceration and those of restricted movement; they are plans of occupation; they show who will be permitted to live in which spaces. Details of architectural drawings, such as the exact depth of a cell or length of a corridor, present particular penal ideologies. For example, cells large enough for prisoners to work within them contain the idea of individual reformation through silent isolation whereas small cells just for sleeping are accompanied by shared spaces of imprisonment in which prisoners practise how to conform to, or in, a society. The architecture itself, the constructed design, gives material form to these ideal operations; power is made manifest in the building. To plan and implement a prison is to assume and maintain power; it is to rule over the lives of others.

H Blocks: a Home Office design

The H Blocks were not a Panopticon. In fact, one prison officer complained to me that it had 'poor sight lines'.[32] It is time to attend to its actual design. Its cell blocks were rectangular, in the form of a letter H (Figure 1.4). The eight H Blocks that comprised HMP Maze contained ninety-six single cells separated into four wings of twenty-four. Each wing was an upright of the H connected to a central administrative area, which formed its crossbar. The Blocks really were blocks: single storey, flat roofed, oblong, concrete structures. They were

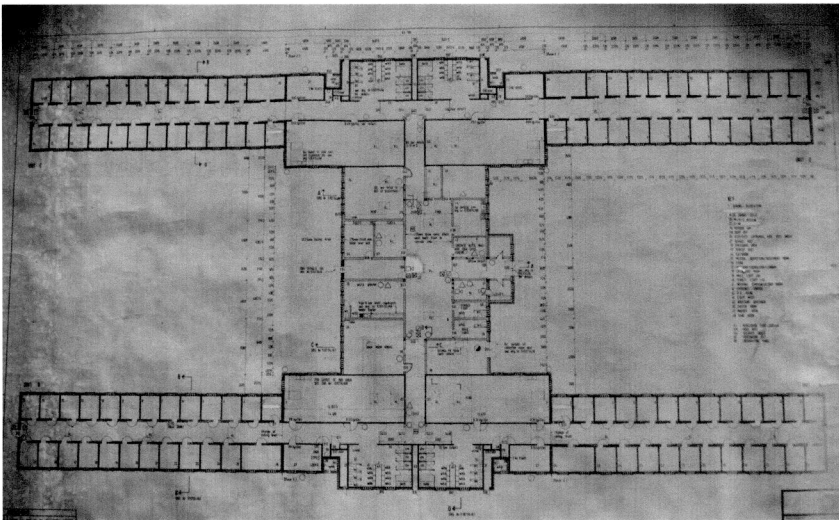

FIGURE 1.4 *H Block plan. Photograph: Louise Purbrick.*

devoid of colour. An external facing of beige bricks was punctuated at regular intervals by square windows with vertical concrete bars.

I was told that the cellular Maze was a 'Home Office design',[33] and the H Blocks do follow the footprint of English prison plans of the 1970s. An existing design was simply pressed into service. A British government department just used what they had to hand. A new jail was needed quickly. In January 1975, a Parliamentary committee chaired by Lord Gardiner and appointed 'to consider, in the context of civil liberties and human rights measures to deal with terrorism in Northern Ireland' recommended a prison-building programme and did so with some urgency. 'The present situation in Northern Ireland's prisons is so serious that the provision of adequate prison accommodation demands that priority be given to it by the Government in terms of money, materials and skilled labour such as has been accorded to no public project since the Second World War.'[34]

Typically, the plans for 1970s English jails were based on repeating rectangular cell units; it was an architecture of connected thin oblongs. A series of prisons were constructed along these lines. Work began on Channings Wood in Devon in 1972, on Deerbolt in Durham in 1973 and Featherstone in Staffordshire opened in 1976, the same year as the H Blocks. All are functional low-rise cubic structures made up of a series of stretches of cell units that duplicate facilities in order to create small prisoner communities within the larger prison population. This design, which disaggregates the prison into blocks and wings, was the dominant model within the Home Office's Prison Department throughout the decade.[35] HMP Maze Cellular, its full official title, is a version of this penal architectural type and there is one surviving architectural drawing for a prison intended for the north Essex coast from which the H Block design most likely developed. HMP Wrabness was abandoned in 1974 when £43 million was sliced off a prison-building programme in England and Wales, one of the first cutbacks in public spending that came to typify the late twentieth-century British economy, or neo-liberalism as it more generally came to be known.[36] Merlyn Rees, the Home Secretary from 1976 to 1979 during the construction of the H Blocks, stated that they were 'copied from plans for a proposed new English prison'[37] and confirmed a 'link' between the Maze and the intended, but never built, jail at Wrabness[38] (Figure 1.5).

The plans for Wrabness were produced by the Architects Co-Partnership, a progressive architectural practice then based in Soho Square, London. By 1971, when the Architects Co-Partnership was working on the Wrabness designs, their reputation for social architecture was well established. Formed in 1939, they played a significant part, especially for a private practice, in post-war reconstruction. They fulfilled County Council commissions and contributed to school building, a programme that relied upon various forms of prefabrication. Their most noted construction was the Brynmawr rubber factory in Wales.[39]

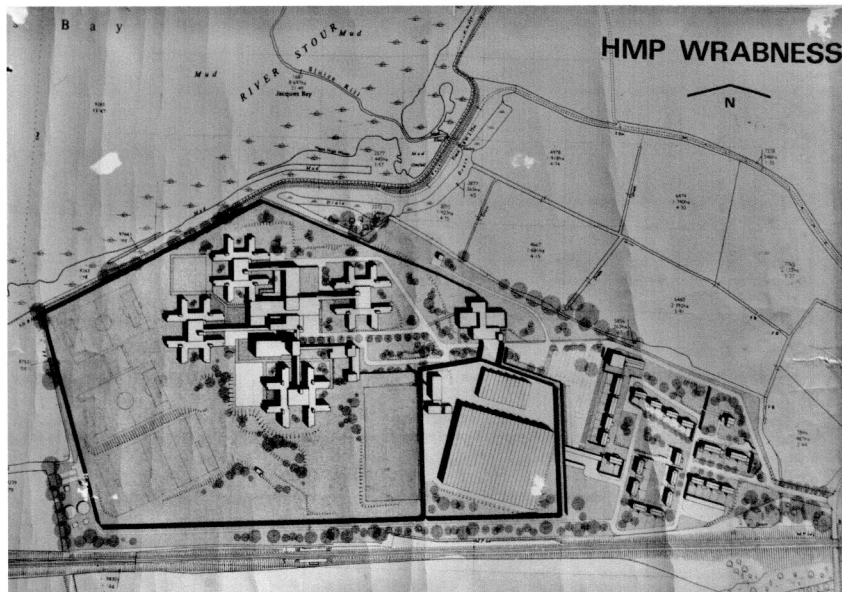

FIGURE 1.5 *Home Office prison design: HMP Wrabness. Photograph: Louise Purbrick.*

Some of the illustrative drawings of the prison at Wrabness present progressive additions to standard prison buildings: it is set in gentle park landscaping. Initially, nothing approximating this was built at Long Kesh/Maze (Figure 1.6). The more instructive drawings, and those that would have directly informed the construction process, are the ground and floor plans. They are remarkably similar to those that would comprise HMP Maze. A comparison between the plans of a block or 'house', as the Wrabness cell units were called, is also revealing. In the Wrabness plan, the cells are arranged in cloverleaf style with double the wings of shorter length (Figure 1.7). To my eyes I see two wings overlapping at right angles comprising each house. On the Wrabness wings and those of the H Blocks, there are the same number of single cells: twenty-four plus a double cell or day room. In both, the size of single cells conform to an English standard of eight feet three inches by seven feet one-and-a-half set by the Development Group for the Design of Prisons in 1959.[40] The cell doors are in the same place. Showers, toilets and urinals are similarly positioned at the top of the wing opposite a large association room. There are four of these rooms in each H Block of Long Kesh/Maze as there were in each house planned for Wrabness. But when the H Blocks were built, the access point was shifted from the central area to the wing, a move that enabled the restriction of movement within a block, the limitation of association to a wing, and thus allowed the enforcement of a rigidly wing-based regime. Another

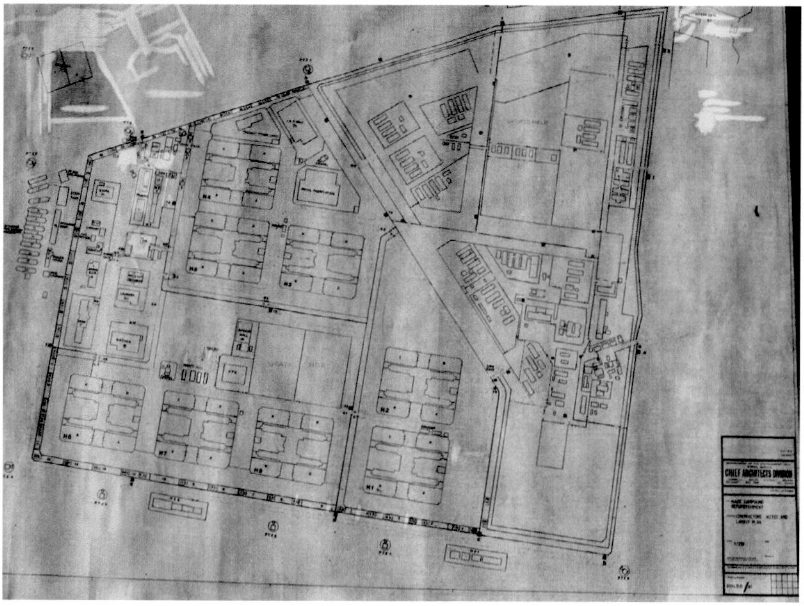

FIGURE 1.6 *Ground Plan: Long Kesh/Maze. Photograph: Louise Purbrick.*

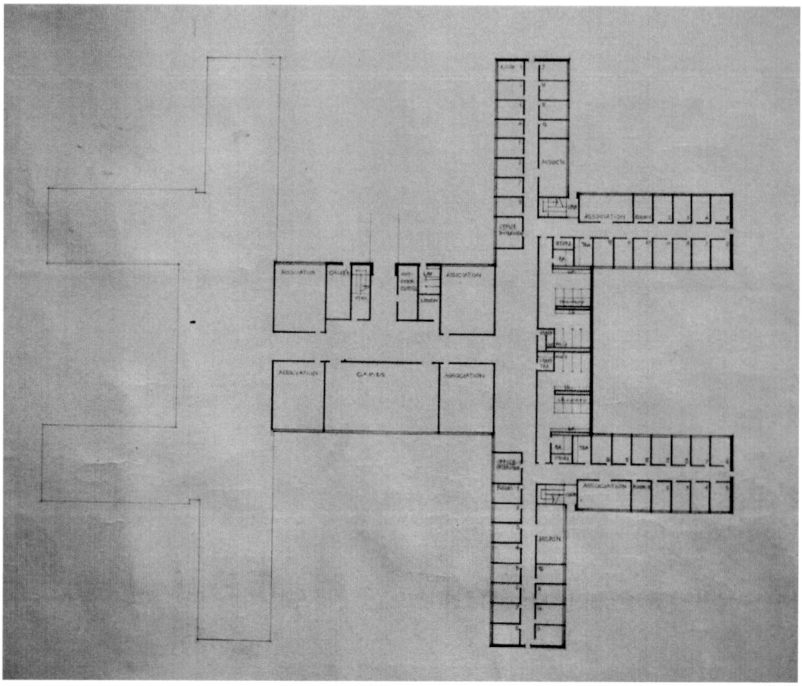

FIGURE 1.7 *Cell units: HMP Wrabness. Photograph: Louise Purbrick.*

adaptation is more obvious: HMP Maze is double the size. There are twice as many cell units within the prison, eight H Blocks to four projected houses, and its external pentagonal perimeter is twice as long. The most important difference is not so easily measured. The Wrabness designs demonstrate the progressive state planning that was becoming typical of 1970s English jails. At this time, softening the appearance of prisons was a concern of the Prison Department. For example, bars had been integrated into the cell window so that they were secure but not oppressive.[41] The H Blocks were stripped of any of these sociable details. The thick vertical bars across the window of an H Block cell are, by comparison, a design from the dungeon. The ground and floor plans of Long Kesh/Maze might be a recognizable version of the post-1945 welfare state penal architecture, but its actual structures are more basic and brutal.

Prison plan and penal regime

Architectural historians trace the development of penal architecture through the changes to the prison ground plan; they chart alterations to the footprint of prison buildings.[42] Two basic types, 'radial' and 'telephone-pole', which were both developed in the nineteenth century, have dominated prison design. In the radial prison, long wings emanate from a central circle; in jails based on the telephone-pole design, they extend off both sides of a central corridor. Eastern State Penitentiary, Philadelphia, opened in 1836, was the prototype radial prison and the first telephone pole was Wormwood Scrubs, London, completed in 1874.[43] From around the mid-twentieth century, a wider variety of ground plans are distinguishable. The H is one of the shapes that emerged from a period of experimentation with prison design. Prisons have been arranged in courtyards (Rustenberg, South Africa, 1968, and Low Newton, Durham, 1978) campus layouts (Fox Lake, Wisconsin, 1962) and in rectangular blocks (Ixtapalapa, Mexico, 1957, Featherstone, Staffordshire, 1976, and Eskişehir, Turkey, 1991).[44]

In principle, the ground plan of the prison is an expression of its regime. Radial and telephone-pole plans embodied a high degree of security; their designs provided prison guards with uninterrupted sight lines and visual command over prisoners. At the other end of the spectrum, a campus layout allows, and even encourages, a measure of privacy for prisoners. Intended to mimic social relationships and thereby create the conditions for rehabilitation, campus prisons comprise self-contained living units. However, prison ground plans can present opposing principles: the rectangular forms found in Louisiana or Wisconsin, at Featherstone or Long Kesh/Maze, were initially designed to reduce the dense concentrations of prisoners housed in nineteenth-century jails. A whole series of relatively short wings extending at right angles from a box-like mid-point administrative area replaced the elongated wings that spread out from a central corridor or circle. It is these shorter spurs of cells that produced symmetrical letter patterns across the prisons, the Hs of Long Kesh/Maze or the Ts at Featherstone, creating a human scale within the prison. But separating prisoners into small groups is also, of course, a strategy of control: divide and rule.

The relationship between plan and regime is not always clear cut. Obviously, it would be difficult to run an open prison along the long wings of a nineteenth-century jail. Nevertheless restricted budgets and rising numbers have meant that very few prisons close when the penal philosophy they represent has gone out of fashion. In practice, contemporary regimes take place in old prisons. Furthermore, regimes designed for different prisoners take place in the same prison. This is especially the case in Britain where a dispersal system operates. Since the late 1960s, high-security prisoners are separated into small pockets spread throughout the prison system; they are dispersed within jails that otherwise operate medium-security regimes and can be confined in High Security Units. Between five and eight prisons in England and Wales have been designated as dispersal prisons since the system began. When the Chief Inspector of Prisons described Long Kesh/Maze as a maximum-security institution in 1984,[45] it was the only one in the entire British system, the only jail where the highest levels of security operated throughout the whole prison.

The design of HMP Maze Cellular, the very form of the H Blocks, existed at an intersection between the faltering development of prison regimes in the last days of a welfare state and the emergence of neo-liberal securitization of the prison estate: long-term imprisonment as a state of exception. It was a manifestation of the denial of war through the attempt to manage combatants as convicted criminals. The conflict in and about Northern Ireland was not, and is not, widely recognized as a war. 'The Troubles' was its euphemism in which 3,665 people died. 'The Troubles' or, to give it its most blandly accurate term, the conflict, was the 'British Army's longest ever continuous deployment'.[46] Indisputably, imprisonment was a strategy of the conflict from the start, following a pattern of typical of conflicts all over the world: it began with the basic and brutal, uncomplicated and unjust, practice of rounding up people assumed to be the enemy and taking them away from their home: holding them in detention. This is internment. Understanding the appearance of the H Blocks involves some consideration of imprisonment in the conflict before they were built.

Internment and 'special category' prisoners

The internment of 'suspected terrorists' was introduced by the Northern Ireland's Stormont government on 5 August 1971. Internment is imprisonment without trial. It is also known as administrative detention because imprisonment is ordered through an administrative rather than a legal process. There were two stages of internment in Northern Ireland. First, a person named on an interim custody order as a suspected terrorist was detained for up to twenty-eight days. Second, imprisonment was ordered by a detention commissioner on the basis of evidence that was usually from an informer and could be 'first hand, second hand and third hand evidence' according to Lord Gardiner, the chair of the 1974 Committee that included the use of internment in its investigations.[47]

The first internees were picked up in the early hours of 9 August 1971, four days after the introduction of internment, in raids that the British Army named Operation Demetrius. They were held in C wing of the Crumlin Road Prison in north Belfast and on HMS Maidstone moored in Belfast Lough. All but two were from Catholic-nationalist communities; 116 were released after forty-eight hours. Most of these had received beatings.[48] In the first six months of internment, 2,447 people were detained and 934 released. Over the whole period of internment, 1,981 people were imprisoned without trial, of whom only 107 were not nationalists or republicans.[49] The first loyalists were interned on 5 February 1973 and their numbers rose to around seventy in May 1974, when the United Ulster Unionist Council organized a general strike against the Sunningdale Agreement and prevented the implementation of a London-Dublin power-sharing government in Northern Ireland.[50]

Internment continued after the introduction of direct rule from Westminster in 1972. A temporary emergency measure had become a permanent feature. However, the number of internees was reduced by successive Secretaries of State for Northern Ireland faced with the illegality of their imprisonment as 'nothing has been proved against them'.[51] Willie Whitelaw, Secretary of State in these crucial early years of using imprisonment in the conflict declared that the Conservative government would examine 'whether changes should be made in the administration of justice in order to deal more effectively with terrorism'.[52] Rather than rely upon internment, his administration created courts for the conflict. 'A trial on indictment of scheduled offences shall be conducted by the court without a jury' as it was announced in the 1973 Emergency Provisions Act.[53] These no-jury courts, named after the Diplock Commission and its aristocrat chairman, accepted uncorroborated and retracted confessions as evidence. Long Kesh internment centre, now re-named HMP Maze, started to fill up with prisoners charged with scheduled offences and sentenced through the Diplock courts. These sentenced prisoners were described as being 'on special category'. They were recognized as political. Willie Whitelaw had acknowledged their political status after a thirty-five-day hunger strike by republican prisoners in Crumlin Road in June 1972. He conceded that all politically motivated prisoners, republican and loyalist, did not have to wear a uniform or undertake work and could receive more letters, parcels and visits than 'ordinary' prisoners. Special category prisoners had more or less the same rights as those who were remanded or interned; that is, they were treated as if they had not, in fact, been convicted.

Long Kesh internment centre: a material form of detention without trial

As part of the preparations for internment in the late spring of 1971, Nissen huts were put up along the runways of the disused RAF Long Kesh airbase twelve miles outside Belfast (Figure 1.8). There were twenty huts at the beginning of 1972 and eighty-eight by 1974. 'Overcrowding was perhaps the worst feature,' said John McGuffin, who was interned in the early days. Most of the huts were used as open dormitories, which slept forty in two-tier bunks with 'not an inch of space' between them.[54] The huts measured 120 by 24 feet. Four were grouped together in a seventy-by-thirty-yard compound enclosed by a twelve-foot wire fence, with rolls of razor wire on top. The compounds were called 'Cages' by prisoners. One hut per compound was

FIGURE 1.8 *Nissen huts: The compounds of Long Kesh internment centre. Photograph: Louise Purbrick.*

used as a canteen, the only interior recreational space for 120 men. None of the huts were weather proof and there was little difference between temperatures inside and out. The International Red Cross, in a series of reports following inspections between 1971 and 1974, continually recommended improvements to the physical conditions inside Long Kesh.

Internees and sentenced prisoners were held under the same conditions. On 19 September 1971, the first internees arrived by helicopter from HMS Maidstone and Crumlin Road prison. Sentenced prisoners were sent to Long Kesh some nine months later, after the creation of the special category for prisoners serving conflict-related sentences. By the time the Gardiner Committee was gathering information in late 1974, internees and special category prisoners were roughly equal in number: of a total of 1,292 prisoners, 513 were detained and 589 were convicted political prisoners.[55] The prison population overall had escalated from 712 people at the beginning of the conflict in 1969 to 2,848 in 1974 when Lord Gardiner was preparing his report on 'measures to deal with terrorism in Northern Ireland'.[56] The number of prisoners per head of population was the highest in Western Europe.[57] Most were held at Long Kesh.

Long Kesh deserved its reputation as a POW camp: it had watchtowers, floodlights, wire fences and soldiers patrolling the perimeter with guard dogs. For one British Army chaplain it was more than a matter of appearances: 'Long Kesh internment camp was really a prisoner of war camp.'[58] Republicans and loyalists were just held, detained, many believed, for the duration of the conflict. No-one was subject to a penal regime. A former prison officer explains that the compound system 'afforded a great deal of autonomy to paramilitary groups in the prison system'.[59] Four prison officers were allocated to each compound: one at the sentry box, two patrolled the fence around the compound with another in reserve. They entered the compounds to carry out head counts, collect prisoners to be escorted for visits and carry out searches. They were often refused entry. Prisoners organized themselves within their compounds without interference from prison authorities illustrated by the fifty-six successful escapes that took place between 1971 and 1975.[60] Indeed, they developed their own political affinities and military structures. The Provisional Irish Republican Army (IRA), the Official Irish Republican Army (OIRA), the Ulster Volunteer Force (UVF), and the Ulster Defence Association (UDA) had their own compounds as did the Irish National Liberation Army (INLA) when it was formed in 1974. The UVF leader Gusty Spence has told how he ran his compound 'on British army lines with made-up beds, highly polished boots, pressed uniforms etcetera'. He described how:

There was a daily regime. Reveille was at eight o'clock in the morning, followed by showers, breakfast then a parade. Then the day was laid out.

Initially we relied happily on military matters, field craft and all those things. There weren't that many fields in the compound, you know, but we practised all those things that made a person a more proficient soldier.[61]

Life in Long Kesh was shaped by prisoners' organizations rather than those of the prison, which did not even decide where those on special category should be placed. An early study of prison routines and structures revealed how sentenced prisoners were offered to the compounds and 'which ever accepted him got him'.[62] There was some occasional contact between the compounds belonging to opposing groups as Billy McKee, IRA Officer Commanding (OC) in the early 1970s recalls:

> The loyalists were in the next Cage to us and we got on alright with them. They were always asking for books, James Connolly books, socialism and things like that. I used to give them extra copies of any books I had. They were more hostile with each other than with us, the UVF and the UDA.[63]

In the spring of 1974, OCs from all the various republican and loyalist compounds presented a joint list of grievances about poor living conditions to the prison governor of Long Kesh. When nothing changed, food protests began. Meals were dumped over the compound wire. Republican compounds were also being subjected to increasingly punitive British Army searches and beatings. In October, republicans set fire to the prison. 'Right, up she goes' went the order, apparently.[64] Eighteen compounds, the interior of the hospital plus some offices were 'wrecked', the kitchen and one of the visiting areas were 'destroyed'.[65] Jim Scullion, a sentenced republican prisoner remembers:

> It was rough afterwards. The first night the Brits didn't come in, they let us run about. They surrounded the perimeter though. At day-break the next they came in. They beat us into the ground. We fought for a good while but they drove us back with the gas onto the football field, which was the only place we could get fresh air. The UVF and the UDA set up field hospitals for us in their Cages. They actually abandoned some of their Cages.[66]

The field hospitals had been created with supplies that loyalists had taken from the prison hospital as the fire got underway. They vacated three of their five compounds grouped together in two, Cages 14 and 19. Following the fire, Long Kesh was a 'shanty town', according to Gerry Adams, who was interned at the time.[67] Prisoners made shelters from the debris and plastic sheeting was stretched over what remained of the huts. British Army construction units rapidly and completely rebuilt the compounds even improving them slightly, using bricks instead of wood for the end walls of the huts.

Lord Gardiner blamed the design of the compounds for the 'total loss of disciplinary control by the prison authorities' within them. The Nissen huts were unsuitable makeshift accommodation that had been over-occupied for four years. Conditions were not, however, Gardiner's main concern; it was the issue of control. The 'layout and construction of the compounds make close and continued supervision impossible'. Rebuilding them would not then fulfil the need, as he understood it, for a proper prison. The flat, official prose of his report could not hide the fact that he found the realities of a political jail quite shocking. 'Each compound is virtually a self-contained community' which 'engages, if it so wishes, in military drills or lectures on military subjects'.[68] Of his forty-seven conclusions and recommendations, twenty were directly related to prisons and prisoners. Essentially, Gardiner argued for phasing out internment but immediately removing special category status, stripping sentenced prisoners of political recognition. No-jury courts would remain. There would be trial procedures dedicated to political acts of conflict without political status within the prison system. The Diplock courts were endorsed while the 'earliest practicable opportunity should be taken to bring special category status to an end'. Equal urgency was attached to prison building. 'The Government should find suitable sites on which to begin construction immediately.'[69] These recommendations were anticipated because they were in line with government thinking, but their publication put some pressure on Northern Ireland Secretary Merlyn Rees, to act quickly. When questioned in the House of Commons by Enoch Powell in February 1975 about ending special category status and implementing the Gardiner report, Rees replied, 'I cannot move in advance of the prison accommodation.'[70] Although a site for a new prison located between Maghaberry Road, Old Road and Hannahstown Road in County Antrim had been agreed the previous November, its construction was being delayed by planning procedures. Rees then decided upon what he called a 'short-term solution' and, on 5 February 1975, informed the Commons that work on a cellular prison adjacent to the Long Kesh compounds would begin.[71] No permissions were required on this military land, a Ministry of Defence estate and an existing site of incarceration.

HMP Maze (Cellular): construction and design

Prisoners in the compounds watched from the roofs of their newly built huts as the concrete floors, walls and ceiling units were cast, set and raised into place. Rows of cells were formed. Dust from mixing sand and cement blew over and covered their clothes. Prefabricated concrete prison construction had been developed in the United States twenty years previously. It was employed in the rebuilding of Louisiana's notorious State Penitentiary at

Angola in 1955. The original prison, one of the worst in North America, was a 'shack camp' that held over 2,500 men. Prison rioting was widespread in the early 1950s and, at Angola, convicts slashed their heel tendons as a protest against the brutality of the guards.[72] The shacks were replaced with a low-rise prison comprising several separate blocks of cells connected by covered walkways. The blocks and walkways were made of precast concrete and erected using a lift-slab system. Flat spans of concrete were formed and set at ground level, one on top of the other. A plywood, plastic or foil 'bond-breaker' separated the flat spans of concrete. These slabs were then lifted into place using jacking mechanisms to form a series of enclosed spaces.[73]

Angola's architect was Nathaniel Curtis of Curtis and Davis, Architects and Planners of New Orleans. The jail was a modern building. Entirely unadorned, it was a functional and efficient form; its simple severity an expression of International Modernism. Arthur Quentin Davis, Nathaniel Curtis's partner, studied under Walter Gropius at Harvard University.[74] Their firm's application of a modern design philosophy to a prison produced a new cell unit arrangement. Angola's blocks were designed in the shape of an H or a 'clover leaf' as Curtis described it. A wing or 'unit' of cells is 'economically repeated four times to form a clover leaf'.[75] Their building received a First Honor Award from the American Institute of Architects. H-shaped cell units were used again in their design for Wisconsin Correctional Institution, Fox Lake, which opened in 1962 and came to influence penal architecture, including that commissioned by the British government, such as the 'Home Office design' for HMP Wrabness produced by the Architects Co-Partnership. The Wisconsin construction and Wrabness plans lost the covered walkways and their cell blocks were completely detached. The Long Kesh/Maze would follow suit. In all prisons, the blocks were built to house the same number of prisoners in the same arrangement: four wings of twenty-four single cells plus a day room.

The Curtis and Davis prisons attracted comment, especially but not exclusively, in the architectural press. Angola was widely praised for its economical design. An article about prison design in the 1961 issue of *The British Journal of Criminology*, which included an H-shaped clover leaf diagram (Figure 1.9), emphasized how prefabrication kept costs per inmate to an 'extremely low figure'.[76] The author echoes the optimism of the US Bureau of Prisons: 'The use of pre-stressed and pre-cast modular units for penal institutions holds out real promise of keeping construction cost within reasonable limits.'[77] Precast forms were 'by far the most widely used type of structural component in British and American architecture of the later 1960s and 1970s'.[78] The concrete load-bearing wall units of construction of the cellular prison, reinforced with a criss-cross of metal bars, were already regularly used for large-scale building projects, from car parks to office towers. Less typically, there were four vertical concrete bars across the window

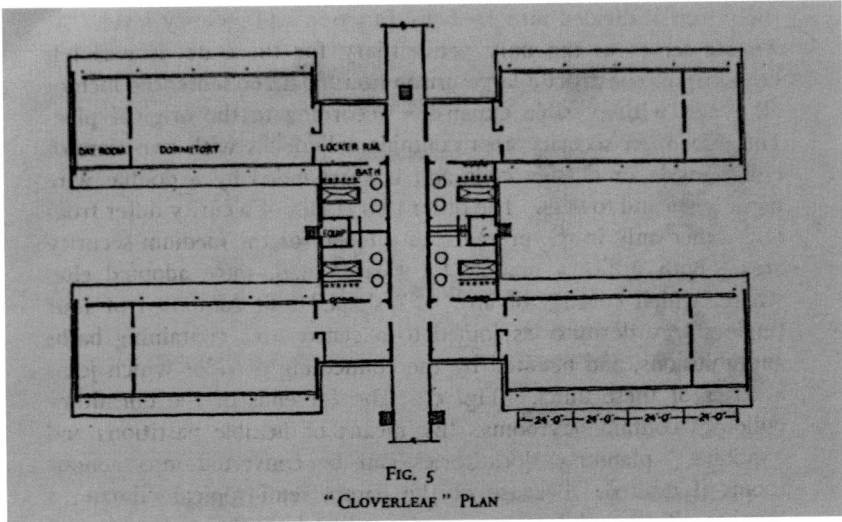

FIG. 5
" CLOVERLEAF " PLAN

FIGURE 1.9 *H-shaped clover leaf prison design.*

openings in the external walls of the H Blocks. This is exceptional in a twentieth-century prison: Wisconsin Correctional Institution was designed without 'security windows'.[79]

By the time the Maze Cellular was being built, concrete was a well-established industrial material. A cheap copy of the density and solidity of stone, its tensile strength is increased by metal reinforcements. The low cost of aggregates, the gravel and crushed stones that is rubble and waste, contributes to its cheapness but its real economy is based on standardization. Whenever a building repeats a series of the same spaces, such as prison cells, concrete becomes an efficient method of construction. Large quantities of standard concrete shapes can be cast in formwork then put into place. Prefabricated buildings can be rapidly erected.[80]

In early 1975, after the Gardiner Report had been published, circulated, and cited in parliamentary debates, delays in the construction of a new prison were, from the perspective of Northern Ireland Office, unacceptable. To those responsible for its building, reinforced concrete must have seemed the ideal material: it was cheap but solid and could be quickly assembled. A courtroom, purpose-built for the trial of the Baader-Meinhof group in May 1975, had been erected in a field next to Stammheim prison, in Stuttgart, for much the same reason: to provide no-frills maximum security.[81] Lord Donaldson, Under Secretary of State for Northern Ireland, was able to report to the House of Lords on 26 June 1975 that: 'we have two blocks of cellular accommodation well forward at the moment at one side of the Maze . . . We hope that these will be occupied by the 1 October.' The two blocks he referred to, H1 and H2, which formed Phase 1 of the HMP Maze (Cellular), were built in the south-east corner of the new prison site and opened in September 1976.[82] Construction work continued as these first blocks began to fill up with prisoners sentenced after the withdrawal of special category status on 1 March. A second phase of three blocks, H3, H4 and H5 was finished by April 1977 and Phase 3, which included the last three bringing the total to eight, was underway. All were completed in less than half the time that it usually took to build a prison and it was twice the size.[83] Hard, high walls were raised with political haste at Long Kesh/Maze to reassert the power of the prison.

The materiality of prison designs is inescapably important. Walls must be impenetrable to perform the work of imprisonment, to continually confront and continually contain. Jeremy Bentham's writings on the Panopticon, which provided the scaffold for a discourse of the power of visuality, encompassed its materiality. Only if you read until the end. In the long, actually long-winded, postscript to *The Panopticon; or Inspection House* Section XIX 'Materials' recommends its construction in brick and stone but with the 'abundant use of iron' for a series of reasons: 'sometimes to admit air, sometimes to save space, sometimes for the sake of strength.'[84] In a further Section XXI concerning 'Approach and Fences', Jeremy Bentham makes a detailed case for a surrounding wall, relatively low but guarded, with only one long narrow walled and gated entrance in which, if a prisoner ever escaped he would find himself 'inclosed in a defile',[85] now known as an airlock. The visuality and power of the Panopticon, so important to contemporary critical understanding of power itself, rests upon materiality, the force of a wall, the brutality of a border.

2

Living in the Cells

When the very last prisoners left Long Kesh/Maze no-one bothered to wipe their number, political affiliation and location off the Control Room white boards. In January 2002, when I was wandering around the deserted prison administration buildings, I noticed a white board, pinned high on a wall. It presented simple notations relating to each of the eight H Blocks. Numbers and letters written inside the H indicated the final place prisoners occupied on its wings: 1 INLA on B Wing of H3 and 3 others on C wing H4 (Figure 2.1) Another board, the 'H Block Roll' contained slightly older information; it also shows the occupation of different wings of H3 by INLA and the IRA and H4 by members of the UFF, UDA, and LVF (Figure 2.2). For the next four years the entire prison stood empty; the artefacts and documents left within it were slowly stripped away, some auctioned, some archived. All were appropriated and some stolen. Some statutory protection was secured for a selection of structures: H6, Cage 19, a section of the perimeter wall, a prison chapel,

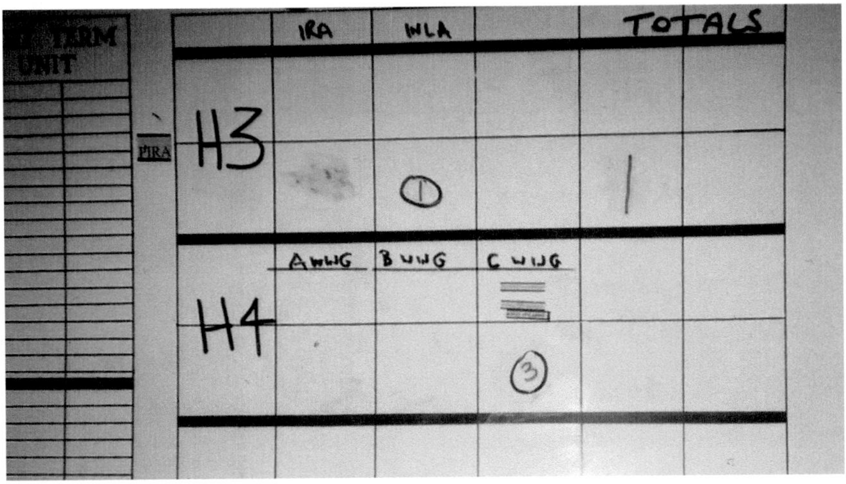

FIGURE 2.1 *Whiteboard, administration building. Photograph: Louise Purbrick.*

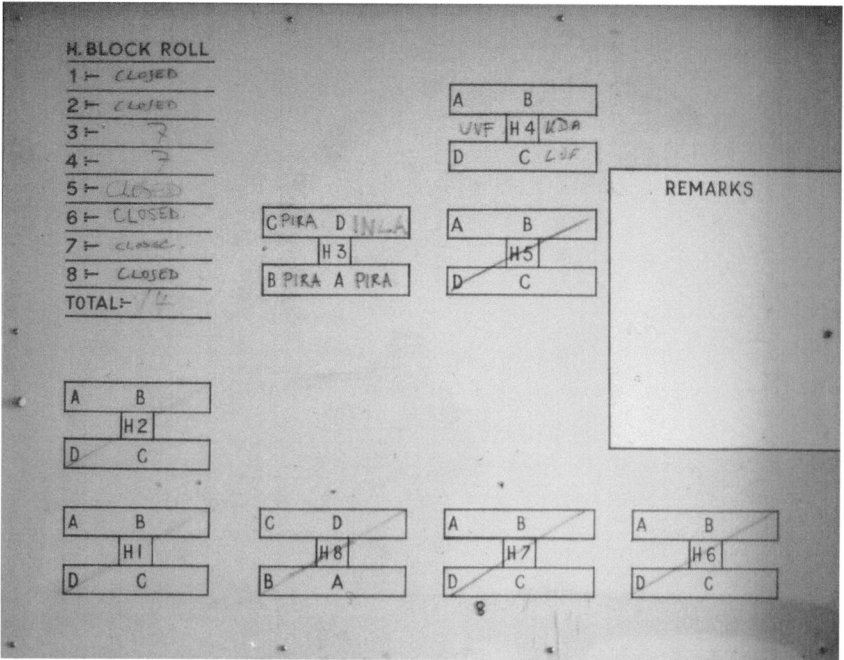

FIGURE 2.2 *H Block Roll, administration building. Photograph: Louise Purbrick.*

the prison hospital and the administration buildings where I photographed the white boards. The rest was demolished between 2006 and 2008. The dismantling and destruction, partial preservation and limited access at Long Kesh/Maze is one of the unstable political compromises of the peace process. The problem this former prison site poses for power sharing is that the unionist half of consociational executive arrangements tends to regard the H Blocks as entirely republican. They were built by the British government, the British Army watched over their walls and were guarded by the Northern Ireland Prison Service, with its determinedly unionist outlook. Yet none of these bodies now command the meaning of its structures. They lost control over their prison.

Fortress

HMP Maze Cellular was a modern fortress. The H Blocks, eight identical single-storey structures, lay within its twenty-foot-high concrete perimeter wall, which stretched for two-and-a-half miles also enclosing the compounds of Long Kesh internment centre (Figure 2.3). Twelve thirty-foot army watchtowers were positioned around both prison systems, five of them along the wall closest to the Belfast–Dublin M1 motorway. The top of their square

FIGURE 2.3 *Perimeter wall. Photograph: Louise Purbrick.*

lookouts were just visible to car drivers. Concrete walls were built within the Maze Cellular itself, separating it into three segments called 'Phases', each sealed off from the other. Within all these walls, wire fences dominated (Figure 2.4). They formed internal barriers, creating blank corridors, no-go areas called inertias or steriles. Behind the perimeter wall was ten feet of empty space bounded by a high wire barrier to leave it inert with sensors inserted at regular intervals to detect even the slightest movement. Within the concrete walls of the three Phases were similar sterile areas. There was so much wire that the prison could appear, initially at least, to be completely grey. Every building in the Maze, from the H Blocks to its administration offices and two chapels, was set in its own wire cage. More wires hung over the internal roadways with plastic spheres suspended from them, a device to prevent light aircraft landing. A sixteen-foot-high wire mesh fence reinforced with corrugated iron and covered with double rolls of razor wire surrounded each H Block.

A repeating pattern of hard walls, high barriers and restricted spaces of Long Kesh/Maze created a system of control. Repetition is the architectural feature of control systems; it allows the regime and routines of incarceration to be planned precisely. The degree of containment and the measurement of movement of prisoners are determined by the walls, their moments of entry and exit decided upon in advance by prison administrators. Prisoners can be

FIGURE 2.4 *Wire fences. Photograph: Louise Purbrick.*

contained in the same prison but isolated in its separately repeating parts. Movement is proscribed and prescribed; it can be prevented completely when a prisoner is locked in a cell, or if allowed, it is exactly regulated, easily monitored; the same route enacted again and again. The duplication of physical structures, the walls, fences, blocks and cells, produces a predictable environment that allows penal regimes to become routines of imprisonment.

Outside the tall, thick perimeter prison wall, a Prison Guard Force of armed British soldiers patrolled, occupying the watchtowers. Inside, the movement of the prison's occupants was choreographed; the walls, fences, blocks and cells determined the destination of prisoners and, although to a lesser extent, prison officers. The space of repeating daily prison routines was the H Block and it was a sealed unit. Located within the concrete Phase walls and their steriles and empty wire-fenced corridors, the Blocks were also fenced, the mesh clad with corrugated iron. A sentry box guarded the double gate entrance; it was an air lock: the first gate shut before the second opened. Within the H Block, the movement of prisoners as they repeated their daily routines was restricted to the wings, A, B, C or D. They were also sealed units. Each of these four wings, which formed the four the stems of the H, duplicated dining areas, bathrooms and exercise yards to create separate self-contained spaces. The adjacent yards were separated by yet another fence, more mesh and more corrugated iron, overlooked by watchtowers, two dedicated to an H Block. Every Block was identical. Distinguished only by the numbers one to eight, they were the same remorselessly repeating structures.

When a prisoner had permission to move outside the Block, to see a member of his family in the visits area, for example, he would have to be checked through a series of internal barriers: the grille at the top of the wing, the gate in the H Block fence, the segment gates within the Phase walls. Every one was an air lock. The Maze Cellular was a prison version of a Russian doll: a small, enclosed space encased by another just a little larger, encased by another, then another and another. Prisoners were accompanied by prison officers as they moved across each space, under escort from leaving the wing and watched from the moment they left their cells. Supervising their movement within and between the H Blocks was labour intensive. There were twenty-four staff to a Block: four on each of the four wings, a total of sixteen, then six monitoring the grilles, entrance and main block gate with two senior officers in overall charge. Prisoners left the Block in the back of a prison van. The size of the prison meant that vans were always used to move prisoners over the long internal distances between its cell accommodation and any of its other buildings: the administration, the visit areas, the workshops, chapels or punishment blocks. The height of walls, length of fences, the amount of wire, the number of airlocks, inertias and steriles, the web of watchtowers, the network sensors are an expression of the level of security in a prison. Fortress prisons make repressive power a visible force and a matter of routine: a daily demonstration of complete control.

Uniform and cell

When the first republican prisoner, Kieran Nugent, was sent to the H Blocks, shortly after his sentencing on 14 September 1976, he did not put on a prison uniform. To refuse to wear a prison uniform is to refuse a place in the prison system; it is a rejection of a prison identity allocated upon entry into it and, therefore, a rejection of the authority of the prison, its power to define its prisoners and claim control over them. It seems a small act of defiance but is full of significance. To choose to wear nothing instead of dress in prison clothing, to leave your legs exposed rather than pull dull blue trousers over them and your chest bare rather than button up a square cut jacket of matching material, announces that this body will not inhabit a prison life. Defying a uniform dress code is often easily assumed to be an expression of individuality; it may, more fundamentally, be considered a claim to freedom. In the H Blocks, it was also an assertion of collective political status within a penal regime that no longer recognized the political nature of conflict.

The construction of the H Blocks announced a new political strategy in Northern Ireland, a change in the conduct of the war. A period of 'reactive containment' was over. Reactive containment was the first phase of the Northern Ireland conflict; it lasted six years from 1969 to 1975 and was, as Kieran McEvoy and Peter Shirlow describe, 'characterised by the state's need to react to the outbreak of political violence' or to get, as they bluntly put it, 'the enemy off the streets'. Suspects were simply removed from the theatre of conflict into jails, ships and camps of which Long Kesh was the largest. 'The prisons' were, they note, 'one element in an overall counter insurgency strategy'.[1] Imprisonment was increasingly important in the next phase, from 1976, known as either 'criminalisation' or 'normalisation'. Both terms capture something of the political strategy of reducing war to violence and occupation to governance exemplified by the transfer of military command from army to the police.[2] If there was no war, there could no prisoners of war. Normalization was pursued through criminalization, the depoliticization of imprisonment. Special category status was now anachronistic, a reminder of state recognition of political actions in a penal system that no longer differentiated between criminal and conflict-related offences. The H Blocks were the material form of a new political strategy, the re-ordering of the collective incarceration of an enemy into the individual treatment of criminals.

Once housed according to political affiliation in shared and overcrowded dormitories, sentenced prisoners would now inhabit a single cell. It was the cells of the H Blocks that distinguished the new jail from the old. They were the reason for its existence. The compounds of Long Kesh internment centre were not only packed with internees and sentenced prisoners, all were held together as political groups. Republicans and loyalists were allocated compounds and they, for the most part, controlled the space within them. Military training took place in the compound yards while the Nissen huts reserved as canteens were used as forums for political education. Separation into cells would begin a process of political disengagement, the republican or loyalist prisoner detached from his organization. Cells were the solution, a material form of isolation: their walls would prevent contact between prisoners. Within them, prisoners would feel no other influence than that of the prison. Any action for which they were imprisoned, perhaps making or throwing a Molotov cocktail, maybe holding or using a gun, could no longer be a shared experience of a collective, but explicable as their own deed. The cell assumed an individual who had committed a crime.

Cells are the basic unit of modern penal architecture (Figure 2.5). Since the late eighteenth century, cells have been the foundation of all prison design, not only of the Panopticon. Cells exert a physical and moral force. Solitude ensured by complete separation in a cell was widely understood to encourage self-reflection, repentance and reform. Pentonville, a radial prison much copied from

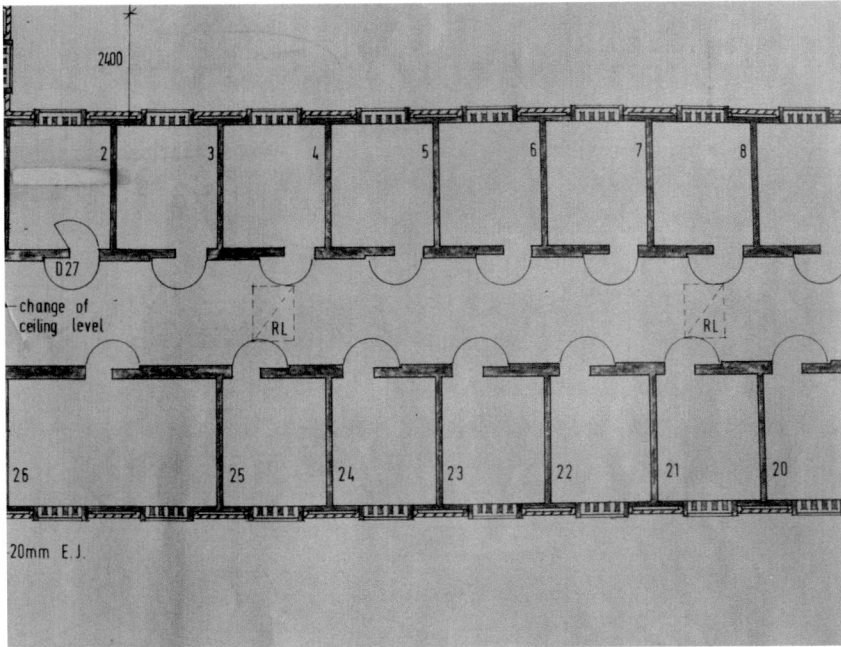

FIGURE 2.5 *Cells, detail from 'H Block plan'. Photograph: Louise Purbrick.*

the moment it opened in 1842, 'embodied the separatist principle'.[3] Prisoners slept in their cells, worked within them, lived in silence and wore masks in the presence of others in order to preserve their anonymity and maintain their isolation. Twentieth-century prison regimes, informed by sociological expertise rather than a mix of evangelical and Enlightenment ideas, seek prisoners' adjustment to society rather than their salvation.[4] With this shift from a reforming mission to a conforming project, restricted socialization was built into prison design: association rooms were attached to a series of cells. The attempt to produce a rehabilitative prison environment is evident, for example, in the design of the Maze as it is in the plans for Wrabness from which the design originated. New spaces were added to the prison as penal philosophies changed but cells remained as rooms for sleeping in and are still used as a technique of separation. Cells realize the separatist principle of simultaneously isolating one prisoner from another and the rest of society; they are held separately but together. As prisoners enter prison cells they are placed outside a community and rendered less able to establish their own identity whilst within the prison walls. Routine lock-up periods, especially those during the day, curtail social interaction and are also intended to regulate, if not control, collective life in the prison. Furthermore, enforced isolation and complete removal of the limited physical freedoms within prison is a punishment, called 'cellular confinement' or simply solitary.

A body may be forced into a cell but the wearing of a uniform is a matter of continual consent. Kieran Nugent was 'locked naked in a cell for three days'.[5] Ned Flynn, sentenced shortly after him, remembers the moment the cell door 'slammed shut' following his removal of all his clothes and by his declaration that he was a political prisoner. He was isolated on an empty wing.[6] Whilst these men were pushed into the space of the cell, they refused to occupy that of the uniform, demonstrating that they did not agree to live within the prison as its architects, in all senses of that word, intended. The plainness of a prison uniform divests the wearer of the assertiveness of personality and previous political allegiance. Putting it on is a physical submission to the prison authority; it is to be incorporated. As such, it would, for republicans, amount to a resignation of their Irish political identity and announce the end of their resistance to British rule. Those demanding recognition as political prisoners announced they 'would not be wearing any prison uniform'.[7] Some stated 'I'm not wearing it' or declared they were 'not putting the gear on'[8] as they entered the reception area of administration building where there were cubicles for undressing: 'six boxes and inside the boxes was a changing area'.[9] Sometimes this declaration was made when they were taken to the entrance of the H Block, which led into an area called the 'circle', the rectangular junction of the Block's four wings. Their verbal and physical refusal immediately instigated a confrontation with the prison; it was met with violence from prison officers characteristic of their response to the protest as it continued. Jackie McMullan, sentenced in November 1976, remembers being put into a cubicle and told to 'hurry up and get the uniform on'. His announcement that he 'wasn't going to wear it' was ignored and he kept his own clothes on until arriving in H2. Encircled by 'seven or eight' prison officers he was beaten then, 'right there in front of them' and ordered to undress. 'I stripped down to my underclothes, but they insisted I take everything off. I did.'[10]

Building and dwelling

How, then, did republican prisoners, with only their undressed bodies, take hold of the structures that were supposed to suppress them? How did the H Blocks come to belong to them? That republican prisoners had inhabited Long Kesh/Maze haunts all deliberations upon its development. It is their building. Explaining such an affinity, attachment, even ownership, one that has outlasted an actual physical presence, requires some reflection upon historical, human and material relationships. It begs the question of how any space comes to belong to anybody. What happens to architecture as it is inhabited or, to be more pertinent, when a prisoner is sent to a prison? What does the building become?

This is not quite the right question, at least not for the theorist of the ecology of architecture, Tim Ingold, because it assumes the building was finished before it was occupied. 'Environments', Ingold observes, 'are never complete but are continually under construction'.[11] Things take their shape through the process of their life rather than according to plan. For him, building is dwelling; thus he acknowledges the writings of Martin Heidegger and Maurice Merleau-Ponty, amongst others, as sources for his re-working of architecture. He summarizes: 'it is through being inhabited, rather than through its assimilation to a formal design specification, that the world becomes a meaningful environment for people'.[12] Ingold's 'dwelling perspective' is brought to bear upon the entire human to environment relationship, rethinking the differences between, for instance, nests and homes, trees and houses, which all demonstrate the untidy borders of human and animal existences. I work with it more narrowly. His perspective, both a relational and a materialist rendering of dwelling, has allowed me to think about how architectural forms emerge and to ask: who built the H Blocks? When narrow lines on the thin paper of an architectural drawing are translated into thick hard walls, a building has barely begun. A building and building, like a dwelling and dwelling, is something that is happening. Ingold insists that it is in the 'practical engagement with the components of their surroundings, that form is generated'.[13] Re-working architecture, rejecting the final duality of an idea imposed upon material opens up space for the consideration of the process, struggle even, that occurs between idealization and materiality, between political projection and architectural existence, between a prison plan and imprisonment.

Ingold's arguments might at first appear difficult to apply to any prison since prison forms are supposed to be a pure expression of their plans. A prison's architectural system is its penal system and thus its operation is dictated by its design, the routines of prison life are determined before a prisoner enters into them.[14] Furthermore, Ingold envisages the generation of form as collaborative and mutually constructive, whereas the architectural relationships of Long Kesh/Maze, as indeed all jails, are characterized by violence and inequality. '[T]he forms people build' he argues, 'arise within the current of their involved activity, in the specific relational contexts of their practical engagement with their surroundings.'[15] Jails are not an obvious example of the creativity of dwelling, for a prison is imposed upon a person who becomes its prisoner: a body is forced into being in this world. In its simplest form, a prison is an act and structure of restraint. Stubborn walls ranged against more malleable and once mobile bodies is not a mutual arrangement, physically or politically. The reinforced concrete that comprised the H Block cells and marked out the phases and perimeter of Long Kesh/Maze were forms of British intervention and occupation of Ireland, designed to manage opposition to British authority and legitimacy; they instil compliance, seek consent through coercion, to borrow words from Italian Marxist Antonio Gramsci composed while he walked within his own prison cell.[16] The 'specific relational contexts' of Long Kesh/Maze were a series of physical and material conflicts between the tissues of human body and fabrics of the prison: heavy cotton, reinforced concrete and numerous metal barriers. Prisoners' 'practical engagement' with 'their surroundings' took the form of daily struggles with the architecture of the prison and the prison officers, who enforced its order. Whilst these engagements were confrontational, not collaborative, they were no less constructive. In fact, Ingold's idea of building provides a very good starting point for a history of a jail that from the very outset was prevented from operating according to its architectural plan.

The rules of clothing

The design of Maze Cellular, its cell blocks in the shape of an H, were built to enable prison authorities to hold sway over prisoners, to make it possible to operate a conventional prison, to implement its penal regime, that is, to follow the Prison Rules. Its spaces were to institute the regular relationships of incarceration based upon prisoners' adherence to the prison, repeatedly demonstrated by enacting the routines prescribed by its rules. These are daily lessons in the benefit of punishment, encouraging individual acceptance of not only the wrongfulness of the act for which they are imprisoned but the way of life of which that act was a part. Routines and rules seek to supplant oppositional habits with a culture of conformity practised in preparation for the moment of release. The work of reforming a character that took place in the eighteenth-century prison cell has been recast over two centuries as conforming to society. This is known, of course, as rehabilitation, to restore to living a normal life.

According to the Prison Rules in operation in Northern Ireland in the mid-1970s, male prisoners 'shall wear' clothing supplied by the prison and 'no other'.[17] Non-compliance was a breach of these rules; the failure to maintain the appropriate appearance was dealt with as an 'offence against discipline', setting in chain a series of 'charges': loss of all privileges, loss of fourteen days remission and the 'award of three days solitary confinement'. Punishment cells, known as 'the boards' because their concrete seat and bed were covered only with boards, located along the perimeter wall behind H1 and H2, were dedicated for solitary confinement with a restricted diet: bread and water. But as protesting republican prisoners consistently refused to wear the uniform and the punishments were continually applied, solitary confinement was so regularly awarded to increasing numbers of prisoners that it was imposed within the cell. All furniture was removed for three days to approximate the conditions of the punishment blocks. Notwithstanding this periodic formalization of the solitary confinement, spending 'almost the whole of everyday'[18] in a cell was routine. It was the effect of always being on a 'charge' for prisoners' incorrect appearance that resulted of loss of privileges and rights. Protesting prisoners had no weekly visits or daily exercise nor did they undertake prison work. They refused to work but their state of undress banned them from doing so anyway. The cell become the site of the republican H Block experience.

For protesting prisoners, the prison comprised a regime of unrelenting restraint. Their freedom within the prison, an equivalent to their range of movement, was limited to its smallest unit of space. Punishments extended the penal principle of separation: cellular and solitary confinement increased the isolation of imprisonment and reduced the already limited distractions of incarceration, enclosing prisoners in bare nothingness. But continuous cellular confinement also ensured that they were not integrated into prison routines; they were able to control their own time, which afforded them a different kind of freedom to that of movement through space. Rather than frightening prisoners into adhering to or conforming to the regime, the removal of traces of everyday existence encourages prisoners to withdraw into their own internal world. '[R]un your favourite memories through your head' as Felim O'Hagan put it.[19] Conscious acts of remembering, calling up moments of a past that project a personal history in a space intended to deny assertions of identity, is not unique to republican prisoners of Long Kesh/Maze. For example, a long-term inmate of Fresne, France, described how he learnt to 'use the memory as a book'.[20] However, for republican prisoners, who regarded individual punishments as shared hardships, their internal world was collective as well as personal. They inhabited space and overcame time together.

Materiality and resistance

Over the period of heightened H Block struggles from 1976 to 1981, the cells were transformed by republican prisoners into sites of resistance. They, furthermore, occupied their cells in ways that reshaped the prison. Its authority, the Northern Ireland Prison Service, attempted to manage the protest and its increasing numbers by separating conforming prisoners from those who rejected the regime. The effect was whole H Blocks housed only protesting prisoners. One entire phase of three blocks, H3, H4, and H5, containing a total of 300 cells, was 'on protest' with many prisoners doubled up in single cells.[21] Maintaining a collective protest radically revised the architecture of the H Blocks; it reorganized its divisions of cells. A cellular structure intended to create individual spaces for an undifferentiated mass of criminal subjects now separated conforming from non-conforming prisoners, instituting a political division. Within the Blocks that were 'on protest', individual cells were collectively occupied. Protesting republican prisoners adopted similar, if not the same, physical appearance. They dressed in two blankets: one twisted around their waist another around their shoulders. A third was folded over on floor to provide a pavement for their bare feet on the cold concrete. They become known as the Blanket Men. The Blanket Men moved as a unified body, sometimes spontaneously and sometimes in a more orchestrated fashion. A year into the protest, they all grew beards. Beards were a collective response to the instruction to shave in their cells rather than in the communal bathrooms. Prison officers were trying to control and restrict numbers using bathrooms and ordered prisoners to wash and shave in their rooms: their response was not to shave at all.

Once republican prisoners were housed together, they re-established their own command structures. Both the Provisional Irish Republican Army (IRA) and the Irish National Liberation Army (INLA) had a political leadership and military staff: each wing had an OC (Officer Commanding) and an Adjutant ('whose role really only came into operation when the OC was taken off to the 'Boards'[22]). The part played by the leadership in coordinating movements of resistance is made clear in former prisoners' accounts of collective action. When Felim O'Hagan joined the protest in April 1978, he remembers that there were still beds in the cells. But only days after he arrived 'it was decided we should break the glass in the spy hole of the cell door. We smashed it with the bed ends on the Saturday night – next morning the screws came in and that was the last we saw of the beds.'[23] Others describe the anticipation of the moment 'when the order came', when 'we got the order' or when 'word came back'[24] to smash furniture and utensils. Acting together and in numbers, prisoners created another spatial organization within the prison.

Collective action that took place within the separate and enclosed space of the cell was dependent upon systems of communication between cells, wings, blocks and 'outside'. The systems that prisoners developed both circumvented the architecture of the prison and penetrated its barriers, creating pathways for the passage of messages and objects, alternative routes for words and things. Prisoners stood at the locked cells doors and shouted; they also banged on the heating pipes that ran along the base of the exterior wing walls and through each cell. Many spent hours 'at the pipes'. Speaking close up to them carried their voices into the neighbouring cell. Plaster filled holes around the pipes were scratched out to improve the sound. However, it was forms of writing, tiny biro script on cigarette papers or the shiny prison-issue toilet paper called 'comms' that have been described as the 'lifeblood' of the Blanket protest.[25] These notes were smuggled on and in the bodies of prisoners; they were pressed into their mouths, noses or anuses. Smuggling was facilitated by supportive or bribed conforming prisoners and greatly extended in 1978 when, after eighteen months without contact with their families, prisoners used their right to half-hour monthly visits for which they covered themselves with prison-issue trousers and jackets. Typically, a parcel or 'beart' of tobacco along with the inside of biros, pencil leads, cigarette papers and comms tightly wrapped in cling film would be passed between prisoners and their relatives then distributed within the wings. This contraband was shared through prisoners' systems, through their alternative architecture of communication and distribution. Ned Flynn describes two ways of moving objects between cells. The first was called 'swinging the line':

> We tore a strip of blanket about 6 foot long and half an inch wide. On one end we tied a dead weight – a bar of soap or a tube of toothpaste – to give enough power to get a swinging action. We put it out of the window and the man in the next cell to put his hand out. Then we started swinging. When he grabbed the dead weight, the stuff – anything from a religious magazine to tobacco – was tied to the other end of the line.[26]

There was a similar principal to the second method, 'shooting the line', which enabled things to move between opposite cells, across the wide corridor of wing, space known as the landing:

> It consisted of a button taken from a prison shirt and 10–15 feet of fine wool which was used to stitch the top of the prison blankets. We tied one end of the wool onto the button. At the bottom of every cell door was a small gap through which the button would pass. It was then flicked with a plastic comb, making it shoot across the wing with the string travelling behind. After a couple of attempts we always managed to get it close enough to the cell opposite for the man in the cell to be able to fish it in using a folded mass sheet as a hook.[27]

Exploiting and enlarging the small gaps in doors and fractures between doors and walls, the architecture of the H Blocks looked different. The view from the cell sees the cracks rather than the continuous shapes of restraint. The prison architecture of Long Kesh/Maze was manipulated into another form.

Cell and body: Collective, individual, personal

The H Blocks are well-known for walls smeared with excrement. The names H Block, Maze and perhaps even Long Kesh, conjure up cells covered in shit for many people who do not know or cannot recall any details of the H Block struggles. The so-called 'dirty protest' had a profound and lasting effect on political imaginations to become what could be called a collective memory. Republicans reject the label 'dirty' and use the more neutral 'no-wash' to describe an uncomfortable practice which, like wearing nothing but a blanket, was a collective action conditioned by the daily confrontations with prison officers. The 'no-wash phase' is explained as both a response to their increasing 'brutality' and as a decision by the republican leadership to 'intensify the form of protest' because there had been no sign that the demands for their own clothes and the restoration of political status were about to be met.[28]

The cells were cleaned many times during the protest and their walls were painted and repainted many times after it was over, yet they were irrevocably altered by the coatings of human faeces. Prisoners made their mark on the walls and in so doing exerted bodily and material control over the space of the cell, which also extended out into the H Blocks. Entire wings covered in excrement were not easily made subject to prison officers' command; they were difficult, even disgusting, spaces within which to work. Protesting prisoners had produced an environment inhospitable for themselves but also for others; they had transformed cells into spaces that were strange to prison officers and estranged from the prison.

Blanket men did not plan to break proximity taboos, putting their bodies in their own waste, polluting themselves; their participation in an abnormal practice followed the logic of resistance to the imposition of a normal order. The good running of the prison was displayed through the clean, tidy cell. Just like the requirement to appear tidy and in uniform, as stated in the Prison Rules, cells were supposed to be kept clean. Conforming prisoners were subjected to cell inspections that imposed the authority of the prison officers in the individual prisoner's space. The no-wash protest abandoned the most basic cleaning routines. 'It began with refusing to brush and mop out our cells', writes Jaz McCann. 'The following week, we refused to wash, then we refused a clean sheet change.' And, as Kevin Campbell explains: 'After a few weeks of not slopping out or brushing out, the cells become filthy. Rotten food was piling up in the corners.' An attempt by prison officers to clear one group of cells of tables, chairs, lockers and presumably clean the emptied space brought about the destruction by prisoners of all furniture. '[W]e wrecked up and put everything out the windows.'[29] The windows themselves were broken to release fumes of disinfectant sprayings carried out while cells were occupied. Only a mattress, blankets, chamber pot and water gallon remained.

Then, prisoners refused to slop-out; they poured urine under the doors; prison officers brushed it back in; prisoners used their rotten food to make dams at the doorsills to prevent it flowing back in. Maggots bred. Prisoners pushed maggots under the doors onto the wing or flung them out of the windows. They threw their faeces out of the windows. Prison officers threw it back in. 'We decided to stop throwing it out of the windows. And seeing that we couldn't let it lie in the cells, we had no other option but to put it on the cell walls.'[30]

One recurring interpretation of the no-wash protest is as a form of self-abasement, a self-inflicted state of degradation,[31] but it may be better understood as a withdrawal into the cell. The refusal to follow any prison routine meant that life was reduced to the fact of incarceration: just the restricting walls, just the cell. From 1978 to 1981, H Blocks were little more than dungeons. Yet, at the same time, in the battle within the jail that began two years earlier and ended with the Hunger Strikes, the cell was a place of safety. Being inside a cell, notwithstanding that it would be, of course, always locked from outside, provided some respite from the initial confrontation over the refusal to dress in prison clothing and the ordeal of moving through spaces controlled by prison officers. Prisoners joining the protest were made 'to run a gauntlet to the cell'.[32] Throughout their protest, prisoners were more vulnerable outside their cells. Beyond them, they were not permitted to wear their blankets. Regulations about fabrics of the cell remaining within it, was enforced at the outset. The prisoner's resolve not to wear a 'convict's uniform' was constantly tested, especially in the first few months following the opening of the H Blocks when there were relatively few protesting prisoners within them. Whenever they used the bathrooms, collected their food, slopped out, went to Mass or upheld their right to exercise, they did so naked. The cell offered protection. It was, Felim O'Hagan states, 'our whole world, a concrete cube of a womb outside of which all was hostile. Wing shifts, going to mass or the doctor were times of nakedness, psychologically as well as physically'.[33] Being naked in front of prison officers was, in the words of many prisoners, humiliating: 'this was all humiliation';[34] 'I was burning with humiliation'; 'we had to undergo the humiliation of having to leave our cells naked to do the things which were essential to our day-to-day living'. Loss of power and dignity have long been associated with disrobing; to have clothes removed is to be put down. Dress is a defence that is simultaneously political, physical and emotional. Without it, a person seems unguarded, too easily visible, as if skin is not surface enough. 'There's an awful feeling of defencelessness when you're standing naked in front of people who are hostile to you.'[35]

When the numbers of republican prisoners 'on protest' had reached thirty, they refused to leave their cells naked and, after a four-day confrontation, were allowed to use a towel to cover themselves when they were outside their cells. The towel offered something of the defence of dress but still there was markedly different bodily experiences without blankets beyond the cell. On the routes to and from the cells, as described by O'Hagan, prisoners were more exposed, both physically and politically, to the power of the prison. They had to face large groups of prison officers as they were moved through each separate space of the H Block. It was monthly visits and wing shifts that interrupted the safety of their cell. Monthly visits were held in a separate building, closer to the administrative complex of Long Kesh/Maze. Prisoners were taken to a double cell, numbered 26, at the top of the wing, where prison trousers and jackets, worn as a condition of the visit and only for its duration, were kept; then, they were escorted through the metal grille air-lock gate leading onto the circle and into a prison van. Wing shifts, a practice of periodical steam cleaning the no-wash cells, involved the transfer of an entire wing, twenty-four single cells often containing two prisoners, to another wing in the same H Block. They were moved cell by cell. In both cases and in every space, but especially cell 26, prisoners were subjected to beatings and body searches. Anal searches for contraband were both confrontational and degrading. Laurence McKeown states that this was their primary purpose.[36]

Being exposed to the prison's power was not just a matter of the increased visibility and consequent individualization of the prisoner's body; that body was open to attack. More immediately brutal than any controlling effect of architecture, the punches and kicks of a beating also individualize. Pain, particularly that inflicted as punishment, intrudes upon the integrity of a person, humiliating and isolating as it does so. The internal nature of pain isolates a person in their body. It is not accurate, however, to argue that outside the cell prisoners were constituted as individuals while inside they were a collective. Although the symmetry of this reversal of prison's architectural plan is rather appealing, prisoners also understood themselves to be a collective body inside and outside the cell.

Republican prisoners describe the physical movements of a search as forced upon a body that is both personal and collective. A rough physical examination is inflicted upon their own bodies but anonymous body parts, which could belong to any republican, are also subjected to this search:

> Arms twisted up my back, legs in the air, head banged off the table, hands probing my buttocks and anus, all to their laughter and jeers. Ears, nose and mouth searched with the same hands, my towel thrown on the floor between two lines of screws, having to run the gauntlet to recover my towel and to hide my nakedness and suffer the beating for it.[37]

Here, Joe McQuillan is recalling the techniques of the table search, which he relates 'grew more savage over the summer of 1978 and was replaced by mirror search 'around November'. His account of this new method positioned a collective body pushed through a violent choreography:

> now at the search point we were asked to squat down over the mirror. We would only stand straddling it, but refused to squat. Our arms would then

be jerked out and back, our legs kicked from below us sending us crashing to our knees, all the while being punched and insulted.[38]

Republican prisoners lived collectively in their individual bodies. They inhabited their bodies in much the same way as they inhabited their cells. From the moment of entry into the prison, they were engaged in a struggle for control over the space they occupied; they fought the enclosure of their bodies within a uniform and redefined the isolation of the cell. Body and cell became sites of resistance to prison authorities. Acts of resistance were coordinated, prisoners responded as part of a larger body; individual and individualizing sites of the body and cell were recreated as collective spaces. Thus, Ingold's 'dwelling perspective', which holds that form is 'generated' through 'practical engagement' with 'surroundings', applies to the body as well as the cell, to the architecture and the person that occupies the architecture. It could be said, then, that republican prisoners dwelt in their bodies as they dwelt in their cells. Cell and body could be considered in Ingold's terms as forms: materials albeit with different properties; soft but resilient flesh, hard but ultimately impressionable concrete are entangled together. The collectivization of both body and cell reveals how neither are inevitably individual, despite their confining designs, but nor were they always collective.

The limited distractions in a cell exposes the matter of existence, draws attention to the act of living in your own body: there is little else except being there. The cell focused attention on the body and it became the centre of the blanket and no-wash protest. The latter, in particular, made the act of living difficult and uncomfortable, or in the words of prisoners: 'awful', 'degrading', 'disgusting'.[39] Peadar Whelan recalled:

The Blanket was full of crises, which were mainly personal. Putting shit on the wall was one such personal crisis. We stopped using the toilet early on in the protest. We used the chamber pots and slopped the contents out into a bucket which the screws brought around the cells. I disliked that. I think it is because going to the toilet is a very personal thing and so slopping a pot out in front of an audience made it public. To me it was an embarrassment. Despite the inevitability of putting shit on the walls, it wasn't any less a conflict of conscience; after getting over all the taboos we still had to come to terms with living and eating in a small cell covered in shit.[40]

I do not want to force an interpretation on this frank account of the difficulties of the no-wash protest but would like to suggest that Peadar Whelan, with remarkable openness, is describing a struggle within himself, between his person and his body. Participating in the no-wash protest threatened the sense of propriety around which personhood is often created. Cleaning your body is a regular, usually daily, practice for most people, a routine repeatedly performed to ensure recognition as an appropriate person. Carried out in private, it prepares the body for public view and protects the person from intrusion.[41] Every layer of excrement that a prisoner added to his cell wall was an act of solidarity with others on the no-wash protest but exposing bodily waste matter made his person vulnerable. In one paragraph with its shifting pronouns, 'we stopped', 'we used', 'I disliked' and 'to me', Peadar Whelan describes how both collective identities and personal feelings were embodied in the blanket and no-wash protest. As a collective and as a person, these were different ways that prisoners dwelt in their cells and were different ways of dwelling in their bodies.

Cultures of resistance: Smells and sounds

Safety within the cell was affected by who controlled the wing landings. There was a varying pattern of occupation by prison officers of the corridors outside the cell. Prisoners spent little time outside their cells; they were hastily, and usually violently, moved along the landings. But, whilst the no-wash protest took place within the confines of the cell, its effect was not contained by its shitty walls; the protest seeped into the wing. It smelt. One young prisoner, sixteen years old when he arrived in the H Blocks described how the smell 'hit me right in the face', adding 'it was like walking into an invisible wall'.[42] The smell was a manifestation of an unmanageable jail, the emanation of disorder. Movement along the wing could be identified by smell. As one prisoner explained: 'The screws often gave themselves away by their aftershave and soap.'[43]

Sound was as telling as smell, if not more so, and specific noises functioned as warnings. 'When the footsteps of the screws were heard approaching and the cell keys rattling, we knew we were in for a hard time'[44] recalled Joe McQuillan. He identified other two other fearful sounds:

> We now came to dread the sound of the table being dragged across the concrete floor. Our stomachs churned and we literally shit ourselves, then smeared it on the walls as quickly as possible before the screws opened the doors for the move. The wait was the worst, a shift could last an hour and if you were left to last it meant having to listen to 44 men being beaten.[45]

Hearing the pain of others is a recurring theme of prisoners' testimony. 'By the time they came to your cell you were nearly glad to get it over with. It is worse sitting listening and waiting for your turn.'[46] Just as smells leaked out so sounds invaded the cell, penetrated through its walls. Sounds and smells along the wings were a register of control over the H Block as well as the safety within the cells. Prisoners used both in the struggle over the space of cell, wing and block. Smells powerful enough to ward off intrusion may have been an unintentional effect of the no-wash protest while sound was more deliberately exploited. The entry of a prison officer onto a wing was greeted with noise: banging 'piss pots'[47] or shouting. Those at the top of the wing, in the cell nearest the air lock that separated one wing from another and both from the 'circle', were strategically placed to pass on calls to action, 'sin é', or shout warnings, such as 'bear in the air',[48] preparing prisoners for the arrival of prison officers. When the confrontation that inevitably followed was over, after the cell search, body search or beating had ended, prisoners reclaimed the space with noise. Joe McQuillan describes the sounds following a wing shift:

> As the last cell door closed, everyone in the wing banged on their doors: no orders, no directives, pure spontaneity, then someone would sing and most the wing would join in. Bawling out the likes of 'Provos March On' finishing with wild cheers and yells getting rid of the built-up tension and aggression. The screws would be raging.[49]

In the evenings, at the close of the prison officers' last shift of the day, once again sound exerted prisoners' control over the wing. Republican prisoners developed an oral culture comprising political debate, accounts of Irish history, Irish language lessons (*ranganna Gaeilge*), storytelling, song and prayer. Kevin Campbell recalls how: 'All the lads would pull their mattresses to the door and settle there for the night.'[50] Physical difficulties are absent from the accounts of H Block evenings. The damp dams of urine sodden rotting foods piled up by the cell doors seemed to disappear as prisoners entered the evening soundscape and escaped from the immediacy and individuality of body and cell.

Oral culture of the H Blocks was collective not only in the sense that many men were doing the same thing at the same time, they were listening and taking turns to speak or sing, but also because the songs, stories and Irish lessons were collectively created. One prisoner might be 'called to the door'[51] to help entertain the wing with a performance of a song, such as those written by Simon and Garfunkel, The Eagles, Harry Nilsson or Don McLean,[52] which had been remembered by many prisoners. The attempt to reproduce the song with accuracy, recreated it from a shared knowledge of popular music, a collected, and collective, memory of words repeated over the radio or on vinyl record players. 'A lot of the songs sung were close to the originals. Different blokes would know bits and pieces and put them together like jigsaw puzzles', explains McQuillan.[53] While some contributions to the evening sounds matched what is often considered an oral tradition, 'yarns about the country',[54] most were an appropriation of a contemporary form.[55] Forging songs from memories of popular rather than traditional tunes were repeated with stories. Entire books were 'told'. Sean Lennon describes how his cell mate, Bobby Sands, 'told' a book:

> One of the yarns made famous was the time Bobby told us the book 'Trinity' (by Leon Uris) out the door. It was while we were in H6 and it took him about four weeks to put it together – it was worth it at the end of the day. Bobby was a perfectionist and to ensure he got it right he asked the lads in the conforming wing which was facing us to help him in his research. He shouted across the yard to them at night with certain questions and if they didn't have the answers he asked them to find out the following day from the lads they worked with in the workshops. This went on until he was ready and it took him three or four weeks to cover it – that was spending two to three hours nightly at the door.[56]

More famously, Irish language teaching was pieced together in much the same way: remembered fragments of spoken and taught Irish were re-assembled and shared. Republican prisoners collectively recalled and revived a suppressed indigenous language. The revival of Gaelic in Northern Ireland can be traced to the prisoners of Long Kesh/Maze.[57] Participation in the soundscape of the H Blocks provided another way of dwelling collectively in a single body and small cell. At the door, their bodies faced outwards, and the cell receded. Pooling remembered song lyrics and storylines, sharing out cultural inheritances, they drew their lives together, creating a common history.

Building resistance

In prisoners' accounts of the sounds of the H Blocks every word is heard. The concrete walls offer no barrier at all. The composition of memory,[58] the processes of which republicans were aware in the midst of the H Block struggle, will be at work here, as Felim O'Hagan explained: '"When this is all over, we'll remember only the good bits." That's what we used to tell each other during the Blanket and in a way it's true.'[59] Certainly, the filth of the cell vanished from recollections of comradeship and 'craic' but perhaps hardships faded in moments of collective participation rather than only later in memory. For the architecture of the H Blocks was materially, really, defeated; it is not just remembered that way.

The transformation of the prison began as soon as it was inhabited by republicans seeking to uphold their 'special category' status and retain recognition of their political identity as prisoners; its normalizing cellular structure was appropriated, overcome, altered and ultimately built again by prisoners living in the cells, often as a collective body, but always without prison uniforms and without adherence to prison rules or routines. The H Blocks were formed through 'current of their involved activity' to borrow Ingold's words once again.

The battles over spaces of the H Blocks, which took place from 1976 to 1981 and culminated in the Hunger Strikes, produced the conditions in which they were inhabited during the rest of the lifetime of Long Kesh/Maze: the wings were run by prisoners' political organizations with their political affiliations declared on the walls in murals and slogans. The physical and material spaces of the body and cell continued to belong to prisoners. On 6 October 1981, three days after the end of the Hunger Strikes, all were entitled to wear their own clothes and, in the following weeks, the collective culture of the Blocks was formalized with periods of free association. Eventually cell doors were unlocked twenty-four hours a day. However, prisoners had never required open doors to communicate with each other and used the freedoms within the jail that gradually increased following from their protest to take control of a greater amount of space and take possession of greater number of things, both newly legitimized objects as well as continuing contraband, significantly expanding the forms of material exchanges within the wings and blocks. The oral culture of protesting republican prisoners became a literate one. Books required for Open University courses and others received from solidarity movements were gathered into a lending library, dominated by texts of revolutionary theory from both a European Marxist tradition or informed by national liberation and anti-colonial struggles (Figure 2.6).[60] The H Block struggle was not, of course, influenced by writings that prisoners did not read until it after it was over; it was shaped, as I have tried to argue here, by the materiality of imprisonment. It was built as it was dwelt in, as it was occupied. Re-occupation might capture the process slightly better. Republican prisoners did not abide in their allotted position as criminal or conforming subjects: they lived outside the prison rules even while contained in its walls. The whole five years of the H Block struggle could be considered as the withdrawal of consent, a continuous resistance to the operation and legitimatization of state authority as analysed by Antonio Gramsci, whose writings, were first studied by prisoners in David Held's 1983 Open University reader *States and Societies*.[61]

Withdrawal of consent began with a small act. Refusing to wear a particular kind of clothing pushed the prison powers, which were ultimately those of the British government, to reveal that the basis of their rule was nothing more sophisticated than force. Protesting prisoners drew the prison into open battle.

FIGURE 2.6 *Republican Prisoners' H Block lending library. Photograph: Louise Purbrick.*

Now exposed, republican prisoners had to face the effects of power: being alone, being beaten, being humiliated, being hungry, being naked and being in just their 'bare life'.[62] In so doing, they made visible the violence of the H Blocks and of the guards who attempted to uphold its order. With its coercive nature exposed, the prison was opened to political criticism. The blanket and no-wash protests were destructive actions that were also creative; the protest was an act of building that reduced architecture, which posed as house of rehabilitation, to the bare walls of restraint. Then the architecture was adapted, its arrangement irrevocably altered and its ownership appropriated. The prison no longer really belonged to those officially responsible for its design or daily operation but to fiercest opponents: republican prisoners.

3

The Global Witness and the Hunger Strike

The prison on the streets: symbolic struggles

On 29 July 1981, an open-top carriage moved slowly through Midtown Manhattan (Figure 3.1). Designed to be horse drawn, its long-maned shires were replaced by six young men. They were barefoot, bare chested and wrapped in blankets. They pulled a crowned and veiled wedding couple up Fifth Avenue. It was the day of Prince Charles and Lady Diana Spencer's marriage in St Paul's Cathedral followed by their triumphant royal procession of horse-drawn carriages and luxury cars through central London to Buckingham Palace. The heir to the British crown and his bride were seated in a State Landau pulled by four Windsor Grey horses. The swaying carriage pulled by people through New York's wide streets was a mockery of the British monarchy; the married couple seated in the open-top were two young men, long haired and bearded, like those that carried them. All were greeted by protesters banging bin-lids, the cacophony that warned of the arrival of the British Army into the catholic-nationalist areas of Belfast or Derry and, in the summer of 1981, announced the deaths of republican Hunger Strikers. This strange performance, staging the oppression of H Block prisoners by young men dressed to appear 'on the blanket' and bearing the burden of the British crown, was the centrepiece of a demonstration outside a British-American lunch at the Plaza Hotel to celebrate the royal couple. 'Outside, armed with colorful placards, rebel songs and angry chants, more than 500 protesters demonstrated that the allegiance and concern of Irish-Americans remained with Irish hunger strikers', claimed Noraid's (Northern Irish Aid) paper, *The Irish People*.[1] On the day of the Royal Wedding, eight H block prisoners were refusing food: Michael Devine, Matt Devlin, Kieran Doherty, Kevin Lynch, Paddy Quinn, Tom McElwee, Patrick McGeown, and Laurence McKeown. Six had already died on hunger strike: Bobby Sands, Frances Hughes, Raymond McCreesh, Patsy O'Hara, Joe McDonnell, and Martin Hurson.

Page 2 THE IRISH PEOPLE August 8, 1981

Thousands Of Protestors In New York Stand With Hunger Strikers

On July 29th, the bells of St. Paul's Cathedral in London pealed for four consecutive hours in celebration of the royal marriage.

On the streets of New York, the bells of Belfast—bin lids—scratched out their own protesting "good cheer" in a mock wedding ceremony alongside the Plaza Hotel on Fifth Avenue.

Inside the hotel, several British-American societies were attending a luncheon lauding their John Bull lineage. Outside, armed with colorful placards, rebel songs and angry chants, more than 500 protesters demonstrated that the allegiance and concern of Irish-Americans remained with Irish hunger strikers.

Staged by Irish Northern Aid and joined by several other metropolitan groups, the noontime demonstration garnered wide media coverage as well as the attention of the lunchtime New York business community.

The highlight of the demonstration was the unannounced and highly unregal arrival of the "royal" couple, seated in a Central Park hansom cab drawn by six blanket men. To the laughter of both passersby and demonstrators, a frustrated Prince Charles urged his "horses" to pull harder, while beside him, "Lady Di" waved effusively to her sidewalk subjects.

Following the Plaza demonstration, the "regal carriage" was drawn by its six protesting horses to the British Embassy on Third Avenue. In front of the carriage several young demonstrators sat on the street. One young demonstrator wore a T-shirt with the legend: "Ireland Unfree Shall Never Be At Peace — Free Ireland Now". Crash went the bin lids. Down Third Avenue canyon the bells of Belfast chimed. More than 2500 joined the demonstration, which was addressed by Dr. Martin Abend of Channel 5 television and New York City Councilman Thomas Manton.

Friday evening, after the death of hunger striker Kevin Lynch on his 71st day, seven caskets took up their dirgeful station at 845 Third Avenue, as a 24 hour vigil began which would remain.

On Saturday, the 115th day of the protest demonstrations, a line of 3500 demonstrators more than two city blocks long marched around the seven caskets. In front of the seventh casket stood a vase with flowers.

Speakers at the Saturday rally included Tony Lynch, a cousin of Kevin Lynch. Said Tony Lynch: "The only reason Kevin was murdered was because he was Irish."

Dr. Martin Abend also addressed the crowd, saying that "what the hunger strikers are doing in the name of Irish unification, the British would not do for their own country if they had to." His remarks were greeted with loud cheers.

The rally concluded with remarks by Seamus Gibney, from the San Francisco Northern Aid Unit. "We have all three governments mad at us — the American government, the British government, and the Dublin government. We must be doing something right."

The crowd cheered, the honor guard stood at rigid attention, and the flowers in front of Kevin Lynch's casket bent low in the evening breeze.

The next day, Sunday demonstrators were saddened with news of yet another death. Kieran Doherty, on his 73rd day of test.

... hunger strike, had died. Immediately, an all-night vigil was announced for the eighth free-dom fighter. As we go to press, a memorial service is planned for Monday evening for Kevin Lynch.

In front of the British embassy, eight heavy wooden caskets pro-

Drawn by blanketmen, "Charles and Di" arrive at the Manhattan demo.

GOD SPARE US Don't Save

The pressure stays on as thousands march in protest.

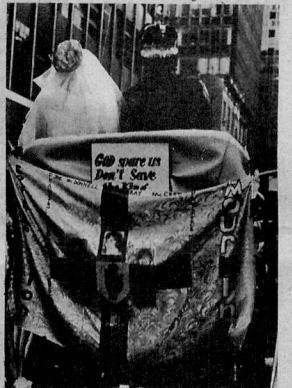

March, Write, Boycott - Support The Men On Hunger Strike!

Reprinted from *New York Post*

OUT OF ULSTER!   JOBS NOW!   IRA   ROT NOW   RELEASE HUNGER STRIKER   UNEMPLOYMENT   INFLATION

"Relax, we're all going to live happily ever after!"

FIGURE 3.1 'Hunger Strike supporters' Royal Wedding, New York', 'The voice of Irish Republicanism in America,' The Irish People, 8 August 1981. Courtesy of The Irish People Collection at the IUPUI University Library.

New York's protest against the British monarchy, or more precisely against the celebration of the continuing symbols of British state power as it was exerted against Irish republicans, was ignored by its mainstream national newspaper, *The New York Times*, while a report from London on the Royal Wedding itself took centre stage. The mimicry that took place not so very far from its midtown Manhattan office, a political performance of opposition to past and present colonial rule so effectively allegorized by the British crown, was ignored. *The New York Times*'s article was devoted to a discussion of the 'patriot festival spirit' as West End crowds waited for the newly wed Prince and Princess of Wales to pass by. Nevertheless, the H Blocks were still present in the reporting on the London landscape. Long Kesh/Maze prison, its concrete blocks on the boggy land of the Lagan Valley, a place quite remote from the cheering crowds of Pall Mall, loomed up in the piece by William Borders:

> Despite the cheery mood, security for the wedding procession was unusually tight, though discreetly so, a reminder of the grim reality that lies behind the fairy-tale world the wedding represented. One of the splendidly liveried footmen on Charles's horse-drawn carriage was in fact a policeman, and so was one of the Queen's. Policemen were posted on the tops of buildings, every few yards along the procession, surveying the crowd. . . . Security officials had been apprehensive about the possibility of some kind of disruption from Irish nationalist guerrillas, who killed Earl Mountbatten of Burma, Prince Charles's great uncle, two years ago, and who are currently conducting a hunger strike at Maze Prison near Belfast.[2]

In the long summer of 1981, the architecture of the H Blocks appeared in global spaces, in the streets of metropolitan capital cities and across the surfaces and shows of the international media. This chapter is concerned with how Long Kesh/Maze prison existed beyond its site, how it was made present as a form of power beyond its foundations, how resistance to its oppressive structures took place many miles from its walls. I ask how the space of the H Blocks manifested itself on streets many miles from their location. The meaning of architecture that can move in and out of its location is investigated here.

The witness and the symbol: the body and the building

This chapter does not re-tell the history of the 1981 Hunger Strikes, that most significant moment in the history of the H Blocks. No-one needs me to do this. That history has been told many times, and most importantly, told by its participants. The Hunger Strikes are the subject of the collective memory of republican communities. This chapter recalls a different history or the same history viewed differently; it considers what it meant to witness what happened inside the H Blocks in the summer of 1981. How did people outside its walls and further afield, far beyond Britain and Ireland, know the details of the lives and deaths of protesting republican prisoners? The punishment of prison is withdrawal from all routine social exchanges, including visual ones: cameras are prohibited in jails. But despite the limited visibility that accompanies all imprisonment compounded with the censorship of conflict in Northern Ireland, the 1981 Hunger Strikes were witnessed across the world.

My reflections upon how the protests in and against the H Blocks were seen in the late twentieth century are written in the context of the heightened importance of witnessing in the early twenty-first: global witnessing through the shared socially networked images is integral to political movements, most importantly those seeking justice from the racist legacies of colonialism and enslavement.[3] Digitized visual information shooting up to satellites then down across so many screens, simultaneously despite their geographical separation, has globalized both refugee solidarity and Black Lives Matter. The global witness, I would argue, occupies the same position that Edward Said attributed to the intellectual: 'a kind of countermemory, with its own counterdiscourse that will not allow conscience to look away or fall asleep'.[4] I also address another question relating to global witnessing. This is the symbolic work of political struggle. The H Block struggle inside Long Kesh/Maze and witnessed outside its walls was fought using symbols: representation was the site of struggle. The shape of the cell units of the H Blocks, the H, became a symbol of the brutality of British occupation in Ireland, and the figure of the hunger striker one of the humanity of resistance to that rule.

The power of the H Blocks was, and remains, both real and representational, material and symbolic. It is not that they were real to those incarcerated and representational to their witnesses; the architecture of the H Blocks is material and symbolic at the very same time. The H Blocks were the forms through which personal freedom and political rights were brought to a halt; their existence ended it. Any person sent to Long Kesh/Maze for any offence, a republican or a loyalist, for a conflict-related sentence or not, had their basic rights withdrawn. All prisons perform this function: freedom of movement and the freedom of political expression, both exercised in the collective assemblies that typify public protest, is withdrawn by restraining walls. For republicans, however, the idea of freedom was also suppressed through the structures of H Block. Their loss of rights was not an individual issue of temporarily restricted freedom but one of the collective freedom of political existence and political identity, the right to the self-determination of Ireland. The building of the H Blocks, an architecture representing the British occupation in Ireland, was the fiercest of the structures, military bases, police stations, the watchtowers and road blocks that stretched across its six most north-eastern counties. To be held within such a structure was a denial of collective political rights of nationality by a British authority; the prison was British power in a solid form: its concrete cells oppressed rights to nationhood as they occupied the land.

This is the context, the physical and political space, in which small details of imprisonment, such as what is worn, is part of larger demand for political rights. Such small details are always material and symbolic matters. The demands of the 1981 Hunger Strike were the same as the blanket and no-wash protests that preceded it: to wear their own clothes, to free association, weekly visits, weekly parcels and not to work. Taken together, these five demands would affect the return of 'special category' status: prisoners sentenced for conflict-related offences would be forcibly detained but not criminalized. The greater freedom associated with being remanded rather than sentenced within the jail allowed prisoners to manage their own time and maintain their organizational structures. But this internal battle about the place of republican prisoners within the prison system was also a rejection of the prison itself; the refusal of details of the imprisonment in the H Blocks demonstrated opposition to its regime as a whole. The material and symbolic significance of such details is best illustrated by the hunger strike that took place in the autumn of 1980, the first and far less famous hunger strike in the H Blocks, whose failure led to that of the summer of 1981. Seven republican prisoners started a fast on 27 October and, throughout December, were joined first by three women republicans imprisoned in Armagh, then by six loyalists – demanding segregation as well as the five existing republican demands – and then by thirty more republicans. On 18 December, as Sean McKenna, one of the initial seven, was close to death, an agreement that conflict-related prisoners could wear civilian clothes was reached. The hunger strike ended but the deal was rejected as soon as its details were known. The clothes were civilian in style only and issued by the prison: it was a choice of uniform but a uniform nevertheless. The style of prison-issue civilian clothing was no match for the dress codes of the youthful membership of the IRA and INLA but fashionable or revolutionary appearance was not the point of their refusal to wear a uniform. Only prisoners' own clothes could demonstrate the limits of the prison's authority over their person: they were not defined by the institution in which they were held; they did not belong there. The close attachment of clothing to the body ensures that the details of its fabric, its cut and colour, its shape and surface, are a most highly charged symbolic form: an articulation of status of all kinds including that described as political status by republican prisoners. Our own clothes carry our autonomy to the outside world. The symbolic order of clothing has tangible force in everyday encounters, sufficient to sustain or sometimes subvert social hierarchies. Dressing in clothes that came from lives before or beyond the prison disrupted the order within it. Their own clothes were an embodiment of autonomy that empowered prisoners against the prison regime and its enforcers, prison officers; they could continually show they had already disregarded one of its most important rules: the prisoner 'shall wear' clothing provided by the prison 'and no other'.[5]

Imogen Tyler's astute summary of power that 'regulates social life from within its most intimate interiors'[6] is at work in the H Blocks in similar ways to the wider 'neoliberal governmentality' that is her focus: the body is the site of political struggle; power is felt here, through the fibres and in the tissues of a person pushed aside or beaten down but resistance arises from the same place: bodies as sites of shared physical exclusion. The H Block Hunger Strikers understood the attempt to exercise power over their bodies, and the blanket and no-wash protest taught them the significance of their own physical forms as sites of resistance. They knew their bodies well; their material abilities and their symbolic force. Those that refused food over the summer of 1981 learnt from those that did so in the autumn of 1980; they knew about the different lengths of time it took different bodies to court death but also learnt to stagger a hunger strike to demonstrate the symbolic power that one body had to represent a collective struggle. The blanket protest, one of the longest prison protests to involve the largest number of prisoners, became focused on a few prisoners who chose to 'go on' hunger strike and did so through structures of their prisoner organizations, volunteering and awaiting selection. One body, which belonged to one person, Bobby Sands or Mickey Devine, Joe McDonnell or Kevin Lynch, came to represent the physical condition of all H Block prisoners and the political conditions of a global Irish diaspora. Their bodies become endowed with the lives and personhood of others: a material symbol of the Irish people. A body is a particularly powerful symbol of the people; it is a recognizable act of political representation, one person stands for the many, their human form is simultaneously analogous and allegorical, indicative and iconic.

Relatives: the route from the prison to the streets

Significant claims have been made about the international support for the H Block struggles. Civil rights campaigners and republican socialist group, People's Democracy, reflected upon its scope as the Hunger Strike continued through the summer of 1981. 'Perhaps the biggest and broadest solidarity movement since Vietnam.'[7] For the British political establishment of the 1980s, a Conservative government twinned with its Tory press, demonstrations of support for the Hunger Strikers were no more than signs of successful IRA propaganda.[8] Sinn Féin's ability to present the political nature of imprisonment in the H Blocks and British responsibility for their repressive regime through news channels and the international press, in particular, led to a debate about media coverage. The news reporting of the Hunger Strikes became a story in its own right that is now part of its historical record.[9] The BBC online GSCE revision site, Bitesize, states that they 'gained huge publicity'.[10] A rather petulant accusation that the small understaffed Sinn Féin office on the Falls Road was an IRA media machine, manipulating foreign journalists who were all too eager to bring Britain down, ultimately led to the 1988 Broadcasting Ban.[11] But the debate about the effect of the media missed the point about demonstrations of support for the Hunger Strikers: street protests are spontaneous actions. Freely, willingly and often determinedly, people gather in a public space. People are moved to come together. This is solidarity. However, naming the time and place of such gatherings does require some organization.

When Bobby Sands refused breakfast on the morning of 1 March 1981, a network of support from inside his H Block, H3, through the visit areas of Long Kesh/Maze to homes of family members, to the streets of Belfast and Derry, to the offices of different republican community groups and into the global media, was well established. The Relatives Action Committees and H Block/Armagh Committees initiated during the blanket protest were very important, an importance difficult to underestimate, in representing the spaces of confrontation inside Long Kesh/Maze to the world beyond its walls. An account of the organization of support for the Hunger Strikes helps us to understand how events within the prison were brought to public attention.

Stuart Ross has convincingly argued that a popular campaign and broad front, wider than the republican organizations to which the prisoners belonged, developed around conditions in the H Blocks.[12] The campaign preceded the Hunger Strikes. Relatives Action Committees were formed in 1976 to 'break the wall of silence surrounding the issue of the P.O.W.s fighting for political status'.[13] Of course, relatives of prisoners had familial and political ties to the republican organizations of their loved ones. Relatives Action Committees included members who were Sinn Féin and Irish Republican Socialist Party representatives but Committees remained 'semi-autonomous'[14] and helped create what Ross has identified as a popular campaign because, I would suggest, they redressed the masculinity of the armed struggle and opened out the opposition to the H Blocks, through a less exclusively gendered politics of prison support. Female relatives were prominent in the Relatives Action Committees; they were composed of 'wives, mothers and sisters'.[15] Relatives of H Block prisoners were affected by imprisonment, as all relatives of all prisoners at all times: the punishment of separation is imposed upon them with the prisoner's sentence. The separation of female relatives from male H Block prisoners was also accompanied by surveillance and harassment from security forces, by the fear and the reality of sectarian violence. The position of 'wives, mothers and sisters' was a structural part of the oppression of the prison regime but, along with that of the girlfriend, it was also strategic in its opposition. Female relatives used family visits with their male prisoners to gather news about worsening conditions inside the jail that was then deployed in the anti-H Block campaigns; they also smuggled tobacco, radios and cameras, occasionally, through the visitor search procedures despite the surveillance of prison officers. For Marie Moore, who led Sinn Fein's POW communications, the work of this 'network of women' was essential to getting information 'out of the jail' and 'to the public'.[16] They delivered the 'comms', the prisoners' writings with the inside of a biro on toilet paper, that sustained the information effort of Relative Action Committees and shaped the content of press releases to the media. The nature of women's role in the H Block struggle was always hidden and it has, to some extent, stayed that way.[17] This is despite the position of the female relative as an important political identity, publicly asserted on speaker's platforms and at street protests. Many women were also highly experienced activists in their own right. Some Relatives Action Committee members had a higher profile; they had been prisoners themselves in Armagh jail where female republicans, who had never lost the right to wear their own clothes, sustained a no-wash campaign to assert their own right to be recognized as political prisoners, to demonstrate their equality with republican men and in protest against the 'sexualised violence' of their prison.[18] Indeed, a 1980 *Irish Times* article by Nell McCafferty about the jailed women's protest, 'There is menstrual blood on the walls of Armagh jail in Northern Ireland', was one of the interventions, according to Stuart Ross, that contributed to the broadening of the movement against the H Blocks.[19]

That movement, it is routinely argued by politicians and historians, journalists and activists, began the journey from armed struggle to the peace process and is considered the turning point in the conflict in and about Northern Ireland.[20] Its significance is summarized as a huge structural intervention or structural shift: 'monumental' and 'seismic'.[21] My point is a little less grand: it was the Relatives Action Committees, and especially the female relatives of H Block prisoners, who caught hold of the force of the forms of imprisonment and carried them out from the high-walled prohibited site of *HMP Maze* into public spaces. Only the flat pale green roofs of the watchtowers could be seen through the windows of a car driving along the M1, but female relatives and activists articulated an architecture of repression, which had, and still has, restricted access; they made the H Blocks visible when they and those incarcerated within them had been removed from view.

The broad front of the Relatives Action Committees was formalized with the election of a National H Block/Armagh Committee, at an open conference in October 1979 involving feminist, anti-imperialist, civil rights and left and trade union groups; it became a more inclusive and expansive activist network. H Block/Armagh Committee 'action groups' spread across both sides of the border in Ireland[22] and were established in global cities with the twinned legacies of British colonialism and Irish migration, most notably, New York, Boston, San Francisco, Sydney, and Melbourne. Existing republican organizations, such as Noraid, played their part in these H Block Committees but the Committees were not theirs alone: it was a broad front that extended across the globe.

Noraid, formed in 1970 to fundraise for the Republican Movement and lobby for a United Ireland, was, argues Brian Hanley, itself transformed by the H Block protests. 'The 1980-81 hunger strikes saw a fundamental shift in the character of Noraid.'[23] It grew in size and scope to include established Irish Americans alongside the core membership of recent Irish migrants with close connections to republicanism in Northern Ireland. It adapted its lobbying techniques to the prison struggle, for example, arranging a speaking tour for Kieran Nugent, the first blanket man, which captured much media attention when he was arrested by US immigration officials as he was about to give a press conference.[24] Courting publicity, creating what is now called a 'media narrative', was a new Noraid strategy that both departed from and developed its standard fare of behind-the-scenes lobbying and the seeking of acceptance in political institutions. Noraid had cultivated political friends in state bodies and now called upon them to them use their influence on behalf of the Hunger Strikers.[25] Chicago City Council, the Ad Hoc Congressional Committee for Irish Affairs, the Massachusetts Legislature passed motions and resolutions, sent letters and telegrams that were designed to put pressure on the special relationship between President Ronald Reagan and Prime Minister Margaret Thatcher. They asked him to ask her to intervene to end the Hunger Strikes. Mrs Thatcher was also directly addressed by some US politicians. In a letter to her dated 15 July 1981, Bernie Sanders, then Mayor of Burlington, Vermont, used a definition of torture to describe her 'government's unwillingness to stop the abuse, humiliation and degrading treatment of Irish prisoners'. Sanders asked Thatcher 'to end your intransigent policy towards the prisoners'.[26] The following day a more mainstream group of thirty-seven members of the Senate and the House of Representatives signed a telegram sent just before midday that concluded: 'Surely it is the responsibility of the British Government to seek every possible means to seek an end to the strike before any additional deaths occur.'[27] Noraid's longstanding lobbying served Hunger Strike international solidarity very well. After years of seeking integration within the US political sphere rather than in opposition to it, Noraid now won support for the H Block struggles from high-ranking politicians. Always rather embarrassed about the IRA's Marxism and Sinn Féin's socialism, it was a long way from being from a left-wing organization[28] but in 1981 became caught up in large-scale street actions such as that along Fifth Avenue on the day Prince Charles and Lady Diana Spencer were married.

Global witness: protestor

The mockery of the Royal Wedding outside Fifth Avenue's Plaza Hotel on 29 July 1981 had been preceded by other protests against the British state. Large crowds gathered outside a Royal Ballet performance at the Lincoln Center on 17 June attended by the groom-to-be and monarch-in-waiting, Prince Charles. Demonstrations in New York had started three months earlier, on the eve of the 1981 Hunger Strikes, 28 February, when Margaret Thatcher accepted an invite to a dinner at the Waldorf-Astoria hotel. They continued through the long summer of 1981. There were regular pickets outside the British Consulate, which often took the form of public theatre with staged opposition to the power of the British state by despoiling or destroying British symbols, burning Union Jacks and political effigies. Sympathy hunger strikes also took place in public; Sister Rosaleen Halloran sat outside the UN in New York in front of a poster of Bobby Sands. All were expressions of solidarity with the Hunger Strikers and part of a wider international movement opposed to the British repression of republicanism mobilized by the H Block struggles. Although the term may be a little anachronistic, the gatherings of people to support the Hunger Strikers were, I would suggest, a social movement; they share the same characteristics of composition and tactics of later twentieth-century political formations: the broad fronts that are now called networks in which supporters of traditional political parties are lost within, rather than lead, wider communities. In the Hunger Strikers support movement, an emergent Sinn Féin and established socialist parties were present but not dominant in the mix of people from the global Irish diaspora. Irish nationalists, political or romantic or both, campaigned alongside anti-colonial, anti-imperial and anti-racist activists of the left. Supporters of the Hunger Strikers followed conventional pressure-group lobbying of political representatives and advocated boycotts of British goods but, more importantly, developed strategies of occupation of street spaces and public spheres. Protests included performances that simultaneously intervened in their local civic arenas and created what Judith Butler has called a 'media event'.[29] The forms of protest practised in New York were reproduced across the globe, not only in cities with large Irish diasporas such as Sydney or San Francisco and, of course, London, but also in Athens, Frankfurt, Lisbon, Oslo, Paris, Tehran, Toronto and Wellington.

The largest street presences followed the death of Bobby Sands. His funeral procession in Belfast was attended by 100,000 people. The lines of mourners that bore witness to a life by walking behind its body extended beyond Belfast across the Irish and Mediterranean Sea, the Atlantic and Pacific Oceans. A thousand people demonstrated outside the British embassy in Athens.[30] Coffins were carried in Dublin, New York and Paris. In Sydney, Bobby Sands' death was marked by 'an estimated 5,000 people' who 'marched from the Irish National Association to the British Consulate and at a requiem mass in the city's St Patrick's Cathedral, 2,000 lined the massive building'. The same number attended another mass in Melbourne.[31] Thousands marched in San Francisco. Irish pubs and bars were shut as if they, too, were on the funeral route of the former OC of the H Blocks. A political practice in Ireland of honouring the deaths of Irish republicans at the hands of British rulers in the funeral procession as a protest march was remembered by its diasporas and shared with their allies.[32]

A global geography of sympathy with the Hunger Strikers and opposition to their imprisonment in the H Blocks was drawn together by simultaneous public grieving and street protests. Despite the distance from the physical presence of the body of Bobby Sands, thousands of people were engaged in the same act of respect for a life as it ended: a public, collective and embodied acknowledgement. This is a form of witnessing, bearing witness through shared presence in space and time rather than through the eyes of an individual journalist at a particular place. Standing together, saying the same words or sharing silence focuses living people upon those who have recently died; the moment of their lives stretched a little longer, continuing the day without them is suspended for a while. The protests that occurred when Bobby Sands died held the Hunger Strike supporters in one body distributed at the same time across the spaces of global streets. From standing together to slowly walking in a group keeps back the immediate distractions of a busy city and delays the return to its everyday demands. The sombre black of mourning that shows restraint, often the dress code of these demonstrations, eschews the trivial interference of daily matters. Distinctions between political protest and funeral procession were blurred, not least because a catholic mass was often the destination of marches for the Hunger Strikers at the times of their deaths. The intersection of the catholic veneration of martyrs with the political power of a hunger strike is the subject of Padraig O'Malley's writing.[33] Without doubt, for the many catholic people within the Irish diaspora that supported the H Block struggles, the funereal protests were an important requiem ritual. But the demonstration of dwelling upon a life unjustly ended, bearing witness to their existence, is an embodied experience not restricted to those who held religious belief.

The international solidarity for the Hunger Strikers was an act of global witnessing. This is my case and in making it, I am reclaiming the witness, redeeming the dominating figure from Foucault's Panopticon: the imperial observer looking over from the outside. All and any witnesses, legal or journalistic, are supposed to be there, occupying a place in the immediate vicinity of any incident and able to see it with their own eyes. The subjectivity and authority of the witness is based on their position, bringing in the same time and same space as an unfolding event, observing it as it happens. Distance undermines the authority of the witness or it ought to do so. A global witness is, then, something of a contradiction in terms unless some consideration is given to the significance of the witness as political body rather than just a pair eyes. Furthermore, the movement to support the Hunger Strikers in the global cities of North America and Australia, in particular, brought the H Blocks into their own spaces; they projected the prison into the political sites that they occupied.

The North American and Australian H Block support groups did seek out places where a real relationship, usually an economic exchange between their countries and Britain, was located. They took action that would affect British trade. A picket of British Airways at Los Angeles International Airport shut it down for a day. The international solidarity of trade unions combined with the boycott tactic promoted by Noraid[34] used economic bans to demonstrate political disapproval. The Waterside Workers Federation refused to load grain onto a British ship at Port Kembla, north of Sydney, keeping it docked for two days.[35] Importantly, local actions asserted global associations; they were intended to initiate a chain of political responsibility for the lives of the Hunger Strikers that led to the door of 10 Downing Street. On 9 August, Eammon O'Connor began a hunger strike outside the British consulate in Sydney 'demanding that the Australian Government and Australian politicians publicly call on Margaret Thatcher to grant the five demands of the Irish political prisoners'. His strike lasted thirty-seven days, ending only a few weeks ahead of those in Long Kesh/Maze itself.[36]

The international solidarity of 1981 is, then, not very different from any other contemporary global protest; it is always the intention to insist upon a connection across a divided geography. Indeed, this is their only task: what happens there matters here. That war fought in another land rich in oil is the concern of this country where multi-nationals selling the Earth's energy trade their shares and where we fill up our cars. That police killing on the streets of another city is the effect of racism everywhere, including here. It is protesters themselves that make these connections; it requires their bodies to be seen on their local streets calling attention to unfolding events taking place somewhere else: the global witness holds separate spaces together by their presence in public. In Newcastle, New South Wales, fifty people picketed a restaurant putting on a Royal Wedding supper.[37] I do not know what they said to the diners as they arrived or what they shouted through the windows as they were seated. My best guess is that it was similar to that expressed by protesters who ended up outside the lunch for Prince Charles and Lady Diana in the Plaza in New York. 'As you fill your bellies on luxury food at this feast inside this showy building to celebrate the continuity of the British crown, others are starving themselves for political status in the struggle to be independent from its power.' Or something along those lines.

The site of protest establishes its political message; as people occupy public spaces as part of protest movements, they also occupy a political position. Polly Ruiz observes that '[w]hen protesters converge on sites of national or global significance, they attempt to illustrate both their own lack of a place within the mainstream and to offer the wider public a glimpse of the view from an alternative political position. Consequently these city spaces become a site of both a physical *and* an ideological struggle.'[38] Halls of national and local government, offices of international banks, the roads lined with these institutions and the spaces adjacent to them are places where the assumption of authority is contested: Wall Street and Gezi Park, Taksim Trafalgar and Parliament Squares. People enter these locations to halt the script of political or economic dominance; to attempt to alter or even overturn the decisions made inside governmental and financial institutions by assembling outside. All protesters need their own Bastille. And, as historians of the French Revolution remind us, the storming of the Bastille, more full of meaning than of prisoners, was largely a symbolic act. The recognition of the relationship between governing power and its representation is the emancipatory element of assembly, the power of protest that can be felt by participants when the real and symbolic are closely entwined in the spaces they have come to occupy. The right to rule expressed in the architecture of old and new political temples, the antiquity of their classical columns or the religious echoes of their spires, in their wide ascending steps or overarching towers of glass is overwhelmed by an organic mass of unruly bodies, the shifting shapes of a human crowd, a chaotic chorus of words painted on placards and a new palette of colours. The architectures of power are adorned differently, disrespectfully, and offer, for the duration of the demonstration, at least 'a glimpse', as Ruiz puts it, of an 'alternative political position'.[39]

International solidarity movements whose intention is making and maintaining global connections start from a position of distance from the seats of power and those who are ultimately or immediately responsible for the injustice for which they seek redress. Sites of significance must be sought out. Supporters of the Hunger Strikers in North America or Australia needed to find appropriate places for people to make an intervention into public debate; they had to occupy space with some association with the British state to present the Hunger Strikers' case; they connected one building to another. In Adelaide, a two-day hunger strike took place on the steps of Parliament House.[40] It was an act of lobbying: I stand here because you as my political representative should represent me and raise the urgent matter of Irish life and death in your building and to those who will listen to you. Beyond the stone steps and behind the high wooden doors of the South Australian Parliament appeared to be a corridor that eventually opened in the Palace of Westminster. It was as if Long Kesh could be reached from the wooden benches and green plush cushions of the House of Assembly in Adelaide. There is also an echo of British power itself in the Australian architecture and a colonial legacy that linked these buildings together. The protesters who refused food as they stood in Adelaide's city centre claimed that an historical connection was now a political responsibility that could be traced back to the British Parliament then through the debating chamber of the British government that had ruled Northern Ireland directly from 1972 and contained the Maze Cellular in its Home Office prison estate. A colonial legacy was the continuous present of the Hunger Strikers and their supporters, the prisoners held in the H Blocks and the protesters outside Parliament House. Demonstrators brought blame to this door or a series of doors that opened like dominoes.

Supporters of the H Block struggles did not simply seek publicity by settling upon a public spot, they developed a spatial politics of protest. The political geography of international solidarity brings separated places into the same view and insists upon their material relation. But part of this political strategy, which emphasizes the real lines of power across global distances, is the use of symbols. The movement to support the H Block struggles and the H Block struggle itself was fought by and through political symbols. Political symbols, bodies as well as buildings, can have a force that exceeds any real effects. Take the figures of the Prince and Princess of Wales. Neither one of the royal newlyweds had any actual influence over the events taking place inside the H Blocks; they had no decision-making power even if they had been interested in exerting it. But their wedding celebrations and the Hunger Strike protests that took place around them, were symbolically charged and fiercely so. The marriage of the next in line to the British throne would have once secured the aristocratic assumption of governance through familial lines and land ownership; such political and legal alliances were at heart of the historical formation of the British state but remained a contemporary expression of the traditional hierarchies of territorial power. In their richly clothed bodies and bejewelled heads, the royal couple were at the centre of a national spectacle of the inherited right to rule. It is the appearance of a legitimate and continuous authority of Britain that the supporters of the H Block struggle opposed, for it had real effects inside Long Kesh. The question of political status for conflict-related prisoners turns upon the use of force within the borders of the British state or against the extent of that border. The Prince and Princess of Wales personified both Britain's past regime and present sovereignty. Supporters of the Hunger Strikers were not only making a political argument about their wedding but also an art historical interpretation about the material power of symbols, especially when the symbol is also physical, or real, like the body of a monarch. Indeed, the Hunger Strikers themselves make the same point. A hunger strike offers up a physical body as the sign of political oppression. Or, put the other way round: political oppression is signified by the physical deterioration of a hunger-striking body. Emaciation is the attrition of restrictions upon the unfree. Of course, hunger strikes are real; the ten men dead in the summer of 1981 is their awful evidence. But the power of the hunger strike is symbolic; one starving body makes visible the suffering of others. Histories of the hunger strike have noted that its practice in Ireland originates in longer histories of fasting at the door of a master as well as the more widespread practice of making a physical sacrifice for spiritual understanding.[41] Republican prisoners in the H Blocks mobilized the morality of fasting, as well as its political history,[42] in an anti-colonial hunger strike. The determination and fragility of the starving physical forms of the Hunger Strikers represented all republican prisoners forced into the hardships of HMP Maze and all Irish people under British occupation.

Necropolitics and the Hunger Strike

Padraig O'Malley argues that 'the strikes were encumbered with the accessories of victimhood'.[43] The Hunger Strikers have been both commemorated and criticized as catholic martyrs. For the republican and Irish nationalist supporters of the Hunger Strikers who held catholic beliefs and belonged to catholic communities to fast was an act of faith and hope that served others through the sacrifice of self for the belief in their future and in doing so redeemed that self, their self. Bobby Sands' 1 March 1981 announcement as he began the Hunger Strike and embarked on his own fast entwines religious argument and political sentiment:

> I am standing on a threshold of another trembling world. May God have mercy on my soul . . . I am a political prisoner because I am a casualty of a perennial war that is being fought between an oppressed Irish people and an alien, oppressive unwanted regime that refuses to leave our land. I believe and stand by the God-given right of the Irish nation to sovereign independence, and the right of any Irishman or woman to assert this right in armed revolution. That is why I am incarcerated, naked and tortured.[44]

The 'victimhood' associated with the early Christian saints is certainly echoed in some of the imagery of the anti-H Block campaigns if not adopted by the protesting prisoners themselves, and for good historical reasons. The importance of religious beliefs and practices within a political struggle recruited from the discontents of institutionalized sectarian discrimination against catholic people should never be dismissed. Catholic identity was politicized through discrimination in the economy and geography of Northern Ireland that is exemplified in the architecture of Long Kesh/Maze: its daily operation was upheld by an almost entirely protestant unionist prison service. The H Blocks' culture of resistance existed at an intersection of catholic belief and republican politics. Rather than being weighed down by victimhood, 'encumbered' by religious associations or its 'accessories', as O'Malley argues, the Hunger Strikers and their supporters understood the role of suffering as resistance to power and the material form of the fragile body as a political symbol. Whilst fasting is a religious practice, and one associated with all global belief systems, it cannot be reduced to individual spiritual achievement. It is contingent upon material conditions and often called up by incarceration. Hunger strikes occur in prisons everywhere. Some have attracted historical study and global attention, such as those by the suffragettes, members of the Women's Social and Political Union in Holloway Prison between 1909 and 1913 or those by Muslim men in Guantanamo Bay in 2005 and 2013, but there are others far less famous. The four female Bolivian communists, 'tin miners wives', who began a fast on 28 December 1977, joined by over 1,000 by its end on 20 January 1978, forced the General Banzer dictatorship to release political prisoners and recognize trade unions.[45] Much more recently, 120 women in Yarl's Wood Immigration Removal Centre, Bedford, protested against indefinite detention with a three-day hunger strike.[46] This is one of many hunger strikes in refugee communities. 'Since', as Imogen Tyler observes, 'Britain began to institute its inhumane asylum system in the 1990s, lip-sewing, hunger strikes, self-harm and suicides have become ordinary features of national life for those caught up in the "abject diaspora."'[47] Hunger Strikes are universal acts of resistance to repression in conditions where other forms of protest are not possible.

The withdrawal of freedom of movement and freedom of assembly is the punishment of prison, is the purpose of penal architecture. The structures of walls and cells impose the loss of freedom and with it the right and the ability to exercise opposition. Prisons place prisoners beyond the public domain of protest, removed from the sites of collective assemblies that can appropriate spaces of political power. Prison architecture is intended to overwhelm the strength of prisoners as it isolates each from another: walls too tall, too wide, too strong to overturn. The architecture prevents any escape and avenues through which prisoners can gather as political collectives. Prisoners are reduced to the internal world of their cell and within this space use the only thing that these material conditions have made available: their own bodies. There is nothing else, no pen, no paper, no placard, no meeting, no march that can express their opinion or opposition. A protesting prisoner has only their body as their means of political expression: a physical inscription of the effect of incarceration. A hunger strike is an act of the utterly disempowered. But the physical weakness of a hungry body ranged against the material force of the prison architecture is a demonstration of injustice. The body of the prisoner exposes the arbitrary power that prison's hard high walls were built to hide.

The deaths of ten republican H Block prisoners exposed, albeit momentarily, what Achille Mbembe calls the 'repressed topography of cruelty'.[48] The sum of British sovereignty amounts to the authority to 'dictate who may live and who must die'[49] rather than any other any other mandate, such as keeping the peace or upholding democracy. The Hunger Strikes revealed the twentieth-century necropolitics of British colonialism in Ireland that has been more widely recognized in the Great Famine between 1845 and 1849. Mbembe's project, an unmasking of the consensual idea of sovereignty, argues it is defined by mortal violence. 'What place is given to life, death, and the human body (in particular the wounded or slain body)? How are they inscribed in the order of power?'[50] Under conditions of necropower, everywhere the basis of sovereignty rather than its exceptional state, 'the lines between resistance and suicide, sacrifice and redemption, martyrdom and freedom are blurred'.[51] The 'agency' of death, which Paul Gilroy attributes to the suicides of escaped plantation slaves on their recapture, is acknowledged by Mbembe.[52] The supporters of the 1981 Hunger Strikers, especially those from catholic communities in Ireland and its diaspora, did not accept that fasting until death had the sinful associations of suicide. It is better understood as a 'blurred' form of resistance: to summon suffering, to begin a journey towards the destruction of your own body, entwines a religious notion of a precious life and a body as a symbol of the people. To beckon death is a final and dignified form of a human and a political agency.

H Blocks: material symbols

The symbolic power of material reality is at the heart of the Hunger Strike. The difficulty of separating the attributes and effects of the material and symbolic, the subject of Pierre Bourdieu's many writings on cultural formation of the social hierarchies of capitalism,[53] is an impossibility in highly charged arenas of political struggle: there is no form of power or resistance that is not simultaneously material and symbolic. The restraining force of the H Blocks was found in their obstinate materiality, which became a lasting symbol of brutal treatment: the hard lines of the concrete cell units of Long Kesh, the shape of the H Blocks, expressed the control of Britain and containment of Ireland. The daily routines dictated by the British penal regime were also the detailed script of a larger lack of freedom. Within the architecture of Long Kesh/Maze were the embodied effects of a colonial relationship of repression and resistance that were unmistakable from the outside, from the appearance of this prison. But the jail itself, its exterior as well as interior, was beyond the view of almost all those who understood its meaning. For symbols to be powerful, they need to be seen. They cannot begin their work of reference without visibility. Prohibited public access, restricted entry to all unless employed by the prison service or granted a visitors' permit, the distance of a few or many thousand miles between the prison site and the supporters of the protesting prisoners was overcome with imagery (Figure 3.2).

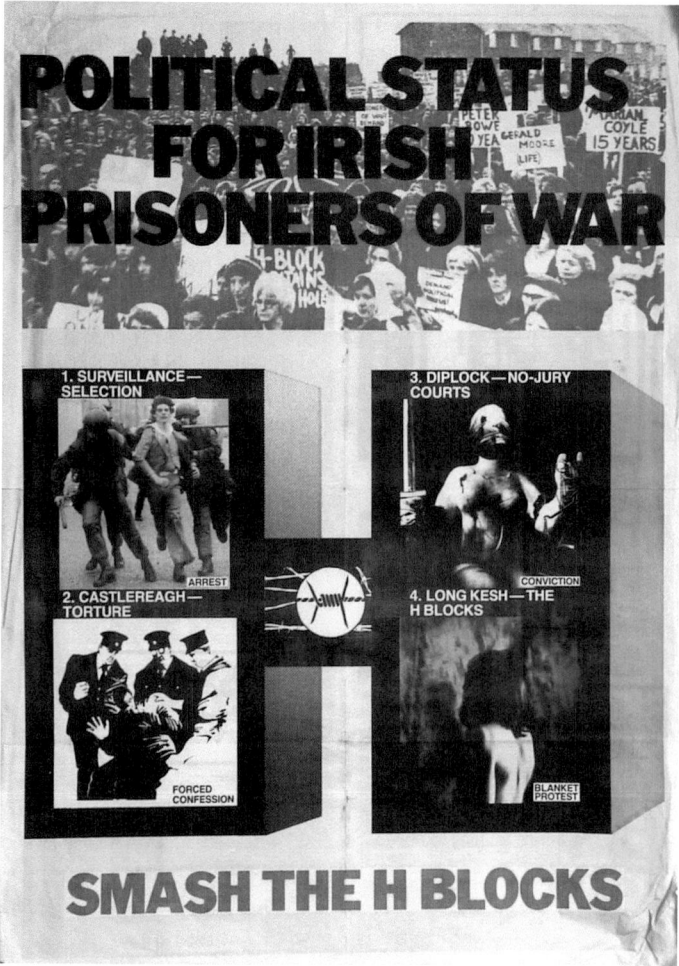

FIGURE 3.2 *'H Block protest imagery'*, Smash the H Blocks: Political Status for Irish Prisoners of War, *Troops Out Movement, 1979. Source: CAIN (ulster.ac.uk/cain).*

The plan of the cell units of Long Kesh/Maze, the H shaped footprint of its Blocks, was reproduced on leaflets and posters calling for demonstrations in support of republican prisoners and their five demands; it was represented on placards initially carried by relatives on the streets of Northern Ireland then later held up by the international solidarity movement at protests all over the world. The H shape testified to the existence of Long Kesh/Maze; it outlined the space of imprisonment; straight hard intersecting lines depicting a repetitively brutal architecture. The political force of such a simple graphic form copied on paper or drawn up on cardboard warrants some explanation.

For Michael Taussig, the power of the protest placard lies in its 'fusion'[54] with the person who carries it. He observed the stillness of the people holding their handmade signs as part of Occupy Wall Street and writes of the 'terrible gravitas'[55] of their pose. Statues mark moments of political change. Protestors may be still and statuesque because they are posing for photographers but, he argues, it is 'the sign' not the 'sign holder'[56] that is presented to the camera lens. For sure, the intention of creating and carrying signs is to call up a camera. I write this as a maker of many placards for many protests. I have been photographed and photographed others many times. But the camera is only part of it. The placard is a wider public address initially made to those in the immediate vicinity of the protest then through a photographer's lens to others further away who are reached when its image is reproduced on a page or across a screen. The demand of all demonstrations is attention. Look at what is going on. Witness it with us.

Photographer of Occupy Wall Street, Nancy Goldring, states that the signs are 'exactly what the sign-bearer wants to say' or as Taussig declares: 'I see the sign as an extension of the human figure.'[57] Protest placards do overwhelm those that carry them; they turn the bodies that hold them into bearers of a message. The political position of the message is absolutely their own, often overwritten to emphasize this, but it is more important than that person who created or carried it. Protesters have already relinquished part of their own personhood to the protest as they join it; their bodies became a part of another body large enough to be recognized as the people, such as the 99 per cent of the Occupy Movement. They use their own form to increase the size of the protest and significance of the people and thus use their physical body, materially and symbolically. They have taken themselves out onto the street as an act of representation, to contribute their own human figure to a cast of the people as political entity. Protesters are symbols. If the placard they carry is 'a sign' that is an 'extension of the human figure' then it is also a continuation of its symbolic work; its content giving shape to the body the specificity to the symbol of the people: global witnesses at the end of British colonialism in Ireland.

Global witness: person

'For a short time', writes F. Stuart Ross, 'the 1981 Hunger Strike, focused the eyes of the world on Ireland's seemingly intractable conflict'.[58] It was the extent of the international media coverage of the Hunger Strikes and its equivocal, if not critical, position on British policy in Northern Ireland that unsettled the Thatcher government sufficiently that right-wing conservatives, for whom free speech was usually a first principle, supported an official censorship process in an attempt to 'deny terrorists the oxygen of publicity'.[59]

But what Ross refers to is not the scope or slant of media coverage but rather its effect: global witnessing. Geographical separation from the site of the H Blocks and prohibited physical access to the cells within its walls in which the Hunger Strikes took place, did not prevent a sense of the proximity and the visibility of the prison. What happened on the flat, wet land where Long Kesh/ Maze was located appeared everywhere as if seen first-hand. The eyes of the world were upon it. Ross's metaphor may have been intended to read as just that, a literary device, rather than an evocation of the ability to actually look into the jail as the Hunger Strikes unfolded, but many people across the globe found themselves in this position: seeing it happen. They felt themselves to be witnesses, no matter what the distance.

Brian Anson, a radical architect and planner from Liverpool who was part of a 'mobile planning aid unit'[60] which travelled through Britain, Ireland and Europe during the time of the Hunger Strikes explained in a letter to *An Phoblacht* how they intersected with his life. 'I know that the tragedy of hunger strike is crucial in the history of the republican struggle, it was also a significant time in my life – and I know I am not alone; there are many non-Irish throughout the world whose lives were profoundly affected by those moving times.' He describes a series of everyday events, recalling visual and aural details, complete scenes of memory. These he calls 'a few memories of an outsider'. He was in Germany with a friend during 'Bobby Sands last days':

> We both wore those cheap button-hole badges – Victory to Bobby Sands. (I still have mine here, pinned to the shelf at my desk; it's followed me everywhere for 20 years – change of houses, change of country even.) We were in a Greek restaurant when the news came that Sands had died. Two strange things happened, which I could never prove – but why would I imagine them 20 years ago? What would be the point? First, a Greek waiter suddenly embraced us – it was out of nowhere. Then the usual Greek music, which we associate with Greek restaurants, Melanie Mercurie, etc. – was suddenly replaced with Irish music. The second memory (which can be vouched for because there were witnesses) relates to the death of Francis Hughes. As I recall, the news came through on the radio at 5pm. I was in the kitchen with my four children drinking a glass of whisky. "The bastards!" I said as I smashed the glass on the floor.[61]

Brian Anson's preface to his account of how his life was entwined with that of the Hunger Strikers is important: 'I know I am not alone.' He was one of many global witnesses to their political fast and his physical reaction to their deaths was also shared: an embodied attachment and anger that often motivates solidarity movements. The technological networks on which global news reporting depended enabled connections between events and audiences and within audiences: a disparate collective was created. The immediacy of information reproduced across the world over the radio, in particular, generated simultaneous effects in separated spaces. A shared instantaneous shock is a well-known phenomenon associated with the global immediacy of, usually, US televised news: the halting of daily routines to watch the footage of the shooting of John F. Kennedy or the hijacked planes ploughing into the World Trade Center's Twin Towers. Everyday actions stop and with them time seems to stop too: an interruption to routines that becomes worthy of recollection. Instantaneous information about the Hunger Strikers, especially the news reports of their deteriorating health, included their media audiences in the timeline of political imprisonment in Long Kesh/Maze: on the inside, they passed another day without food while we, on the outside, waited for a family supper. A lived experience more intimate than most, an internal feeling of a hungry body, spread from the jail across the airwaves. As the words of journalists are sent out across a global geography, immediacy becomes not only temporal but also has a spatial affect: time filters into space, commercial restaurants, domestic kitchens. Sounds reverberates into everyday rooms, the immediate vicinity of lives as they are lived. It is no wonder that Brian Anson felt that the Hunger Strikes occurred in his life. He did not, of course, feel the hollow ache that must be supressed to continually refuse food, but some part of the physical struggle within the H Blocks echoed through architectures across the globe to become embodied in its witnesses. Anson described his physical responses to their deaths: a jolt of sympathy offered and accepted between strangers or shot of adrenalin that released an angry strike of a hand downwards and the glass that it held. These bodily movements indicate that this is happening to me in my moment: here and now. The temporal register of the Hunger Strikers in lives beyond the H Blocks is angrily expressed by Bernadette McAliskey: 'I sometimes wonder how many people stop to count how many seconds make up the hours of the 66 days of Bobby Sands's dying, or the 73 of Kieran Doherty's, or the 46 of Martin Hurson's. How many seconds did it take for all 10 to die?'[62]

The Blanket Man and the rights-bearing body

I may be wrong. F. Stuart Ross's phrase for what I have been calling global witnessing, 'the eyes of the world', is only a metaphor. No-one, except a small circle within Long Kesh/Maze, its hospital staff, a handful of prison officers, close family and catholic priests, actually watched the Hunger Strikers die. Those outside the jail and far beyond its concrete walls and wire fences, heard of their deteriorating condition, listened out for information that combined accounts of their physical health and analysis of British prison policy; they waited for news broadcasts and as they did so measured the suffering of the Hunger Strikers. Some did count the time it took them to starve. Global witnesses did not see it happen; they felt it.

Not only were the Hunger Strikers out of sight, but the physical body in pain is always acutely difficult to confront or contemplate. The individual protesting prisoners refusing food came to be represented through a collective figure. The visual form of the Hunger Striker was the Blanket Man. Throughout 1981, blankets were worn by participants, often young men, in the H Block protests across the globe. However, it was women, often the mothers of republican prisoners, who first wore blankets in protest at the conditions inside the H Blocks. They covered their undressed, partially or fully dressed bodies in a variety of institutional or domestic blankets and stood in front of significant addresses, interrupted public events or walked at the head of marches with the names of their sons hung around their necks (Figure 3.3). Mary Nelis of

FIGURE 3.3 '*Women wear the blanket: Relatives Action Committee, Falls Road Belfast* c. *1977*', Republican Prisoners and the Prison Struggle in Ireland, *Ireland Information Fact File, AP/RN Print, Dublin, n.d. Reproduced with thanks to Kaye Page.*

Derry's Relatives Action Committee recalls the first time she wore a blanket. It was 1976. 'We said "We have to do something about this." We said we'd strip naked, just wear an old army blanket. We'd made up some placards, we got a taxi and stood outside the Bishop's door, in the freezing cold.'[63] For the next 'two years' this strategy of solidarity was female: 'women had marched, held vigils, appealed to priests and bishops, written letters. Wearing only blankets and in bare feet like prisoners, they had gone around Ireland and Europe.'[64] Wearing the clothes of another, always a process of identification, was the purpose of all political performances by either young men or older women. Female bodies also bore their family connection and heightened the significance of a used or worn square piece of cloth. I stand here in place of my son, my brother, my husband; their absence has not ended their attachment to me or me to them. I am wearing this humiliating blanket to make their hardship present to you. Look at me and you look at them: be my witness.[65]

Inside the H Blocks, the 1981 Hunger Strikes had brought an end to the collective and sustained blanket and no-wash protest, but its imagery remained a powerful representation of protesting republican prisoners. The rejection of food by a small number of prisoners escalated the refusal to comply with the prison. Not wearing its uniform, not undertaking its work, not leaving its cell, not washing in its bathrooms and now not eating its food. The decision to go on hunger strike, debated and agreed through the IRA and INLA organizations within the H Blocks, also recognized the physical and mental hardships of being 'on the blanket' through both the assault upon protesting prisoners' bodies by prison officers and the depressing conditions of cells. It allowed prisoners to 'come off the blanket' but continue the campaign for political status. It individualized, even personalized, the H Block struggle, evident in the importance attached to the name of Bobby Sands, but it was, and still is, the collective body of blanket men that provided powerful imagery of both the Hunger Strike and Hunger Strikers.

Dressing in the drab cloak of an H Block prisoner, was another strategy, like carrying an H, of displaying the prison in public space. The Blanket Man remained an important part of the visual repertoire of the H Block/Armagh Committees. In Australian Aid for Ireland's magazine, *Toward 32*, Chris Raleigh describes a demonstration on 1 May 1981. 'As Bobby Sands entered the 61st day of his Hunger Strike, over 200 people held a silent, candlelit vigil in the centre of Sydney. Two men wearing nothing but blankets stood at the head for six hours, providing powerful imagery for the city's seething masses, weaving their way home.'[66] The effect of a person in the midst of the routine urban rush hour eschewing contemporary clothes, is eye-catching, of course. The H Block/Armagh Committees and the variously named groups established along the same lines across the world understood the need to be media-savvy. More than this. Re-staging the H Block struggle on busy city streets with people wrapped in blankets did not merely play for the media but reached through it. 'At the appearance of any assembly or even just a "crowd,"' as Judith Butler has pointed out, 'there is also a media event that forms across time and space, calling for the demonstrations, so some set of global connections is being articulated'.[67] These connections are not only those of the technologies of photojournalism, the prints and pages of newspapers or the pixels and clicks of social networks. A gathering that attracts attention, two nearly naked men, can set in motion a media event that moves people, as Brian Anson was moved when Bobby Sands and Francis Hughes died: distance is overcome in that shared moment in time and shared sensation of historical significance.

Although addressed to dispossession rather than incarceration, Butler's observations about bodily presence on the streets of twenty-first century cities, reveals another layer of meaning in the wearing the clothes of an H Block prisoner. It makes a claim for political inclusion and historical relevance. It uses public space of places far from the prison, and Sydney is ten thousand miles away, to assert what she calls 'thereness'. Butler states: 'Bodies on the street are precarious – they are exposed to police force and sometimes endure physical suffering as a result. But those bodies are also obdurate and persisting, insisting on their continuing and collective "thereness." '[68] The task of the H Block protests was to make immediately present the 'thereness' of others.

I have tried to argue that international Hunger Strike solidarity asserted connections between places, but more importantly perhaps, they did so between people. Dressing in the same way is to claim connection. This is obvious enough for any dress historian or cultural studies scholar. Connection is the fundamental physical and symbolic function of cloth: skin to identity, body to representation.[69] The wrapped blankets drew together the bodies beneath them, those in Sydney and those twelve miles south of Belfast in the H Blocks. The 'translocal commitment to the alleviation of suffering' that Paul Gilroy recognized in the early twenty-first century 'cosmopolitan solidarity from below and afar' is also at work earlier, to some extent, in the global support for the Hunger Strikes.[70] 'Rights-bearing bodies' use their freedom of movement and assembly on behalf of 'rights-less people', who remain disempowered even 'after empire'. To appear as prisoner when not imprisoned asserts a human association that transcends both the act and the place of incarceration; the clothing of a captive on the body of the free announces: this is happening to another person in another location but a person like that before you now. I am on an historical and geographical journey with Gilroy's rights-bearing bodies. The ones about whom he writes are the human shields that travelled from Europe to the Middle East in the late twentieth century and early twenty-first in the hope of preventing the airstrikes and other acts of war against civilians. Their 'translocal commitment to the alleviation of suffering' was also a 'practical transfiguration of democracy which is incompatible with racism and ethnic absolutism. It is only racism that acknowledges the difference between their rights-bearing bodies and the right-less people they protect by their presence.'[71] Human shields recognized universal rights and their denial; they knew that rights are relative to the place of a person, their territory, their identity, their 'race', not recognized in everyone everywhere. But they should be, they say with their bodies. The Hunger Strike supporters who presented their bare physical forms covered only by a blanket in public spaces made a similar claim about the rights-bearing and the right-less bodies. Gilroy states: 'These gestures of solidarity proceed from the assumption that translation will be good enough to make the desired experiential, political and ethical leap. Purposive vagrancy and exile, albeit in temporary forms, are again the order of the day. Once more, suffering rather than autonomy and self-possession has been located in the center of the public culture.'[72]

The H Block street protests represented the provocative act of human suffering of the Hunger Strike itself. The body beneath the blanket evoked the fragile form of the starving body but the blanket itself was also a display of the downtrodden. The rudimentary shape and rough surface of a blanket evokes a lowly status. This was, no doubt, the intended effect of the six men pulling the British monarchy along Fifth Avenue: the mockery of the Royal Wedding satirized but also simply expressed British state power: the visual hierarchy of the seated crowned figures carried by barefooted, bare-chested men in blankets below illustrated Britain's rule over Ireland: ancient and oppressive.

Importantly, for many of the Irish diaspora, the gatherings to support the Hunger Strikers were not only a show of solidarity with them but was, to borrow Butler's phrase again, an articulation of 'a set of global connections' associated with the colonization of Ireland by Britain. At protests in New York or in Sydney that which is shared is an historical as well as human condition. To be part of an Irish diaspora and wrap around your body the fabric of a republican in the H Blocks uses the rights-bearing body of protester to reveal a rights-less prisoner; but this 'translocal commitment to the alleviation of suffering' is pierced with a specific claim to a colonial condition held in common. Street-protesting blanket men sway between the rights-bearing and rights-less body. Here I am in my body that is usually safe from harm but there is another like me whose life is not considered important enough to save. They perform the hunger-striking prisoner and themselves. With the claim that the prisoner is a person who is a person like me lies another. This is not me, but it could be. This could be my destiny. This would be my condition if I was still in Ireland. This body wrapped in a blanket is an interpretation of me. The blanket, being 'on it' in jail and wearing it in the streets, makes visible the oppression as a condition of the H Blocks and of Irishness itself. The cloth creates shared conditions of life, protestor and prisoner, inhabiting, albeit differently, British colonialism 'after empire'.

The Blanket Man as Hunger Striker:
media, art and memory

The Blanket Man has become the most lasting image of the Hunger Strikes: its visual reference. It is through this figure that the H Block struggles are remembered despite the shifting strategies of resistance of prisoners in Long Kesh/Maze. Prison escapes and prison art practices, collective political reflection and individual education, which extended beyond 1980, have a less lasting visual presence. The faces of the Hunger Strikers themselves, particularly that of a smiling Bobby Sands framed with 1970s hippy-style shoulder-length hair, are part of an H Block imagery mobilized to mark anniversaries, but it is the Blanket Man that is most widely reproduced in commemorative forms: in paint on walls as a mural, placed in plinths as a public sculpture, drawn and scanned as a graphic for numerous leaflets, photocopied and circulated in newsprint, cast in theatre productions and captured on film[73] (Figure 3.4).

Much of this cultural production coalesced around the twentieth anniversary of the Hunger Strikes in 2001, just a year after the final release of prisoners convicted of conflict-related offences under the Good Friday Agreement and the closure of Long Kesh/Maze as an operational prison. Former prisoners were prominent in this early period of the peace process, their stories part of

FIGURE 3.4 *Blanket Man as Hunger Striker: recurring images. Photograph: Louise Purbrick.*

its media narrative[74] as their organizations consolidated community support for the consociational constitution of Northern Ireland. For both the IRA and Sinn Féin the peace process was the ultimate outcome of the H Block struggles, the Hunger Strikes in particular; their twentieth anniversary celebration was of a risen people that had endured but overcome oppression. The Blanket Man carried their history.

As commemorations began in March 2001, marking the announcement of Bobby Sands's 1981 strike, a mural was unveiled in the estate on the edge of Belfast, Twinbrook, in which he grew up. It features two Blanket Men. They are positioned in the lower foreground overlaying the mix of myth and history, symbolism and realism, of the mural form.[75] The dates 1981 and 2001 are painted on the left and right top corners of the gable end. Between these historical marks and the spreading wings of a phoenix rising from flames is an H Block, its solid structural form in perspective. A dove has flown from the broken vertical bars of a cell window. Below another cell window is the setting for the Blanket Men; its bars, still intact and covered with a grill, lie between the dark outlines of their half portraits (Figure 3.4, bottom left). This composition is repeated and repeated. Just take one example. On the evening of 1 March, around the same time as the mural was unveiled, a public discussion about the historical significance of the Hunger Strikes took place in a community centre in the Short Strand, East Belfast. Blanket Men were its backdrop. The same figures, the head and torso of half portraits defined by the contrasting black shapes of long hair, beards and blankets, are positioned in the same way, either side of the vertical bars of a cell window (Figure 3.4, centre left).

A commemorative calendar has punctuated the practices of memorializing the conflict between Britain and Ireland. A decade of centenaries, 2012 to 2022, that mark the Ulster Covenant to Partition, intersected by the First World War and the Easter Rising, also contains other significant anniversaries: fifty years since the deployment of British troops and forty since the Hunger Strikes. Remembering the Hunger Strikes is the most continuous practice. Large-scale public events were concentrated on the twentieth anniversary, so relevant for reflection upon the origins of the Good Friday Agreement, but memorial works existed before and continued after, often accompanied by imagery of Blanket Men. A poster announcing the unveiling of a statue of a Blanket Man in May 2002, a monument dedicated to the ten men who died in the 1981 Hunger Strike, presented the two now-familiar figures, half-length portraits of protesting republican prisoners. They are differently rendered, sketched to show folds of blankets and lengths of hair but hold the same stance either side of the cell window (Figure 3.4 bottom right and right).

The Blanket Man image has ossified over time, solidified into a consistent form. The male prisoner stands against a wall, his body gently angled towards the right. His eyes look downwards in the same direction and are enlarged and darkened, his own forehead creating shadows on his pale oval face contrasting with a black beard below his chin and black hair curling around and away from his neck. A blanket falls from his shoulders and another is wrapped around his waist. His chest is bare, exposed by the dark lines of the blanket. Prisoners who went 'on the blanket' and who participated in the no-wash campaign did, despite differences of human form, assume a collective appearance. Standard cell-bedding fabrics of the same rectangular shape and same rough weave were their only clothes and created a uniform of resistance. Their collective refusal to leave the cells to use the shared bathrooms at the top of the wing without their modest drab dress meant that their uniform appearance extended to their person: their hair and beards grew; they assumed the same uncut, unkempt style. But the figure of the Blanket Man, so widely reproduced and constitutive of the collective memory of the Hunger Strike, does not derive directly from prisoners in their cells or from the performance of protestors who made their imprisonment public. It is a media image (Figure 3.5).

On 27 October 1980 BBC2's Newsnight programme broadcast 'The first TV pictures of the "dirty protest" in the Maze prison'.[76] The report by Robin Denselow, also included in Granada Television's World in Action programme, *The H Block Fuse*, shown a month later, begins with elevated exterior views of Long Kesh/Maze accompanied by a steady monologue introducing the official name, 'Non-Compliant Prisoners', for protesting republicans in an authoritative British accent, the distant voiceover added with the edit. The opening shots are blurry. There is a gloomy mist over the camera lens as it follows guarded movement along walls, fences and then stops at an H Block.

FIGURE 3.5 *Blanket Man media image, BBC2 Newsnight (27 October 1980)', frame grab.*

A shot held on an exterior cell window cuts to its other side: barred, grilled and set in cell walls covered in brown smears. Human excrement. Sounds and sights of high-pressure cell cleaning elsewhere in the prison cut in before the camera and the distant voice, disembodied presences, return to the cell. The camera pans in a circular clockwise motion around the interior cell taking in the smeared walls and scanning slowly across to two figures who stand along its back wall, the window between them. Then there is a change of direction. The camera moves forward, closer to the two men, the lens lowers over the body of one at the farther side of the window. It pans down to his bare feet. The circular motion of the camera around the cell continues across the wall, over a pock-marked sponge mattress, pieces picked out to wipe the excrement on the walls, and a bucket for piss. Another circuit begins but this time the camera lens is lowered over the body of the man on the window's nearside. The thick air of awkwardness of this encounter is retained in the film that was viewed on terrestrial television sets in 1980 that I replay on my laptop screen. For a brief moment, the atmosphere is broken when both men turn away from the camera, exchange glances, hide smiles, and speak in Gaelic through the grilled barred window. Most, and my good guess is almost all, viewers did not understand their words but were still relieved that their embarrassment was shrugged off, if only for a few seconds. As I watch, I am grateful forty years later for the relief from just looking. No verbal exchange between the camera crew and prisoners was permitted. 'We were not allowed to talk to them', Robin Denselow explained as the cell sequence came to end. Without dialogue, the staring effect of the camera was amplified. The two Blanket Men, Hugh Rooney and Kevin Toal, are trapped in their H Block cell and captured by the camera positioned just inside the door, a spatial and visual snare. Both often adjust their stance, if only very slightly, in the few minutes of filming, arranging their bodies into a shield of pride. They successfully deflect any of their own awkwardness onto those that keep peering at them. The effort of holding themselves, exerting control of their bodies, can be seen momentarily in a close up of Hugh Rooney: his shallow adrenalin-fuelled breathing is shown in the rapid rise and fall of his chest.

The position he and Kevin Toal held as the camera made its first sweep around their cell and over their bodies is the source of the widely reproduced commemorative Blanket Man imagery (see Figure 3.5); these are the forms most often used to evoke the 1981 Hunger Strike although they held them for the television report on the earlier, unsuccessful and almost forgotten strike of 1980. A black-and-white photograph of this moment, which has the grainy quality of a photograph of a television screen, was reproduced inside a *Republican Resistance* calendar and on the front cover of an Australian Aid for Ireland journal, both 2001 Hunger Strikes twentieth anniversary editions (Figure 3.4 centre and left). The form of the figure of the Blanket Men, the half-length portrait either side of the cell window, determined by the distance of a film camera in the enclosed space of an H Block cell that was too small to take the whole body in one shot, has been recreated in many media: drawn and re-drawn, painted, printed, photographed, rephotographed. Their image is now composed of layers of analogue and digital copying, yet it is possible to find a 'tiny spark of contingency'[77] in Kevin Toal's suspicious upward glance, an instant in the actual time and real space of the H Block struggle that was documented as he got the measure of the presence of the camera that had entered his cell.

The importance of this particular image, a television still from autumn 1980 (Figure 3.5), is an effect of the absence of all others created by the general prohibition on cameras within the prison system and compounded by the culture of censorship of the conflict in and about Northern Ireland. But its reach across different media and into collective memory is not only a matter of rarity but also of the significance of the body of the Blanket Man as the site of meaning of the H Block struggles. The power of their physical forms as symbols, understood so well by those who participated in the global movement of Hunger Strike solidarity, was endorsed in art.

The citizen (1981–3), a large 2 metre by 2 metre oil-on-canvas diptych, painted by Richard Hamilton, was exhibited six times between 1983 and 1988 in prestigious galleries in New York, Derry, London, Edinburgh and Oxford, and was widely reviewed (Figure 3.6).[78] Hamilton, an early British Pop Artist, is most famous for his 1956 collage *Just what makes today's homes so different, so appealing?* that remounted US lifestyle magazines to mock US consumer culture. *The citizen* also reworked media imagery. 'After obtaining some of the film shown on TV', footage from Robin Denselow's H Block encounter, he rephotographed it.[79]

The left panel of *The citizen* is an abstract of swirling brown lines that reproduce the excrement smeared on the walls of H Block cells occupied by the Blanket Men, the natural hues of the curving lines of shit-stains evoke eroded parietal art: petroglyphs, rock art, cave painting. The right panel is a full-length portrait of a male figure raised above the floor on a small podium, the colour of creamy stone. Representation in oils has lent the yellow sponge mattress, which held the prisoner's feet off the messy black cell floor, a ceremonial edge. The fabrics, two white towels discarded below the figure, one grey blanket gathered around his waist as a skirt and another in brown tones over his shoulders as a cloak, all present the falling folds of drapery of classical portraiture; their depth, soft texture and gentle movement shown on a canvas surface also demonstrated the virtuosity of a painter appropriate to the task of celebrating an historical subject. Indeed, the figure is classically rendered. One foot in front of the other, it is poised; the body balanced at the back and prepared for viewing at the front. The Blanket Man's body is

FIGURE 3.6 *Richard Hamilton,* The citizen *(1981–3).* ©*Richard Hamilton. Photo: Tate.*

displayed slightly angled, his face turned over one shoulder with the other sloping away. Richard Hamilton reveals in oils a bare and well-defined chest, the muscles of a male torso symmetrically balanced to create a statuesque form endowed with the status of allegorical figure. Hugh Rooney is no longer one of the two republican prisoners whose cell was selected for a 1980 television documentary but recast as a political subject named in the painting's title and engraved in capitals on a brass plate at his feet. The title, as the image overall, is a reworking. *The citizen*, which Hamilton insisted should have a lower-case 'c' when written, is a reference to and redefinition of James Joyce's caricature of a Fenian in *Ulysses*.[80] However, the literary devices and the play of artistic style, between abstraction and classicism, non-figurative and figurative, should not, I would suggest, distract too much from the political significance of the work that resides in the forms of history painting deployed in the diptych's right panel in contrast with those of pre-history in the left one.

Hamilton's contemporary classicism is an artistic strategy that directly addressed the demands of the H Block struggle.

The award of elevated political status, always the effect of oil paint, is applied to a Blanket Man, whose individual body was already invested with a collective representative force, a symbol of republican prisoners in the H Blocks. The H Block struggle against their criminalization, the withdrawal of special category status for those serving sentences for conflict-related offences, had been won within the visual circuits of contemporary art, at least, and through the painting of a rights-bearing body.

The classical pose and statuesque qualities of *The citizen* are fashioned from Hugh Rooney's full-length portrait. His complete form is not an imaginative projection from a camera closeup, the lens too near to capture his whole body across the small space of an H Block cell, but a composite from the television film. Hamilton produced 35mm colour negatives from the 8mm colour film from which he sized hand-made prints, 'Cibachromes'. *The citizen* is a collage of prints – Hamilton explained he worked with an 'enlarger to get a better relationship between parts of the figure'.[81] Then the prints were painted. The work of painting, its devoted attention and laborious dexterity, announces the symbolic significance of its subject. Richard Hamilton's *The citizen* has helped commit the televised form of Hugh Rooney to collective memory but Hamilton alone did not turn the Blanket Man into a symbol. That had already been done through the international solidarity for the H Block struggles. Hamilton was just one of their global witnesses. His painting began, he explains, when 'I was struck by a scene in a TV documentary'.[82]

4

Women Visitors:

Waiting to Understand Prison Architecture

For most of September 1970, Black September, Leila Khaled was held in Ealing Police station. Her second airplane hijacking had been less successful, but probably more dramatic, than her first, which had already made her famous. She was recognized before she made her move to the cockpit to announce the hijack of the delayed 11.20 El Al flight 219 from Amsterdam. Air marshals began shooting at her. When Patrick Arguello, the other Popular Front for the Liberation of Palestine (PFLP) hijacker on the plane, returned their fire, he was killed. The Boeing 707's pilot dived down into lower airspace. Khaled lost her balance, then was kicked and beaten by four people, two passengers and two air marshals. The plane made an emergency landing at Heathrow.[1]

Beautiful and eloquent, Leila Khaled caught media attention. Her detention in Ealing Police station, emptied of all except those that guarded and questioned her, while the PFLP negotiated the release of hostages on hijacked planes for those of Palestinian prisoners was widely covered in the British press. Khaled's name and her image, one in particular, a 1969 Eddie Adams photograph of her wearing a keffiyeh, holding an upturned AK47 while looking down gently away from it, became well-known. But she was not the first female hijacker and far from the only female fighter in the Palestinian national liberation struggle or PFLP.[2] Women are always present on the frontlines of conflict and especially in the unofficial armies against occupation. Only a few have been recognized, recurringly represented as exceptional, and thus without altering the gendered conduct and understanding of conflict.

Operation Demetrius, the internment swoop that started the strategy of imprisonment for the management of conflict in Northern Ireland, and led to the construction of the H Blocks, was straight out of Frank Kitson's *Low Intensity Operations: Subversion, Insurgency and Peacekeeping* (1971), a text full of lessons learnt from fighting anti-colonial struggles, such as that in Palestine. Internment usefully displaces combatants, in Kitson's words, 'insurgents', from both the contested territories and the communities that sustain and support them. The fear caused by the arbitrary arrest of members of communities profiled as 'insurgents' or their suspected supporters is as useful as picking up actual combatants. The raids on catholic-nationalist areas of Belfast and Derry began in the early hours of 9 August 1971. Black September and Leila Khaled's stay in Ealing was less than a year ago. Three hundred and forty-two people were lifted. All men. No women.[3] I am not arguing that women should have been detained or deserved to be detained; arbitrary arrest on the basis of suspicion rather than evidence is a violation of human rights. The issue is the invisibility of women's 'insurgency' in a defining moment of the conflict. Operation Demetrius was an example of the 'armed patriarchy'[4] that kept women in their place in war. Doreen Massey's succinct summary of how 'the identities of "woman" and of the "home-place" are intimately tied up with each other'[5] is a spatial politics perpetuated and even extended through conflict despite the disruption to everyday life that centres upon the home. When the British Army barged into houses off the Falls Road in Belfast and in the Bogside of Derry, they searched through their rooms for men, violently hauled them away to leave women behind broken doors with damaged furniture and traumatized children to begin their 'exclusive job': 'to wait and worry'.[6]

Prisons were very much part of our lives for a long, long time[7]

The armed patriarchy of war, accompanied and recorded through the patriarchy of the pen, has positioned women outside the theatre of war but affected by it: passive victims of the violence of others. Feminist scholarship seeking to reclaim the agency of women in war and reinstate their role in the conflict in and about Northern Ireland has registered different experiences of republicans and loyalists.[8] Female fighters were far more prominent in the republican movement; those sections or factions informed by politics of equality in left-wing struggles for national liberation had some influence over the whole. From Constance Markievicz, the Price Sisters and Mairéad Farrell to name only a few, Ireland had its own famous female fighters. But it is the unarmed activist, the female political campaigner that was, and is, much more representative of republican women's experience. Loyalist women were less politically visible despite a longstanding feminist endeavour to uncover the role of women in loyalism. In 1985 *Fortnight* invited Hester Dunn to write about the problem women faced in loyalist paramilitary groups. In response, Dunn outlined the wider context of gender relations in the 'loyalist community in general'. For her, female acquiescence to patriarchy was part of the problem:

> Women in Ulster have been their own worst enemies. They have been reluctant to stand up for themselves and on the whole this has been encouraged by the men in our society. The idea of the man being the boss, the head of the household, while the woman is at home dealing with children and housework, still prevails. Attitudes are changing, but very slowly. Some men accept that women go out to work and share the financial burden of the household; yet they refuse to share the financial burden of the household; yet they refuse to share the household duties.[9]

Whilst she continues to blame loyalist, Ulster or Northern Irish women for the double burden that has characterized conditions of heteronormativity across the globe, she observes that there are some that have empowered themselves:

> Northern Ireland women have allowed themselves to be used in this way and although things are changing, women here should realise their own potential. Some loyalist prisoners' wives have discovered this after their husbands had been imprisoned, and have had to become responsible for their own lives and those of their children. They have had to cope with making decisions and running the home independent of their men. Many have surprised themselves at just what they can do, and how capable they have become. I wonder if the situation was reversed and we had loyalist women in prison, would the men keep the household going, the children cared for, the bills paid and go up to the prison regularly with a smile and a parcel?[10]

The prison to which she refers is Long Kesh/Maze. Hester Dunn reserved her praise for the female relatives, wives in particular, of loyalist prisoners in the H Blocks. She identified the emergence of an important form of female agency through the conflict. But the female relative of a male prisoner remains a secondary subject. They are a stronger 'domestic stereotype'[11] but domestic nevertheless. They exert more control over their lives and homes but remain in the same place: a secondary position. They hold the fort, if you can forgive the military metaphor, and take up that exclusive role of waiting and worrying. A focus on female fighters may appear to be a better attack upon the armed patriarchy of war. For example, Sandra McEvoy concludes her study of loyalist women combatants by arguing that failure to understand 'women who wield political violence' is an underlying failure of conflict-resolution processes.[12]

My argument is different. I want to reject the binary and the hierarchy that the binary holds in place, then re-think the secondary category of conflict. From this position, it is possible to suggest that the supportive subjectivity of conflict, exemplified by a female visitor to a male prison, is the defining experience of conflict. It is an argument about waiting and war. Waiting is a dominant war experience and most of it is carried out by women. I arrived at this argument by listening to the voices of women. Much of this chapter is an invitation to read the spoken words of women visitors. They are followed by some analysis of my own about waiting and about feeling the effects of architecture, but their words are not a description to my analysis: my analysis derives from theirs.

This chapter is indebted to work of, and the work held in, the Prisons Memory Archive (PMA). Laura Aguiar, the co-director of the film *We Were There*, compiled from 23 interviews of women visitors to Long Kesh/Maze collected by and for the Prisons Memory Archive, has already challenged 'the idea' that women had a 'secondary role within the prison's history'[13] and argued that 'women played a key role not only within the prison walls but in the wider conflict context'.[14] Place is important in Aguiar's work and that of the Archive itself: returning to the site of conflict triggers story-telling processes that can contribute to conflict-resolution at personal and political levels. The audiovisual holdings of the Prisons Memory Archive are active documents addressed to the place of the past in the peace process. My re-examination of the footage of female relatives, female teachers, female probation officers and female artists also tracks between past and present but with a particular focus. Returning to a space, re-visiting the same space at a different time, going back into its buildings and re-tracing the routes in and out of them, produces not only stories but sensations. From 1971 until 2000, from the hasty establishment of an internment camp at Long Kesh to the emptying of the H Blocks, women visited the prison site; they visited monthly, weekly or daily to see loved ones or to teach prisoners or provide professional support. They felt dislocated within the prison site, out of place as visitors and as women in a prison full of men, most serving life sentences. It is their alienation from a space to which they returned time and again that produced a profound understanding of the jail (Figure 4.1). Women, I want to argue, knew the jail better than the men. Their voices begin to answer questions that I have asked myself since I first walked through the structures and spaces of the H Blocks. How do its walls, its barriers and borders, exert such power? What are the effects of an architecture upon those who walk within it and those who are refused entry? These questions of spatial politics are addressed through a practice of feminist writing that I, in the following pages, have tried to craft.[15]

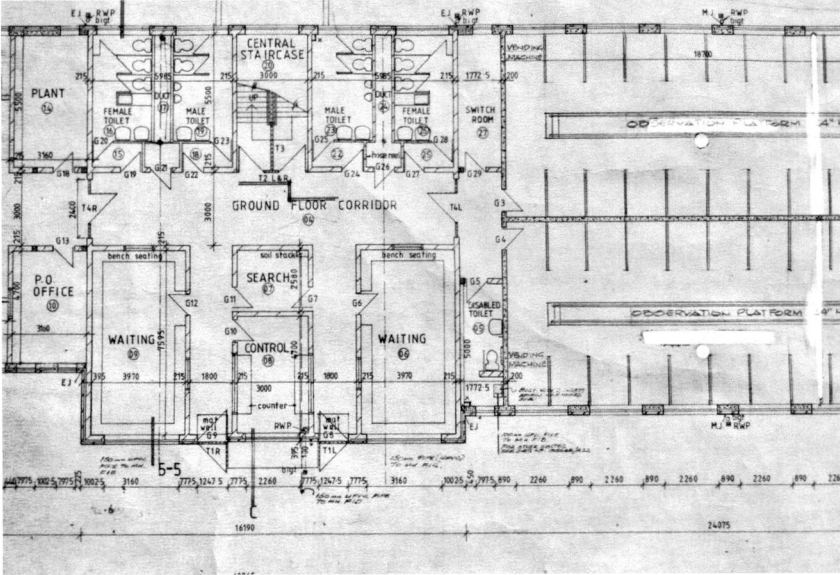

FIGURE 4.1 *Visiting spaces of Long Kesh/Maze. Photograph: Louise Purbrick.*

From the audiovisual documents in the Prison Memory Archive, I have drawn the words of Fionna Barber, Amanda Dunsmore, Louise Little, Siobhan Maginn, Joanna McMinn, Mary Nelis, Bernadette O'Hagan, Elizabeth Rea, Margaret Skelly and Sandra Spence into a single text and reordered them into one journey through the jail.[16]

* * *

It was always a cold place

Just grey, just grey.
And yet you'd go into this environment that was very grey and very, very intimidating.
I remember when I first came up here and feeling quite frightened as well.
All grey. No colours whatsoever.
The kind of greyness of it, just going into this place that is all tarmac, and concrete and wire and everything and the complete absence of colour. This lack of colour.

Not a green leaf in sight, just concrete and tin and so on.
It always seemed to be a grey day every time I came in.
It was always bad weather.

It was I just always felt really tense even on the brightest day coming into this place. I always thought it was dark.

You look at the metal and you look at the concrete. The barbed wire and the hard edges and all these hard, human . . . emm . . . permanent. Y'know, they are permanent. They are made to do what they do, right?

Yes, so you'd come in here

I'd come in here.

I would've come in here.
So this is how you'd come in.
You'da come down the Bog Road or you could'a come down that road as well.
We came in on the bus from Derry.
The bus brought you in these gates.
You had to depend on the community buses. There were stupid wee minibuses and they used to break down all the time and then you weren't getting home til ten or eleven.
You'da pulled up here.
I'd drive up here.

I'd park here.

And really it's hard to remember coming here every day and taking it for granted because it is a very strange environment.

It takes you a long time to get in and out of these places.
You'd come into this door.
You'd come out here.
I would've come in here. After doing the security gate stuff.

This is the security entrance and that's where teachers would have come, we would have come through this building before we were allowed to go up to the education block.

And this area where you'd come in was, I felt it as a teacher, very intimidating because there were a lot of prison officers standing around. Later on there was a screen thing where you could put your bags through and everybody was standing around looking at you. I'd put my equipment through the scanner. My equipment and I would be talked to and looked at.

Then they introduced a conveyor belt system where things went through and I remember once, later on after a few years teaching here, that a Marks and Spencer opened at Sprucefield and I used to pop in and buy a packet of fancy chocolate biscuits as a treat for teatime breaks and I always thought it was funny that you could smuggle these little things in. You'd start this process of coming into this incredible goliath of a building.

It is a very affecting place

It was a very strange environment to work and it didn't seem so at the time.
How strange. So many strange buildings in here.
This is a very, very, very vivid place here to me.
It's very vivid, very vivid.
It's very harrowing coming in here now.
This horrible place here.
Really, a prison is a horrible place and the security in this place was so tight.
It was a living place, tho', a living, sort of breathing. This huge, groaning, cold beast. It's a beast of a place. It was an absolute beast of a place.
Despite the hospitality and the people trying to make you feel at home and everything, you were still in a very regimented environment and there was a lot of oppression and regulation and everything that was going on beneath the surface. I sometimes used to feel a bit paranoid about that as well. Just that whole sense of this whole kind of machine that was at work, kind of prison service in some ways plus the whole kind of physical environment being in here. Just the oppression of the architecture.
It's dreadful.
It's really a dreadful, dreadful place.
But prison has a really severe effect on people. There's no doubt about it.

Through the turnstiles

You'd come across that yard down there, through the turnstile.
And coming across the yard, I used to have this knot in my stomach, really awful tension.
And in through the turnstiles.
You'd come in the turnstile.

When you'd come in, again, there's prison officers everywhere

It was actually quite full of prison officers hanging around, to me, they looked as if they were hanging around in this area.

There was always a lot of prison officers in this space. There was always a big presence.

My memories is that there was always a conflict situation going on between myself and prison officers.

You'd go through. The prison officer let me in.

The attitude was: 'What are you doing here?' So, as I say, it was a bit intimidating when I first started coming into the prison but after while you got used to it.

They were a bit critical of teachers coming in anyway.

Because when you came in, often some prison officers would be disparaging. At one level they were resentful of students getting free education but they would depict people as, y'know, murderers, they killed this person or that person and they were animals, there was a real attempt to dehumanize people. And it was actually quite difficult at times to manage that and then you would be sitting with people having a very human interaction and then coming back to this whole environment that is so dehumanized really.

I remember coming up with a priest one day. They treated, they really humiliated him. Prison officers went out of their way to humiliate us, too.

And what was so degrading about it is that this big warden would have walked in and said whatever prisoner you were visiting you were never recognized as a person. You got up and followed them like a nobody. I never felt like my own person when I came in here.

Every visit was an absolute battle between ourselves and prison officers.

All very formal. All very locking and unlocking of gates

One person at a time, y'know.

I would've walked up here and these gates were shut.

Them gates weren't open.

You'd walk through the gates.

You'd walk up to here.

This was always locked here. This lock. That was always locked.

You go in here.

And this was a closed off door. And the screw would have come in through this door. There was that many chains and rattles and keys. They made an intimidating noise opening these doors.

All these noises.

The sound of that now. That's what I remember. Clicky gates.

You had to buzz in at the front and walk. There was somebody at the front, a prison officer at the front there, in a hut.

So, I would've come in, stood outside the side gate there and wait for somebody. Now somebody would have been watching me, ok, watching me coming up and I would've been let in there and then you come in and there's another gate so I would then have to wait for that to open so you are constantly coming in and you'd be in between two gates, so you were confined. And then that gate, the first one would close and then someone would come and open that gate and I would walk up here to the door of the block.

These two gates, which were electric, the prison officers wouldn't open and close them themselves.

They were electric and there would be this nnnrrrr and this buzzing and the ck . . . ck . . . ck and sirens going off. As one opens the other one is shut, y'know, and this shuts, that one opens. So its an airlock.

You'd come in here and there'd be here, there'd be somebody, there's a room just in here to the right, there'd be another prison officer there, so you've got here, again, you've got the same thing, you've got these gates all of which would have been locked and then you come through one, another one would open.

Your parcel would have been given in

And you went in here. We would'a come through in here. We would'a went through up there.

You'd put your pass in.

Then you went in through this here door to hand in the permit. This was where you put in your permit and further down was the search. They also checked your ID. This was where you could'a left money in. You left a few pound in.

This is where you put your parcel in.

From Tuesday and Wednesday you planned what parcel, what you could afford. You done without yourself and you planned their parcels and you made sure you had everything in for them. Unknown to us, screws were stealing stuff out of it. But we had to . . . money was very scarce in them days but you made sure the prisoners had their parcels.

You went to an office with a parcel that nobody ever accepted. You'd have to give a name and address and I'd say Derry. They said back to me no, Londonderry. I used to insist I lived in Derry.

In here. Actually. The parcel would have been very meagre. A few apples, oranges. You'd to go in here with the apples and the oranges. Handed it over. The screw checked it. And more than often, there was something wrong depending on what form the screw was in that day. You would'a bring that back. But that was, this was, the fruit, papers, shampoo.

Then you went into the other end, out through this door, in through the next door to leave in the clothes. This is when the fun started. In here. It had the different wee sections with your clothes in it and there was another screw stood behind here. And he put the stuff in.

That was the clothes in and then you went on through here. You had to head over here then.

And you were searched. There was a body search. You went through search

You'd come in here and, here, this is where you'd get searched. I think there were tables. They might have had some machines, you know like they'd have in an airport. Search your bags and stuff again. You were searched outside and you're searched here.

You might have been bodily searched. There were female officers here that's for sure.

And then you went in through search and the search was very, very thorough. This is where you got searched.

This was the actual search area.

You got called here. You would have got called here.

And then you were called through into the searches. Then you were called through in there.

There used to be a table.

A desk.

At that stage, there was a table here, two chairs and two females.

There was two of them. The way they searched you here. They took your bag. There were women officers as well who'd do a body search.

The security was very strict and there was, y'know, a quite intimate body search. It felt like to me because I hadn't experienced it before and bags were searched and all that.

You were brought in one at a time.

If you had a small child with you, the child was allowed with you but I would have been what about ten or eleven when I went in on my own.

They weren't allowed to search kids but they pretended to play. 'Hello, wee love. How are you?'

And you emptied everything out of your pockets. There was, to be quite honest, there's many a day you would'a come in here and . . . sanitary towels, anything, it was very demeaning. And often you were asked, maybe, to take your trousers off or whatever. But it was all, I suppose, to try and . . .
You got totally, nearly stripped.
They absolutely stripped your bag and absolutely stripped you. I mean, it wasn't just a body searched like that. It was all this, right up, all over. Right up in between your legs.
My memories of the search was that the people doing the search were just hostile people. You could almost feel or sense this hostility. You weren't never treated as if you were a human being. The female searches, they were also obscene. They way they put their hands down your body and felt you and stuck their hand up your jumper. I just felt they were really degrading.
And because the situation was so bad. Mothers, wives, sisters, we tried to bring in things. We tried to bring in things that they needed. So you'd smuggle in vitamin tablets, you'd smuggle in a bit of tobacco. The searches knew. You'd smuggled in the tops of biros or you'd smuggled in ciggie papers. All those things. The searches got very extreme. A lot of us were getting pulled and told to go sit in a certain place. I remember them searching me one day. 'You go into Box A, Box number 1,' I think she'd said 'because you are a problem'. The problem was we were trying to make what was a situation of intense horror a wee bit easier for our own children, for the prisoners.
You used to go into the toilets after the search and take out whatever you had then, so you did.
And later on maybe it became more relaxed as I was here more and more at least I didn't take so much notice of it.

Always busses. We were always on buses. You never just walked though

And then you were called by a number. Never your name first.
So then you came through here.
You would have gone down into here. We got on the wee bus. It was the wee small minibuses at that stage.
Then you got into the bus.
Directly here was a minibus with blacked out windows. You got into the back of the minibus. That gate was always locked up. The bus was locked off and then out through the gate.
You went out into a van with all these other people and the van had darkened windows. You couldn't see where you were going. You just drove somewhere.

You got out through these gates and you got head counted and you got to the other place and there was another head count before you got off the bus.

You got out of the van and came across a yard and you went into another room there and then you waited until you were called for your visit.

There would be vans moving all the time, shifting prisoners.

And sometimes when I was coming in there might have been a minibus out here when prisoners were going on a visit so I'd have to wait for them to come out or they'd have to wait for me to come in. But it was always a strange thing. They were always, they'd get dressed up really smart and clean. They looked immaculate. It always struck me how immaculate they were when they went on visits.

And then when you were actually called for the visit you went into this visiting room

But at that time that was your life. We only lived for Thursday. That's when me and our mummy went. You live from one Thursday to another Thursday. That's what you lived for.

Well, exactly half an hour. When the half hour was up, if you were in the middle of a sentence you had to get up and come out, they made you get out. They actually allowed us a visit. Thirty minutes. Thirty minutes, once a month. At the beginning it was ok I recognized my son although the day he was sentenced they shaved all his hair off but after a while, they all looked the same. They had these unshapely sort of trousers and, maybe, like denim jackets, and they all looked exactly the same. Hard to find your own children because after 1978 when the no-wash began my son had blonde hair but that got dark.

Everyone of them had these white faces and these black sort of rings under their eyes.

And you sat down at the table and you tried to, you tried to, to be normal, if that is the right word for it, you tried to act as if you were normal and you were sitting there in shock. And you didn't want your children to see the look on your face.

You're trying to conduct, you know, 'How's things?' You're trying to be normal and there are seven or eight prison officers standing around you listening to everything you are saying, watching everything that you were doing.

A screw would have been standing, leaning over like this, listening to every word.

There used to be a warden for every cubicle.

It was very, very tight. There is no doubt, very tight. You just weren't allowed any contact at all.

You're trying to pass wee notes and things and the screws are standing over you. You had to give your son big hugs and kisses and they would be pulling you away.

If I had two passes for the two of them on the one day. I would have had to come and see whoever's name was on the pass first, and then come in, go through the search, stand in the waiting room, go into the van, come down, go into the other waiting room, go in for the visit and then come back out of the prison, into the van, away down as if I was just, I was just coming in and go through the exact same thing all over again.

And it was cruel, you know.

I expected to see the two of them together. All that time waiting and they wouldn't let us get together.

So, that was the type of little cruel things that they would have done at that stage. Some prison officers poking their head around the door and saying 'No visits for them naked boys.'

They turned you down the visit. And you'd have to stay all day because there was no way of getting home.

So you waited for hours

We would have been leaving at eight o'clock in the morning for a visit which was strictly half an hour but you weren't getting home till four o'clock or five o'clock at night, so you weren't, because you had to sit there for hours upon hours.

You were up here from early morning, you were here all day. For a fifteen minute visit. Now, you put your pass in and you stood in the car park.

Your Saturday was completely finished.

There was just a hut. There were no seats in it. People standing for hours and hours and hours. Four or five hours.

There was still no where to go, nowhere to sit.

You still had to stand there.

And then you went in here. It is in later years they have obviously put these pictures up. But believe it or not, it hasn't changed. It was as grubby and as dire looking to be honest. The floor was the same colour, the same dirt on it. The ceilings. Nothing has changed. But there were seats, you know, like a hospital waiting room, and you had your rows of seats all along here, so you did. Took a lot of time. But that was before you went to another waiting room and you took a bus and went to another waiting room. And you could sit there, maybe, half an hour. You'd leave, maybe eight o'clock and get into the visit due at eleven. And it was a very scant thirty minute visit.

And you went in and you waited in it.

That could have taken anything up to half an hour depending on, you know, how many people and what form they were in, whatever.

And you waited in here. And you sat along here and you coulda sat for . . . you never got out of it in under twenty minutes. On a good day. It could have easily been thirty-five minutes.

They took you back to another waiting room. You could have sat in the other waiting room for up to another two or three hours, so you could.

And then you went through into this other room then second room and you waited there and everybody smoked. My goodness, the place would have been full of smoke. You waited until your name was called.

I was always tense. There were nerves in my stomach. The only consolation that you had was maybe talking to the other visitors but very few people spoke in those visiting rooms. Everybody smoked. Because I think everybody was feeling the same apprehension.

That was the long wait.

Here for hours.

Plastic seats.

There were plastic chairs.

In the summer, in the summer you were melting. This would have been jam packed. No seats left. The kids squealing. They wouldn't open the windows and you could have been sitting here up to three to four hours.

I do remember sitting in this room because they kept me sitting here so long. I was so tired. It had gone on for hours and they were calling everybody else and kids were running around and my head went back because I was so tired and they kept me here all day.

I seem to remember taking a long, long time to get there and having to go quite a convoluted route.

You'd go into the education. You'd have to sign in and say you were there. There was almost like a teachers' common room where you had to wait before you were allowed to go up to the blocks. Sometimes you could be waiting for ages. There was a lot of bureaucracy in the education department but you never really knew what the hold up was so you just sat waiting.

It would take you about an hour or more to get to where you wanted to go.

It would take me two hours or three hours to get to the men to do an hour's work.

But you see the outside of the cells here. I know from afterwards that students told me if they were waiting for a tutorial, if they were waiting for a teacher, they might be looking at the window to see you coming up.

Eventually I'd get to what was called the circle. You come in here. This is called the circle even though it is an oblong and down here there would've been the Block PO and again you'd be kept waiting but basically you had to report to him to say which student you were going to see at that time.

And then whatever side of the Block you were going to then you'd have to wait for someone to come and open the door for you.

I would have stood there waiting. A student would be here waiting for me and I would be here waiting for him.

So, I'd come in here anyway, and again, it's the same thing. You're waiting in the middle as one door closes and another opens.

And, not only architecturally, and a very male place as well

But it was a very male place, you could feel the maleness in it.

There was an issue about being a woman in a prison, in a very, very male environment. But it wasn't about any kind of danger or threat. It was about being conspicuous, I think.

This is the thing. If you are a woman in a prison everybody knows you because you are conspicuous.

There's all these men, y'know, and they may . . . not that I felt uncomfortable. And just feeling you didn't want to do anything to draw attention to yourself and of course you are already drawing attention to yourself as a woman going into this kind of very all male environment as well, which sometimes seemed to be a problem, and the problem tended to be, I have to say, mostly with the prison officers, some of whom I felt very, very uneasy in their company. I had a sense they resented me, coming into this male environment, who had a very, very different type of life from them as well and it would be taken out on you as a woman in kinds of subtle ways. Sometimes I would feel very uncomfortable in their presence.

Prison officers would often say in a disparaging that 'they' liked women coming in and there was always this kind of, y'know, implication that it was, that prisoners like having this . . . it turned them on or something but I think, erm, that may have been the case, but I think it was much more the human connection was valued by people and I grew to then be very conscious of that and take some kind of responsibility in being as compassionate or something to be with people as a human being.

I would go out here

And then again, coming back, you would have been dropped off here and you walked up here. Now, at that stage you still could have been pulled in and searched and you came up here to collect your driving licence, your car keys, your, you know, that kind of thing.

I remember when I used to come out here, I used to feel exhausted. You're not conscious all the time of the level of alertness that you have. When I used to come out I used to feel relieved and I used to feel exhausted. I couldn't wait to get down that motorway again. Get away. There was a sense you left a little bit of yourself behind.

You're very much aware of this whole environment, an atmosphere of surveillance that kind of still lasts here. But the amazing thing was that this feeling, the sense of being watched and feeling uneasy would stay with you even when you left. It stayed with me for a couple of days. You begin to get used to it but you never really get used to it.

You had this sort of complex human being in a place that was very, very restrictive around expressing that. So, it was, at times, quite a charged atmosphere in here and I remember, y'know, coming in. It was a little bit scary at times, and I had my own life going on, but then you came out you were just so conscious of it. I felt a relief getting out and also drained of energy it took to actually be in here.

Imprisonment is an awful thing

I can hear the M1, which you could always here.
It's full of ghosts here, isn't it?

*   *   *

Understanding architecture

There is no need for me to interpret or reinterpret the voices of the female visitors to Long Kesh/Maze. Their analysis is evident in their words without my voice. However, I would like to emphasize two aspects of their journey through the jail already foregrounded in the collective account of their visits: the effects of the architecture of H Blocks and the act of waiting.

Feeling power

A strange environment, a horrible and a dreadful place, a cold beast, a machine and a charged atmosphere: women visitors recognized and registered the overall effect of Long Kesh/Maze. They did so, I suggest, because they were female in a male space; women were out-of-place and from that isolated position were able to absorb and to acknowledge the effects of the prison upon them. They did not expect, nor did they come across, any friendly encounter that could deflect the power of the architecture, at least until they met their prisoner, their student, their relative. Without distractions, female visitors felt the prison's full force. Also, as visitors, they entered and exited the jail; they moved through spaces and structures that were prohibited from prisoners. They did this often: daily, weekly, monthly. Their regular journeys through Long Kesh/Maze enabled them to understand its thresholds; they became familiar with the systems and sounds of the turnstiles, gates and doors but this did not necessarily soften the effect of the architecture. Most revealing within the female visitor documentaries in the Prisons Memory Archive is the identification of the effect of being inside the prison and outside it: the 'apprehension' ahead of a visit and the exhaustion, being 'drained of energy', upon leaving. The prison produced fear. The bodies of its female visitors were at work inside the jail controlling its physical effects; they must soothe their own adrenalin defence system in order to see their sons or their students; they were aware of being 'conspicuous' but remained calm on the surface; they sensed the power of prison but their appearance, in each moment and in every repeated visit, was an act of resistance.

'It was a very affecting place.' Maybe women visitors can speak about the sensations of oppressive architecture because an emotional response is an easily accepted performance of female identity, while it remains much less permissible for a man. But their ability to articulate the sensations of architecture, to express the effects of Long Kesh/Maze, is not because they fulfilled the Victorian female stereotype of naturally submissive and sensitive creatures. The opposite was the case: every time women entered Long Kesh/Maze they walked into a confrontation with the architecture and those who upheld its order. '[T]here was always a conflict situation' and '[e]very visit was an absolute battle between ourselves and prison officers'. Relatives recall that confrontations began early in the visit with the rejection of contents of parcels, followed by intrusive observations during visits and physical intervention when they passed small parcels of tobacco and 'comms' (Figure 4.2). They recount the humiliations and cruelties of prison officers. Teachers talk, with some difficulty, about verbal sexual abuse. All female visitors remember the degrading body searches.

'Very, very intimidating.' 'A bit intimidating.' 'Intimidating.' Women visitors identify the intention of prison architecture: the use of fear to influence a person, to control their behaviour. They describe how Long Kesh/Maze intruded upon them. Bodies tensed. The place had an intimate physical effect upon those who entered; it altered a sense of self. 'I never felt like my own person when I came in here.' These effects were not just felt once, understood and put

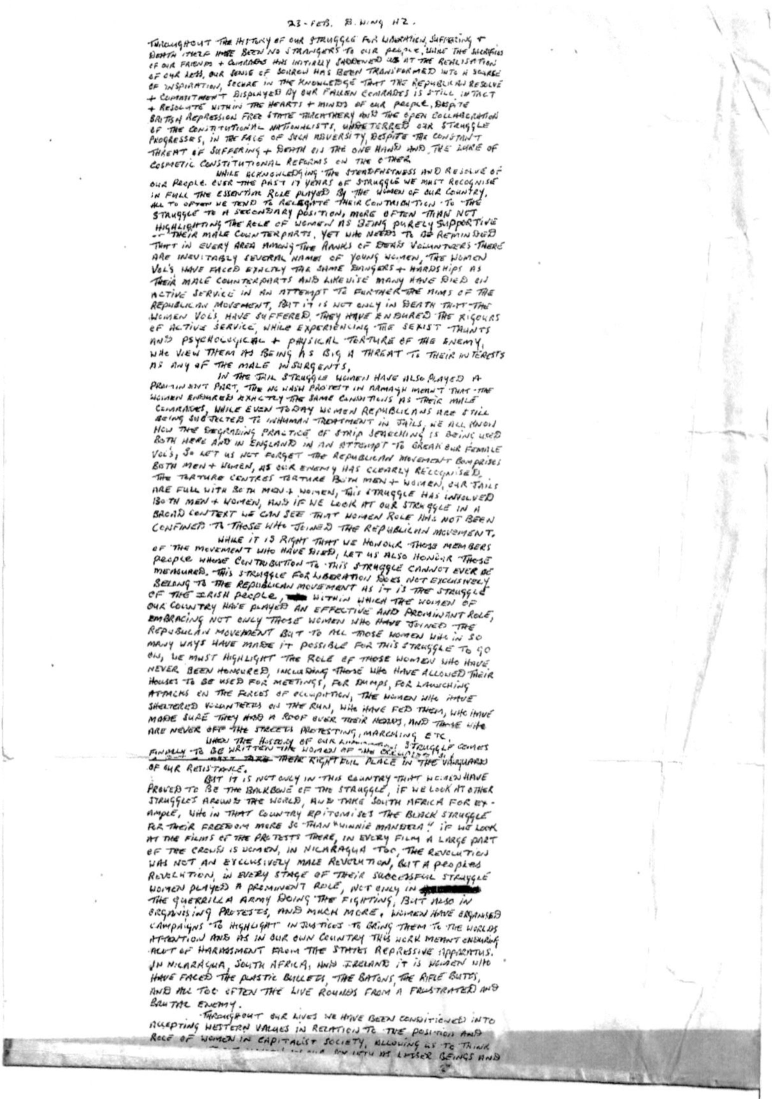

FIGURE 4.2 *'Comms', dated 23 February D Wing H2. Reproduced with thanks to Kate Page.*

aside but enacted with each visit to produce a lasting relation between person and place, body and building. 'You begin to get used to it but you never really get used to it.' The power of the prison took hold of the bodies of visitors, or part of their bodies, and it remained within them beyond its buildings. '[F]eeling uneasy would stay with you even when you left.' Long Kesh/Maze took something from them. 'There was a sense you left a little bit of yourself behind.'

On waiting

If all the hours of waiting in conflict were counted, it would be an easy bet that waiting, not fighting, would be conflict's mode: its most frequently occurring activity. Waiting to be called up; waiting for orders from high in the hierarchy of a military bureaucracy to take action; waiting to return home. The most well documented European wars of the twentieth century are dominated by waiting: in the trenches of France and Belgium in the First World War or in the army bases of the English countryside in the Second. A memorial marks the spot in the New Forest where the Royal Canadian Army Service Corps waited until mobilized for D-Day, 6 June 1944. More relevant to this history of the H Blocks is that the British soldiers that occupied the watchtowers along its perimeter wall came from an otherwise waiting force. Those that undertook six-month tours of duty in Northern Ireland were drawn from units stationed in West Germany: the British Army of the Rhine. Whilst the female visitors to Long Kesh/Maze uphold, and stoically so, the gendered oppositions of war, they 'wait and worry', their words also reveal an underlying experience beyond any gendered binary opposition: the imposed passivity that large-scale wars produce settles upon combatants as well as their relatives, men as well as women. Waiting is widespread in war. When I came across the memorial that recorded the weeks that Canadian soldiers waited before D-Day, a friend reminded me of a famous saying about boredom being nine-tenths of war. Boredom is the obvious and perhaps most depersonalized effect of waiting and not one that is felt or named in any of the interviews of Long Kesh/Maze's female visitors. Waiting in war may be widespread but is differently embodied. To try and shake off the boredom of off-duty routines in a barracks is part of the paid work of an armed patriarchy and far from the heightened emotions of attempting to control the apprehension of entering a jail to wait to see your imprisoned sons.

Waiting is part of modern life: the routines of everyday life in modern societies involve waiting. Both the speed of life and its separations are characteristic of modernity; bureaucracies of capitalism organize time into production lines; commodification requires the repetition of regular rapid movements, which also increases the amount of waiting: getting ready for the action to begin. 'Waiting is constructed as an in-between experience' writes Breda Gray.[17] Waiting can be extended into exclusion: the waiting person is prevented from moving from one part of life into another: not yet, not now. They are halted. Stilled. The modern punishment of a prison is enforced waiting as exclusion from society. Prisoners are removed from the rhythms of everyday life. A prison is a waiting chamber and its architecture a complex, compartmentalized waiting room. Cells are places in which prisoners wait for their release, for the interruptions in the routine of waiting, such as visits, and ultimately for their return to the outside world. But as described by female visitors to Long Kesh/Maze, prison architecture is composed of many spaces of waiting. The rooms demarcated as waiting areas in the prison's design (see Figure 4.1) are only some of the spaces dedicated to waiting, which takes place outside every gate and inside every airlock system, by and behind each door.

On the table beside me as I write this chapter is a book called *Border Country* (2007), its author and photographer, Melanie Friend, gave it to me. She saw a connection between her work on Immigration Removal Centres and mine on the H Blocks. I agreed. At the time, around *Border Country*'s publication in 2007, I believed that connection to be the use of architecture as a system of containment, which it is. 'Security is tight at IRC's' writes Melanie Friend. Her words echo those of female visitors to the H Blocks. She describes being 'escorted across "the sterile area", which acts as a secure buffer zone between the Gatehouse (administration block) and the Centre (visits room and detainee living quarters)'.[18] Such steriles and inertias are characteristic of the architecture of the H Blocks. But now after listening to the female visitors to Long Kesh/Maze, I understand another connection, just as close: prisons, like immigration detention centres, are places of waiting. A review from *Border Country* applies to the architecture of either:

> Not only do we confront the banal and mundane aspects of the architecture, where the impersonal visits rooms . . . conceal the extraordinary suspension of everyday life, but we also encounter people who are waiting. The detainee's experience is re-inscribed. These are people who may be subject to processes which aim to take away their everyday visibility, their political presence.[19]

Waiting is one of those processes. The waiting person becomes bound to the very processes that prevent them from participating in their own lives; to wait is to be held back in time and space, to be detained, to be imprisoned. It enforces an inability to act until the moment of release occurs and that moment is not determined by the waiting person; their agency is restricted to the ways in which they wait, how they accept their own waiting. 'Pushed to wait' is Deirdre Conlon's summary of the treatment of asylum seekers by European authorities.[20] Waiting is thus 'imbued with geopolitics'.[21]

A recognition of waiting as a power relation demonstrated all too clearly by the buildings that exclude refugees from the movement of modern life has helped me understand anew the architectural effects of the H Blocks. Immigration Removal Centres, such as those photographed by Friend, are sites of the geopolitics of waiting and are an architectural type, which includes prisons. Their structures are strategies of exclusion from the rhythms of everyday life and political rights of persons. Female visitors to the H Blocks felt the loss of both. In the wait to see their relatives or work with their prisoners, all was suspended except for time. Time passed and nothing else. 'Here for hours' and 'for hours upon hours'. [S]tanding for hours and hours and hours.' Days were lost. 'Your Saturday was completely finished.' In the empty time, personhood receded and identity deliberated overlooked. 'And then you were called by a number. Never your name first'. 'You got up and followed them like a nobody'. 'You weren't never treated as if you were a human being' and 'were never recognized as a person'.

Waiting within the architecture of exclusion becomes embodied in the people who inhabit it. Breda Gray, who examines the social norms of waiting in the migrant nation of Ireland, states that 'waiting produces disharmony between inner-life experience and the expectations associated with the progression of mechanical time'.[22] Most people have waited for another person to turn up in a particular place and at an agreed time. I know the experience of waiting for a friend all too well. For me, 'disharmony' is more like disempowerment. You long for an end to waiting or even an escape from your immediate environment but must continually impose your own passivity upon your own body if you want to see your friend. You are dependent upon another for your own freedom. You feel frustration with your unchanging surroundings and within your body. A sensation of enforced inertia moves from the buildings that may enclose you, or the view that does not alter, and your own irritated body. Time slows. Seconds stretch. Another minute gone and no-one is here. Passivity becomes the easier alternative to impatience.

But my waiting is not on the same scale as women visitors to Long Kesh/Maze. Female relatives waited for the release of male relatives for same length of time as their sentence, the same amount of time as the prisoners themselves. As women visitors entered the architecture of the prison, they could feel its power as theirs drained away into the passivity of enforced waiting. Its spaces take control over the time that belonged to a person before they arrived. Obedience, accepting the abeyance of your own agency, a subtraction of self, is demanded in order that visitors move so very slowly through the building towards the person and the time for which they wait: seeing a loved one, working with a prisoner. To feel the disempowerment of the prison system, to experience its intrusion upon a body, to understand how personal agency is removed then enter its architecture again and again is an extraordinary act of resistance to power. To understand the effect of Long Kesh/Maze and not walk freely away is, actually, to withstand it.

5

Erasure:

The Last Murals and Final Performance of Long Kesh/Maze

A series of sixty images of the empty spaces of the H Blocks were exhibited by Donovan Wylie at *Belfast Exposed*, the city's contemporary photography gallery, located on Donegall Street.[1] *The Maze* opened on 12 March 2004. The sixty images had been selected from eighty-five in his book of the same title, and those in the book from many hundreds more that he took in visits he made to the site in the previous year.[2] Both exhibition and book focused upon the voids of the prison site: the inertias and steriles that lay between the walls which were essential to an architectural system that monitored all movement; the blank dark grey tarmac of the roads; the deserted H Block yards; uninterrupted views of the long corridors of the wings and uninhabited and depersonalized cells. Emptiness served Donovan Wylie's photographic account of the scale of the structure of Long Kesh/Maze very well, enabling a visualization of the capacity of architecture to contain and control. *The Maze* appeared as 'a figure of political technology' that Michel Foucault had attributed to the Panopticon, 'a diagram of a mechanism of power reduced to its ideal form'.[3]

One exhibition visitor, a former prisoner, remembers it differently. 'The cells used to be packed with stuff', he told me.[4] There was a time when H Blocks were full of people, highly decorated, filled with things. The busy social and material life of the jail was recorded by Peter Taylor's film crew for the BBC 1 documentary, *The Maze: Enemies Within*, broadcast on 20 November 1990.[5] On the walls behind prisoners interviewed inside their cells, sitting on their beds, were pinned posters, magazine pictures and newspaper cuttings; framed photographs were supported on ledges (Figure 5.1). Some prisoners sat at their tables to talk to

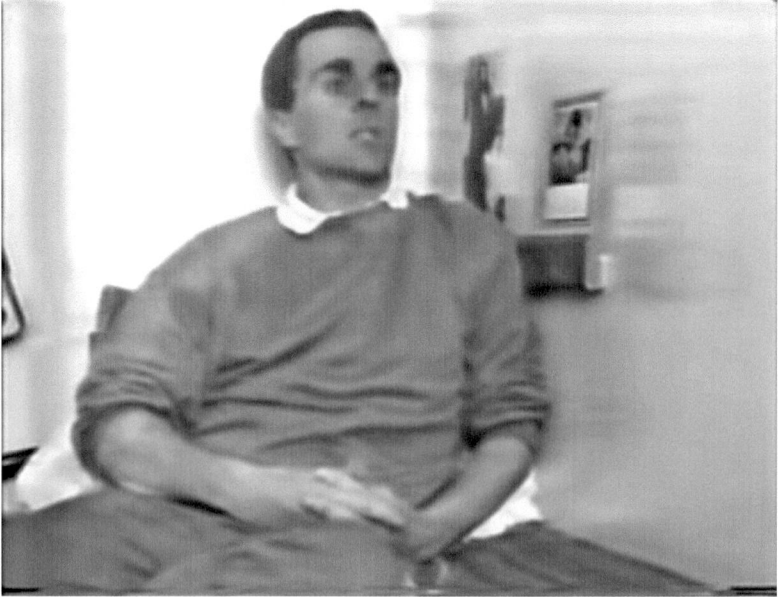

FIGURE 5.1 '*Cell interview*', *Raymond McCartney in Peter Taylor's*, The Maze: Enemies Within *(20 November 1990)*.

journalist Peter Taylor with writing materials in front of them, mugs and cups pushed aside, books squeezed into the shelves above. The spaces of association where republican prisoners watched television, studied their curriculum or that of the Open University, sang rebel songs or heard mass, were painted with murals. Behind prisoners who sat elbow to elbow as they crammed into seats, a large phoenix was visible in one room and two gently billowing flags, a tricolour and starry plough overlaid with outlines of the leaders of the 1916 Easter Rising, in another. The corridors of the loyalists' wings bustled with activity, were colourfully adorned and, in one place at least, substantially altered. An arch had been constructed in the emblems of Ulster; the space above transformed into a pediment, a union jack at its centre, Ulster and Scottish flags on either side. Under this arch and along this corridor that ran the length of the stem of the H was the most striking scene of the *Enemies Within* documentary: C Wing Long Kesh Protestant Boys Flute Band, led by a colour party of two prisoners carrying large flags, marched three abreast in reproduction Orangemen regalia from its far end to its airlock gate.

The absence of control over the collective organization and movement of prisoners within the wings of the H Blocks, amply demonstrated by Ulster Volunteer Force (UVF) prisoners marking the 12 July Battle of the Boyne with their own Orange parade in H8, was typical of the regime inside Long Kesh/

Maze for most of its operation. The contradiction between a high level of freedom in a high-security structure was intended to shock a British television audience but it is characteristic of internment aimed at managing a war rather than running a rehabilitative prison. The prison regime of simply detaining political prisoners started, albeit a little slowly at first, after the end of the Hunger Strike. As the fast began, Northern Ireland Secretary Humphrey Atkins stated in the House of Commons 'in case there is any doubt anywhere about the government's position . . . we shall not give way on the issue of political status'.[6] He had spelt out that position many times. 'They will not concede that they should now establish within the normal Northern Ireland prison regime a special set of conditions for particular groups of prisoners. They will not surrender control of what goes on in the prisons to a particular group of prisoners.'[7] This is, however, exactly what happened.

Liberated zone

On Tuesday 6 October 1981, three days after the Hunger Strike ended, the Northern Ireland Secretary, James Prior, announced that prisoners could wear their own clothes. Weekly parcels and visitors would return and the government would 'take steps' towards 'free-time association'. Later that month, he explained to the House of Commons that the 'arrangement for a limited increase in the opportunities for association will take longer to implement, but necessary work is proceeding'.[8] It was free association between prisoners of the same organization in segregated wings of the H Blocks that was the most distinctive feature of *Enemies Within*'s coverage of Long Kesh/Maze.

Segregation had been the persistent demand of loyalist prisoners. It was particularly important for them because they were initially fewer in number than republicans and therefore less able to control the wings. In the early 1980s, the prison population in the H Blocks was around 850, of which approximately 550 were republicans and 300 were loyalists.[9] The demand for segregation had often been made through sporadic no-work protests. In the summer of 1982, 200 cells were systematically wrecked and protesting loyalists were put in separate blocks establishing a de-facto segregation that became a lasting feature of life in Long Kesh/Maze. All prisons are based on segregation. Prisoners are defined by their offence, length of sentence or level of risk to themselves or others; the separation of prisoners according to assumptions made by prison authorities about their type is standard practice. But segregation along the lines of prisoners' organizations, separation according to prisoner and not prison categories, undermines, indeed overturns, official classifications that underpin management techniques and rehabilitation schemes. For example, Lord Gardiner in his 1975 report that led to the building of the H Blocks advised that 'detainees whose involvement in terrorism is weak and detainees who are fully committed, should all be kept apart'.[10] The influence of republican or loyalist organizations should end upon imprisonment of republican and loyalist prisoners to allow a process of rehabilitation to begin. This was never the case in the H Blocks and accepting that allegiances were unchanging reduced the function of Long Kesh/Maze to a holding operation, which was a realistic recognition of its role in political confinement. For some prison officers, the prison had been surrendered to the prisoners. One told Chief Inspector Hennessy: 'If they continue to get their demands met then the prisoners will soon be running the prison. Either you have a prison or you don't.'[11]

Nevertheless, the prison authorities pursued an increasingly pragmatic approach to managing the prison. The H Blocks had become as autonomous and self-contained as the compound system they were built to replace. In the last years of Long Kesh/Maze, this was openly acknowledged. It was noted in The Northern Irish Police Services Annual Report and Business Plan 1998–2000 that 'prisoners largely manage their own lives'.[12] Their cells were unlocked twenty-four hours a day. That amount of individual autonomy is, of course, exceptional within the prison system but more significant still is that individuals were also treated as members of a group. A mission statement I found on the floor of the circle in H6 in 2003 declared: 'We will operate a secure, safe and humane regime which recognises the individual and the organisation to which he or she claims allegiance' (Figure 5.2). Being part of a collective, as a loyalist explained in an *Enemies Within* interview, empowered prisoners within the prison system:

H.M.P. MAZE

> ### MAZE PRISON
>
> ### MISSION STATEMENT
>
> This Prison serves the Community by holding prisoners who have been sentenced by the courts for acts of terrorism and other crimes linked to para-military organisations. We will operate a secure, safe and humane regime which recognises the individual and the organisation to which he or she claims allegiance.
>
> For our staff, we will provide a working environment which reflects their difficult role and minimises the risk to their physical and psychological well-being. We want to develop and use their tallents to best effect in delivering the work of the Prison.

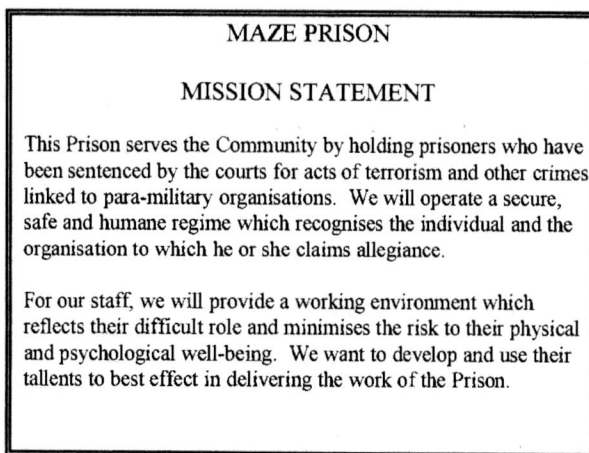

FIGURE 5.2 *Mission Statement, Maze Prison, found in H6. Photograph: Louise Purbrick.*

Prisoners here, whilst they are individuals, are part of a group. The fact that we are a group in the broad loyalist sort of sense gives us a certain negotiating power and a certain amount of freedom which we wouldn't have in an ordinary prison environment where everyone would be very much an individual.[13]

Furthermore, the prison administration actively sought the consent of prisoners to the implementation of prison routines through their representatives. The Chief Inspector of Prisons endorsed this way of working:

[T]he current Governor's approach to managing the prison, which involves a series of monthly meetings with the Officers Commanding of each of the five prisoner factions, is founded on an honest recognition of the unique nature of the Maze. There is no point in pretending that it is a normal prison.[14]

Bill Rolston has called the H Blocks a 'liberated zone' in a study of its murals.[15] The autonomy and agency of prisoners within the prison enabled them to amass their own material culture inside and on its walls. Their organization, being a group and working as a group, was realized in large-scale imagery and collective performances, in murals and parades. However, the historical record of prisoners' collective material culture is partial. That which could be sent or taken out of the prison by prisoners has been preserved and is now preponderant in the historical record but these are individual pieces, objects and texts, artworks, writings, letters and books that were made by or belonged to particular prisoners.[16] The collective material culture created, practised, that is, performed inside H Blocks and on its walls has gone. A visual record of the material culture of the 'liberated zone' of Long Kesh/Maze persists but the material culture itself has been erased. Bill Rolston's mural photography and Peter Taylor's television documentary are crucial parts of this record on which this chapter draws, alongside the fragments I have compiled, to interpret a material culture now absent at the prison site and to reflect upon, in particular, the collective performance and mural painting of loyalists in its final years.

Performance

The Orange parade along C Wing of H8 was a ritual performance. 'The right to perform a particular ritual does not usually become a central political issue in a modern industrial European state' observes Dom Bryan.[17] Yet, it is in Northern Ireland. Orange Parades became explicitly a matter of state intervention following the confrontations at Drumcree in 1995 between the Orangemen, the Royal Ulster Constabulary (RUC) and local catholic residents who lived along the Garvaghy Road route of the returning march. The Public Processions (NI) 1998 was passed, appointing a Parades Commission as a means of resolving disputes.[18] The ritual of the Orange Parade which commemorates the 1690 Battle of the Boyne when the armies of protestant King Billy defeated those of catholic James II is contested across the street spaces of Northern Ireland. Orange parades appear as a display of power of Protestantism over Catholicism: a re-enactment of the origin of its ascendancy and reassertion of its continuity. Why, then, parade along a wing of an H Block? Who sees the display of power? In a closed space occupied only by members of the same group, for whom do you march? To whom do you parade? But loyalist prisoners always held 12 July commemorations inside Long Kesh/Maze and did so without being recorded on camera.

Rituals require repetition which is often called tradition: dressing in the same costume on the same day to an assembly along the same route. 'Rituals are by their very nature repetitive performances', writes Dom Bryan.[19] Simply holding an Orange parade of any kind inside Long Kesh/Maze on each 12 July was important in itself; it fulfilled the ritual function of repetition. Judith Butler's account of the assertion of 'thereness' of global city occupations could be extended and adapted to the 'hereness' of commemorative parades.[20] We were here at this time and so we must return to mark that time and that to show we are still here. And, we will be here again at the same time. The effort of reconstruction of the dress, decoration and instruments of an Orange parade in the materials available inside a prison is also attention to repetition. To wear the same things invests the occasion with the same significance; repeating appearances is a claim to continuity and legitimacy. Despite its unconventional route along an internal corridor, the date and the dress of the H8 Orange parade established itself as a real ritual. 'Rituals', argues Bryan, 'not only give the appearance of lack of change but their imagined lack of change is often held by the participants to legitimate the events'.[21] But Bryan is alert to change or, if not change, at least adaptation, of the ritual of Orange parades whose repetitious forms clearly have a political dynamic and are a 'political resource'.[22] Rituals are always a resource for the formation of a group and the legitimation of that group as a community, recognized through their coherent representation.

Collective identity was the key 'political resource' of imprisonment in Long Kesh/Maze; it was the premise of prisoners' organization in the H Blocks: shared with one group, segregated from another. Prisoners as recognized communities could withdraw from the immediate reach of the prison authorities; resistance was based on membership of a group. Dressing in the shared orange colour of a T-shirt, pinning an imitation suit cut from the same black paper onto the T-shirts then wrapping over both equally flimsy sashes and putting on reproduction piper hats is to seek conformity to a group. Those who wore these things required no audience: loyalists were performing their own collectivity to themselves. But there is irony, if not parody, in the performance of an Orange parade in H8. The respectable symbolic order of Orangeism[23] to which many Long Kesh/Maze prison officers adhered as members of Orange Lodges was flouted by prisoners supposed to be under their control. Locked-up loyalists on parade were breaking prison rules. Whilst free association within a wing granted the Ulster Volunteer Force (UVF) the right to march together in their own clothing, uniforms other than the prison uniform were banned. The unofficial loyalist parade reclaimed a Protestant ascendancy from the official Unionist state forces who were failing to uphold it. Their carefully prepared and well-ordered display was a declaration along these lines: we were here at this time and dressed in our contemporary copies of your ancient regalia: we are more real than you.

It is the work of imitation that instigates the formation of identity within Judith Butler's hugely influential theory of gender performativity. The parody of drag plays upon the location of gender on the surface of appearances: 'an imitation without an origin'.[24] Gender identity, as other identities, is not hidden within a body, decorated for display or just dressed for everyday, but constituted in a series of constant actions: '*a stylized repetition of acts*'.[25] Performativity is ritualistic. Butler's understanding of ritual is shared; similar to Bryan's, from the same source. She summarizes Victor Turner: 'repetition is at once a reenactment and a reexperiencing of a set of meanings already socially established; and it is the mundane and ritualized form of their legitimation'.[26] Meanings, such as loyalty or masculinity, can be disempowered if the 'bodily gestures'[27] that uphold them are stilled, silenced, shut-up, removed from view, then erased. If they are imprisoned. Meaning cannot be left alone even in jail. Judith Butler helps to explain why loyalists need to parade out of sight along a corridor of an H Block wing or in its exercise yard. As 'politically tenuous'[28] as all other identities; it is made present through performance.

Murals

It was written on the walls. The walls of the H Blocks announced who ran them. Murals representing the collective identity of the prisoners' organizations that occupied entire blocks or particular wings covered their walls. Although some can be seen in the background of *Enemies Within* filmed in 1990, mural painting accelerated four years later, after the ceasefires that preceded the Good Friday Agreement. Bill Rolston's study of the H Block murals in the prison's 'final phase' from 1994 to 2000, from ceasefire to prison closure, is based on the examination of over 100 paintings on its walls. Rolston, who began documenting the gable-end murals that have defined the visual culture of conflict in 1981,[29] feared those inside the H Blocks murals would be 'painted out' as prisoners were released. He was right.[30] He recorded them on the eve of their erasure and his interpretation of that record gives an indication of why the authorities would remove them. The H Block murals were an example of how 'politically aware prisoners can collectively create the space which allows politically articulate art to be produced despite their confinement in a total institution'. They were 'an attempt by politically motivated prisoners to win back the space in which they are confined, to control it, to aspire to creating a liberated zone in the most inhospitable of environments'.[31]

That environment was still occupied in 1998 when Bill Rolston began his documentation of the H Block murals. He negotiated with both prisoners' organizations and prison authorities for permission to photograph and was invited onto the H Block wings controlled by IRA, INLA, UVF and UDA. His images were made while he was 'locked in with prisoners'.[32] The only murals not photographed in an inhabited H Block are those of LVF, who did not reply to Rolston's request. He returned to their empty wings in 2000 to complete his study. It is a comprehensive and inclusive account from which he asserts that 'all the murals mirrored the equivalent murals in loyalist and republican areas outside the prison'.[33]

H Block mural painting followed that established on gable ends; it reproduced both the form and content through which opposing political traditions have been, and to some extent still are, visualized. Republican murals most often deployed mythological, historical and contemporary portraiture to depict the subjects of Celtic legend, Irish revolutions, national liberation and socialist struggle, and their own respected figures. IRA murals tended towards more mythological subjects and those of the INLA to historical ones. The representation of the Hunger Strikers has been the preserve of the IRA, although three of the 'ten men dead'[34] were INLA members. Instead, the INLA depicted their lesser-known leaders on the H Block walls.[35] Loyalist murals inside the prison, as those on their streets outside, were largely emblematic, dominated by flags, crests and mottos. The history and the human figure are not entirely absent but always abstracted. Soldiers of the trenches of the First World War, an important historical referent for the formation of the UVF and the valour of the loyalist volunteer more generally, appear in conventional poses of commemorative stone or action movies, statuesque silhouettes or uniformed figures charging over the top with an open bayonet. But the most common generic form was that of contemporary paramilitary: a masked man engaged in conflict, shooting a gun.

Murals mark out the segregated and sectarian geography of Northern Ireland; they announce the boundaries between catholic, nationalist republican and protestant, unionist-loyalist areas and ensure the separation persists. They define the space; they declare its allegiance. For those from both near and far, a resident who lives alongside them or a neighbour who views from a distance, they can invite or deter entrance. 'They are', Jonathan McCormick and Neil Jarman argue, 'expressions of power and they are attempts to demonstrate control over space and place.'[36] But murals are no straightforward reflection of unfettered loyalist power in a protestant estate or uncontested republican control over catholic streets. Mural painting exists in a relationship between communities and those who claim to represent them. A large-scale image spanning the architecture of an urbanized area ensures that a visitor is acutely aware of being in a space that belongs to someone else; but their precise location in that area, their specific imagery and their pattern of upkeep is bound up with the political struggles within their localities. A newly painted or re-painted mural may be roundly welcomed or quietly tolerated; it may simultaneously demonstrate support for a particular political or military group or the suppression of opposition to that group. It can articulate the collective identity of a particular space and impose it upon a population whose lives may be less fixed than the paint on the bricks around them. Neil Jarman maintains that a mural's intended audience is, or at least it was during the conflict, local. 'It targets the image at people who will more readily understand the nuances and allusions.'[37]

Murals are coded. I would suggest that they are compositions of a series of codes. Their form alone, pictorial-style street painting on two-storey end of terraces, is an historical and geographical code of 'The Troubles' and of Belfast or Derry. The colours of the flags of Ireland, Ulster or Britain included in a mural or providing its decorative border are the generally understood codes of national belonging; the acronyms of political or military affiliation are less widely shared and the hierarchies of the pantheon names and portraits, their inclusions and exclusions, often unreadable and easily overlooked by those who do not possess these specific codes. They just get the overall picture.

Murals are a visual shorthand for 'The Troubles' despite their layers of unintelligibility. Those covering the gable ends of housing estates across Northern Ireland are recognizable to those who have never set foot in them. Their forms are a tool of recognition while their content is not fully comprehended. 'The media', as McCormick and Jarman point out, 'use murals to convey a sense authenticity to films and dramas ostensibly set in Belfast, even when this requires the painting of a paramilitary mural in Dublin, Cardiff or Manchester'.[38] Murals provide instant historical and geographical associations required by television and film script writers and offer the experience of proximity to the time and place of 'The Troubles' for post-conflict tourists in Northern Ireland. However, murals change, have changed. They are renewed, replaced, removed. Processes that accelerated with the process of peace. Murals were never petrified in architecture nor have they become calcified in the landscape. But they are now often buried behind another layer of paint.

Loyalist Eddie: interpretation against erasure

In 2002, I stumbled across one of the murals documented by Bill Rolston in 1998. A UDA/UFF mural based on a graphic design of heavy metal band Iron Maiden was in pristine condition and good lighting when photographed by Rolston. Faded with patches of paint blistered with damp, it was still intact and undisturbed by the processes of prison decommissioning when I viewed it in the dark, empty C wing of H7 four years later. Rolston described it as the 'most striking of all the UDA/UFF murals' of which there had been at least twenty across their six wings. The 35 mm black and white film in my borrowed single lens reflex camera that I carried without a flash attachment or expectation of undertaking any systematic visual documentation, captured the mural very poorly (Figure 5.3). Its significance as a record of imprisonment in Long Kesh/Maze exceeds this incomplete record; its scale and its strategies of representation, the deployment of allegorical and indexical symbols that reference real events, are those of a history painting. Drawing on my dim image with the clarity Rolston's reproduced in the *State Crime Journal*, alongside the written record in my field notebook (Figure 5.4), what follows in the next few pages is an attempt to address the incompleteness and absence of the mural with an art historical reading, attending to how formal composition of a painting reconstructs social reality.[39]

A battlefield has been transformed into a graveyard. A skeletal figure, a death mask for a face, is clothed in the uniform of a nineteenth-century British soldier: pale trousers, a jacket of a darker stronger colour, belted and crossed with white straps, epaulettes on the shoulder. He charges out of a dark landscape. Carrying a tattered flag like a spear in one bony hand and an AK47 in another, the skeleton soldier appears in the desperate and determined stance associated with 'going over the top' and the uneven ground behind him suggests the muddy mounds of trench warfare. But the mounds are newly dug graves whose wooden crosses read: Greysteel, Sinn Féin, IRSP, INLA, IRA. A grim reaper stalks in the background, behind the skeleton solider. Above him is a large fist encircled by 'UFF 2nd Batt'. 'Shankill Road', on the radiator below the mural, completes the image and confirms its ownership. A text painted on the wing wall also explains the mural's purpose and to whom it belonged: 'This mural is dedicated to all the brave men who have fought with "2nd Batt" West Belfast UFF. Since 1973 they have taken the war almost single-handedly to the Republican Movement. From having so little to achieving so much that their memory must forever live on. *Quis Separabit.*'

The skeleton soldier is an adaptation of Eddie, heavy metal band Iron Maiden's mascot. His stance and, indeed, the composition of the entire mural draws upon the cover image of the band's 1983 single *The Trooper*, a rock music interpretation of Alfred Tennyson's, *Charge of the Light Brigade*. This

FIGURE 5.3 *UFF Mural, C Wing H 7. Photograph: Louise Purbrick.*

misdirected, disastrous but most famous advance of the Crimean War is a less important historical reference for loyalists than the Battle of the Somme, expressed through the First World War landscape that has replaced the dry rocky background of the original image. However, the incarnation of Iron Maiden's Eddie as a doomed trooper of the Crimean War does articulate the reckless courage of the last defender of Empire, whose appeal to loyalists is demonstrated by its duplication in mural form: there are several different versions painted on gable ends in Derry and Belfast.[40] These were later copies, Rolston points out, of that painted on C Wing of H7.[41]

The trooper Eddie is unmistakably a loyalist; the tattered flag he carries displays the red hand of Ulster. The UFF's mural of loyalist Eddie is layered with meaning typical of history paintings that provide contemporary political readings of an honoured past: his skeleton figure screens the masculine nihilism of heavy metal music with the selfless bravery of nineteenth-century

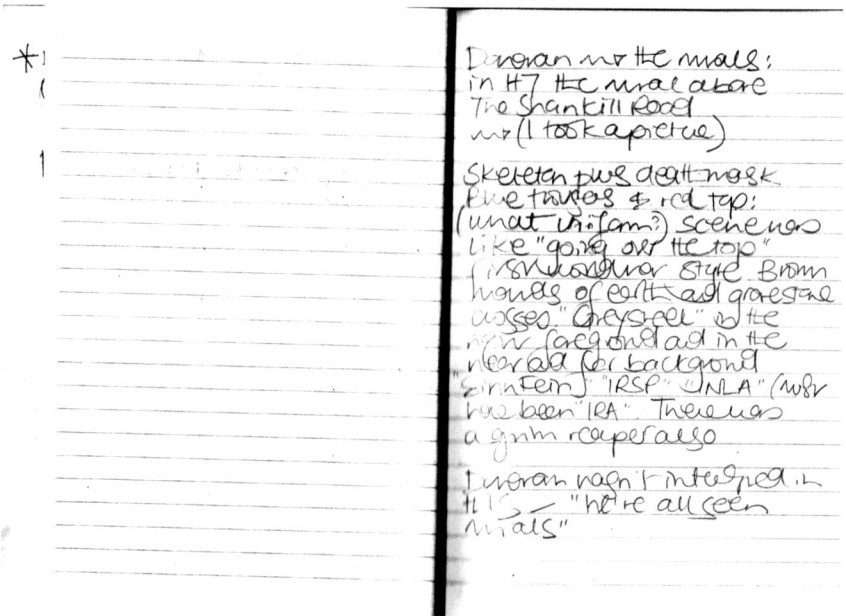

FIGURE 5.4 *'Field notebook entry on UFF mural, C Wing, H7', photograph: Louise Purbrick (2022)*

trooper; the reverence for the trenches of the First World War is projected onto the sectarian landscape of the conflict in and about Northern Ireland. There are also echoes of the Winston Churchill's Second World War speech of national gratitude to the Royal Air Force in the dedication of the mural to the '"2nd Batt" West Belfast UFF': 'so much' is compared with 'so little', a substitute for 'so few'.

The loyalist Eddie mural was part of a series of wall paintings within H7. The other interventions and inscriptions on the prison walls were less visually sophisticated but part of the same circuit of meaning. Loyalist Eddie was located at the top of the H7's C wing, near the entrance to its dining room. On the walls in the dining room were painted four male forms that represented UFF 2nd Batt. All were shown in black combat uniforms distinguished by balaclava headwear as opposed to the more conventional helmets or caps. All displayed guns and were accompanied by the repeating line, 'Simply the Best', from the love song, *The Best*, recorded by Bonnie Tyler in 1988 and covered by Tina Turner the following year. The latter's more famous and more bombastic version was easily appropriated to celebrate military as well as masculine prowess.

In the floor plan of the H Block, dining rooms are found at each corner of the cross bar that forms the H and is its administrative circle, but they are entered only from the wing. Dining rooms are located at the top of each wing, four to a block. C wing continues through double airlock gates into D wing to complete the stem of the H. In the D wing dining room of H7, a poem was painted in large script under the headline, '2nd Battalion on Tour'. The headline appeared on a banner, paint trying to capture the appearance of the folds of a ribbon created when pinned to a wall. The poem read: 'I First Produced My RPG. / Then I Produced My Rocket / I Shouted No Surrender and Connelly House Got It / We'll Kill Them at Their Work / We'll Shoot Them in the Head / We'll Kill Them in Their Bookies / Then It's Home To Bed / Freedom Fighter' (Figure 5.5). Below the poem, a kneeling figure in a black uniform, balaclava and gloves provides a pictorial illustration: he holds a shoulder-fired rocket propeller ready to launch its grenade. Bordering the poem and completing the ensemble were two images. To the left was an adaptation of a red-edged triangular 'men at work' road sign, featuring a silhouette in the same kneeling pose as the central figure, aiming another rocket propelled grenade. 'ON HOLD' was boldly displayed in black capitals along the bottom. Below the road sign image, were three place names also painted in black capital letters: 'ROCK BAR / CONNELLY HOUSE / LOWER FALLS SF. To the right was a shield shaped emblem displaying a clenched fist, a version of the Red Hand of Ulster, surrounded by a repetition of military affiliation: 2nd Batt West Belfast (see Figure 5.6 below).

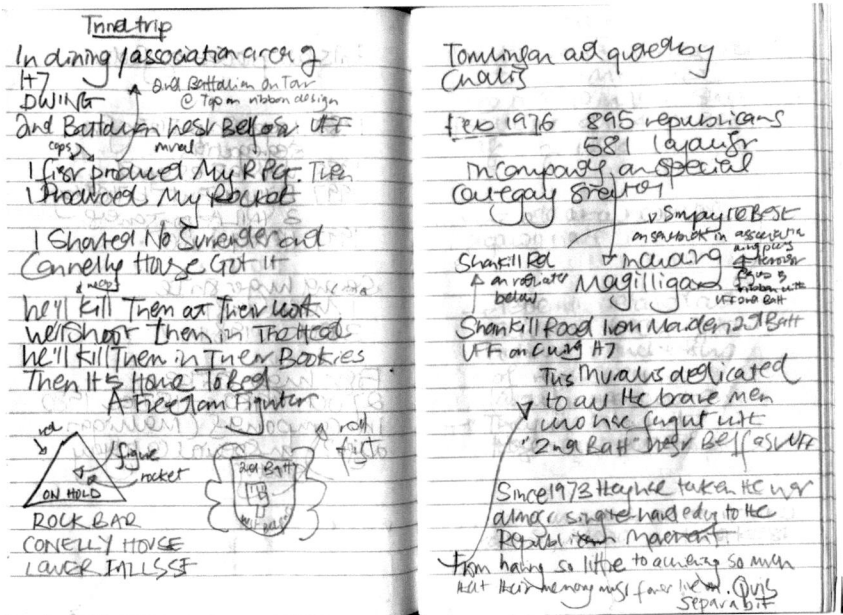

FIGURE 5.5 *Field notebook entry on UFF poem, D Wing dining room, H7. Photograph: Louise Purbrick.*

The H7 mural series is, obviously enough, targeted, as Jarman phrased it, at a local audience, at those who lived within the walls on which they were painted, the UDA/UFF prisoners. No 'nuances and allusions'[42] would be lost on them. Most murals contain acronyms and place names that assume intimate knowledge of the conflict. They are one of its codes. UFF is the regularly used shortened form for the Ulster Freedom Fighters, the loyalist group described as the 'nom de guerre' of the Ulster Defence Association (UDA), its 'flag of convenience' and its 'cover name' used 'to claim responsibility for the killing of Catholics'.[43] The UDA, formed in 1971, was the largest loyalist organization: estimates place the number of members in the mid 1970s at 30,000 or 40,000, many of whom were also members of the part-time British Army force, the Ulster Defence Regiment. The UDA is identified in the Sutton Index of Deaths as being responsible for 112 fatalities;[44] it was not proscribed, however, until 1992. The UFF was established two years into the life of the UDA, in 1973, to be, in the words of one of its founders, 'more effective' than its parent organization and 'willing to take the war to the IRA,'[45] a phrase repeated on the walls of H7. The Sutton Index lists 147 people killed by the UFF.[46]

Of the acronyms written on the crosses scattered over the graveyard cum battlefield over which loyalist Eddie stomps, perhaps only one requires no explanation to those outside the H Block walls: Irish Republican Army (IRA). The shortened form of Irish National Liberation Army (INLA), the Irish Republican Socialist Party (IRSP) and SF for Sinn Féin are less commonly used. This collection of letters blurs the political with the military and elides contested republican traditions. All are also encompassed by the pronoun repeated three times within a poem attributed to A Freedom Fighter: them. Them is the other side, the entire catholic community and any of its representatives. The mix of acronyms and pronouns on the walls of H7 are indications of the dual sectarian strategies of the UFF. On the one hand, they targeted representatives of the republican movement aided, as the Stevens Inquiry revealed, by the receipt of intelligence information from British security forces including the Special Branch of the Royal Ulster Constabulary and MI5.[47] On the other hand, they engaged in the indiscriminate killing of catholic people. Deliberate attacks on those who could be described as uninvolved, non-participants, civilians, bystanders or innocent, and I use these difficult exclusive terms because I have no better others, have been defended by UFF members as a 'clear strategy and methodology' of pressurizing the IRA by attacking the community assumed to give it 'support'.[48] The dedication on the wall next to loyalist Eddie claimed both strategies for the UFF who 'have taken the war almost single-handedly to the Republican Movement'.

Acts of war are commemorated all the time. They are the subject of cycles of large-scale national ceremonies of which Remembrance Sunday is just the most regular in western Europe and far from an isolated affair. Artefacts of violence are also everywhere. Bomber aeroplanes and assault tanks, guns and bullets, torn uniforms and abandoned shoes, dead bones and bloodied walls are found in international peace museums and those of national war, regional displays of everyday life and collections of single communities.[49] However, the violence of war is often, almost always, distanced from those who carried it out. The people who flew the plane, drove the tank, shot the bullet from the gun appear opaque and their acts of war are represented as inevitable and ranged, rather vaguely, against human integrity. Actual victims do have greater presence in commemorative practices in museums or around monuments but their suffering is universalized as a condition of war rather than the outcome of a particular confrontation or imposed by perpetrators of violence. The significance of the series of wall paintings in H7 is that they do not adopt the dominant commemorative practice of generalizing the acts of war. The gleeful routine of killing expressed in the words and rhythm of the UFF's wall poem represents war as the actions of some people against others. The celebration of weaponry and of the victory over the dead glorifies violent actions. Staring straight out of the walls of H7 is an account of the relationship between superiority and hatred, violence and conflict. This is a rare record of sectarian warfare that reveals motivations for conflict that are rarely, if ever, addressed.

The presence of 'the military activity' of the UDA/UFF in its wall paintings is carefully considered by Bill Rolston. He argues that the subject matter of the loyalist and republican H Block murals 'speak of a differential relationship to the state'. The British state and its forces are the obvious opponent of republicans and this requires no explanation, particularly in one of its own fortresses, the H Blocks. Loyalists are in a contradictory position and place. 'Believing themselves an extension of state forces in combating republican terrorists, loyalist muralists express a sense of indignity that loyalists should be locked up for expressing their loyalty.' Thus, Rolston writes, their 'guns are pointed clearly towards republicans and nationalists'. Their murals need to 'spell out more directly who the enemy is'.[50]

There are a number of references to UFF actions in the mural series. 'Their Bookies' is an allusion to the killing of five catholics in Sean Graham Bookmakers, Belfast, on 5 February 1992. The place names, 'Greysteel', 'Rock Bar', 'Connolly House' and 'Lower Falls' work in a similar way. On 30 October 1993, two Ulster Freedom Fighters opened fire on people drinking in the Rising Sun bar in Greysteel, County Derry, killing seven. They shouted 'trick or treat' before they used their weapons, an AK47 and a Browning pistol.[51] The attack was a retaliation following the premature detonation of an IRA bomb in a fish shop on the Shankill Road a week before. The intended target was the Loyalist Prisoner Association offices above the shop run by the UFF but ten people downstairs in the shop were killed in the explosion: the IRA member, the fish shop owner, his daughter and seven of their customers.[52] The other UFF actions indicated on the walls of H7 took place the following year. On 10 January 1994, Ulster Freedom Fighters launched a missile at a public house called the Rock Bar on the Falls Road, Belfast. They used an RPG, the celebrated shoulder-held rocket propelled grenade device of the H7 poem. The grenade ricocheted off the pub's protective metal grille exploding in the street. The UFF men drove away firing shots.[53] The attack on Connolly House, Sinn Féin's offices in Andersontown, another catholic-nationalist area of West Belfast three months later was very similar: the same type of weapon was used, damaging the front of the building.[54] There were no fatalities from either UFF action; Sinn Féin's Andersontown offices were empty at the time of the attack, but both were a significant show of force, a threatening display of loyalist armoury and their ability to invade nationalist areas. These actions are claimed as the achievement of a particular UFF unit, West Belfast 2nd Battalion C Company, led by the notorious Johnny Adair, who was arrested in relation to at least one of these rocket attacks. All are indicative of his leadership but also of a longer period of loyalist assaults on a so-called 'pan nationalist front'[55] that included representatives of constitutional nationalist parties as well as supporters of the republican movement. The UFF actions that took place in the early part of 1994 could also be considered both a backlash and a series of warning shots in the months following the signing of the Downing Street Declaration, regarded by loyalists as political pincer movement against Northern Ireland by a British Prime Minister and an Irish Taoiseach, John Major and Albert Reynolds. Eddie as loyalist trooper is a record of a specific historical period: one of political uncertainty felt by loyalists and unionists as they anticipated some form of British withdrawal from Ireland, and the intensification of violence preceding political change.

Murals: appropriation and erasure

The H7 mural series works in the same way as the gable-end murals. Although the relationships within the H Blocks were rarefied with these highly structured spaces of solid separation, their murals still perform the work of demarcation. The geographical segregation between loyalists and republicans that extended and deepened during the conflict in and about Northern Ireland was an organizing principle of the prison. You could be forgiven for thinking that murals were not necessary or were the decorative form to the prison's functional structure. But their proliferation within the H Blocks in the 1990s suggests otherwise; their 'attempts to demonstrate control over space and place',[56] mirroring the wider sectarian geography of Northern Ireland, intensified in this period. The poem, slogans, battalion badges and mottos, black figures with their balaclavas as well as the loyalist Eddie in his graveyard battlefield are all declarations of the territorial limits of the UFF within Long Kesh/Maze, the extent of their power over the wings of the H Block and the individual cells attached to them. To those who visited C and D wing of H7, including any prisoner officers, the mural series demonstrates that the space is that of the UFF; only they have the authority to manipulate and dominate it. The wall paintings of H7 depict protestant supremacy over catholic people and from this visual platform, they then assert UFF dominance over prison officers as well as other loyalist groups, the Loyalist Volunteer Force (LVF), the Ulster Volunteer Force (UVF), and even other battalions within the UDA/UFF itself. To those prisoners who are affiliated to the UFF, the array of emblems would be a familiar sight, a daily welcome back into the group, reassuring them of their place within it and a reminder of its authority. Images are as performative as the bodies to whom they are addressed. Thus, whatever reassurance of superiority the wall paintings might offer members of the 2nd Battalion of the West Belfast UFF, they are also a command and warning to those members to continue to adhere to its organization.

Since the high point of mural painting across Northern Ireland in the 1990s, its practice has altered considerably and been bound up with peace process attempts to produce neutral urban spaces. The redevelopment of mural sites, the removal and relocation of murals or their replacement with officially commissioned public art has been debated by local communities, university academics and political representatives, sometimes together in the same forums.[57] The position of mural painting in power struggles within and between communities means that they are unstable art forms, the objects of conflict rather than simply its record. Their instability, their availability for alteration and removal, is debated by Neil Jarman and Jonathon McCormick who shared Bill Rolston's concern and interest in the disappearance of historical records of the conflict.[58]

Murals are, therefore, never permanent; they are temporary interventions into public or shared space, which were, and in some cases still are, maintained while they remain relevant to the community who lives close by. What matters is who cares for them. Much like conventionally commissioned public art, responsibility for the work and its physical condition does not reside with its creator but the commissioner. There are a few mural painters, Bobby Jackson and his family, The Bogside Artists or Gerard Kelly also known as Mo Chara, with reputations as muralists sufficient for them to claim ownership and exert some control over their work. But most wall painters are unnamed and unknown beyond the groups who commission the mural, those that ask them to paint it, and the communities who live alongside it. The anonymous community wall painters may adapt trade skills, use self-taught methods or practices acquired from other local painters in the production of pieces to support, with their creativity, the group that seeks control or has control over the spaces where the mural will be. There must be a negotiation before the first brush of paint. Yes, you can use my wall but I should consult my neighbours. A community, and one which is relatively small, made up of the occupants of a few streets and those who walk through them, must agree. The relationship between paramilitaries and communities determines the destiny of murals: their existence, upkeep, or abandonment.

The effacing of the H Block murals as the prison was cleaned up in preparation for re-use or closure is another wall painting lifecycle. With no nearby community interested in maintaining them, they disappear. Their paint fades and flakes. The signs of neglect are also those of disinterest and prepare the way for replacement or removal. Painting over murals within the prison may follow a similar pattern to that in a housing estate but the power relationships in the process were not the same. Clearing the walls of the H Blocks of the political signs of republicanism and loyalism was the endgame of a long confrontation within the prison between its prisoners and the prison authorities. At the site of incarceration, the incarcerated resisted the forces that incarcerated them. The walls showed they had won. Covering the wings of the prison with the images and words of prisoners, their marks of identity, was a rejection of the prison regime announced in its architecture and a reconstruction of prison life from within its confines. Painting on walls makes a material change to the spaces within them. Paint may not be permanent but its spans of colour and manipulations of shape are long lasting enough to challenge the permanence of the power of the buildings on which it has been laid. Its visual effects extend across rooms and corridors to their inhabitants who can feel the freedom of political recognition.

Bill Rolston knew the H Block murals would be painted out because he understood their purpose. 'Politicized prisoners', he explains:

> . . . were intent on maintaining their political beliefs and organization as a challenge not just to the system of imprisonment itself but to the wider system of power which gave rise to their imprisonment in the first instance. In that battle for control, cultural artefacts such as the murals became both a sign and means of the prisoners' appropriation of space and power.[59]

At Long Kesh/Maze, erasing prisoners' wall paintings reasserted the authority of the prison and that of its prison officers where they had relinquished their control. That the Northern Ireland Prison Service accepted that prisoners ran their own wings was a pragmatic policy but routinely embarrassing for those who were supposed to enforce a prison order. 'Painting out'[60] it is an act of repossession of space. A hollow victory, perhaps, in an empty jail.

I noticed that the clearing and cleaning of the H Blocks removed all substantial signs of a republican presence within the prison despite the fact that the single largest group always had been the IRA. I found one fragment that might have been associated with a republican prisoner: a tiny green and red image cut from a newspaper was taped above a cell door. It was an advertisement for a car accessory made to dangle on the inside of a rear windscreen. Two small paper reproductions of card reproductions of football kits, Celtic and Manchester United, embraced each other. It is a long way from a direct reference to either the IRA or the INLA and relies on an association between Irish identity and football fandom but it was the only trace of any republican prisoners. And you have to take my word for it, because the 35 mm black-and-white film had run out in my camera.

The absence of republican imagery allowed the remaining inscriptions, such as the UFF murals, to dominate a deserted space that was once bounded and contested through opposing political imagery. Why did the H7 UFF wall painting series remain when all others were erased? Bill Rolston accurately predicted that the H Block murals would be covered up; these were the exception. One of the maintenance workers responsible for clearing the cells explained to me that they just 'didn't get around to this block'. But notes left in the administration buildings show that H7 was not the last block to be emptied of prisoners. Photographer Donovan Wylie surmised that the explicit sectarianism of UFF series justified the role of the Northern Ireland Prison

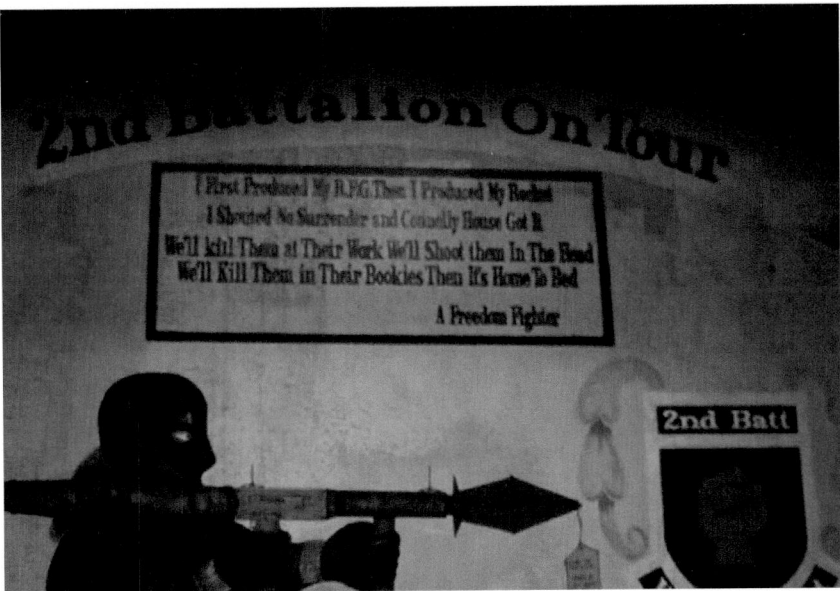

FIGURE 5.6 *The UFF H7 mural. Reproduced with permission from the Prisons Memory Archive.*

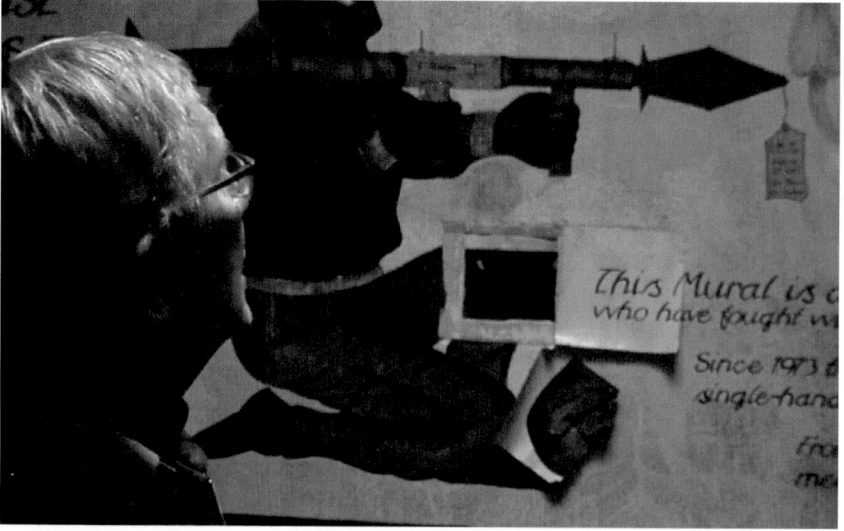

FIGURE 5.7 *Peter Taylor in front the UFF H7 mural, close up. Reproduced with permission from the Prisons Memory Archive.*

Service at the Maze. For a brief time, from its closure to its demolition, H7 was their 'museum' and displayed why imprisonment was necessary. When Peter Taylor returned to Long Kesh/Maze to record his experiences for the Prisons Memory Archive he halted in front of the Freedom Fighter poem in D wing H7 (Figure 5.6 and Figure 5.7). In the hesitant phrases that indicate thinking aloud and trying to be truthful, he said: 'These murals should really be, should really be, these murals really should be preserved. Because they reflect some of the darkest days of "The Troubles" and the UFF, who were the so-called military wing, the killer wing of the UDA.'[61] But to leave such imagery in place is also an act of acceptance of its content. The poem celebrating loyalist violence and weaponry, loyalist Eddie charging over the graves of republicans and catholics, mottos announcing the supremacy of the UFF all remained on the H Block walls until they were brought down by the wreckers.

6

On eBay:

Who Owns the Keys of the H Blocks?

There's stuff you find along the way and stuff you leave behind
And it all ends up as stuff that you can buy
On eBay, from Babylon back to Babylon
On eBay, from Babylon back to Babylon

In old Baghdad, they're dusting off the antiques (sad, so sad)
It's the fourteenth Guernica we've had this week (sad, so sad)
I got twenty-five dollars for a Persian vase (sad, so sad)
Hold the critique, I think I'll go large (sad, so sad)

That stuff inside your houses and that stuff behind your eyes
Well, it all ends up as stuff that you can buy
On eBay, from Babylon back to Babylon
On eBay, from Babylon back to Babylon

They're building a tower out of wrappers and cans (sad, so sad)
Now we speak in a language that we all understand (sad, so sad)
Tongue-tied and starry-eyed (sad, so sad)
It's the ancient history of old school ties (sad, so sad)

There's stuff dressed up as truth and then there's stuff dressed up as lies
And it all ends up as stuff that you can buy
On eBay, from Babylon back to Babylon
On eBay, from Babylon back to Babylon.[1]

Babylon back to Babylon

On eBay, a melodious critique of the sale of looted antiquities from Iraq, following the war prosecuted by George W. Bush's US administration and supported by the British government of Tony Blair, was released by Leeds-based anarcho-punk-folk band, *Chumbawamba*, in 2004. The words, sung with ironic innocence, refer to both acts of war and works of art: 'In old Bagdhad they're dusting off the antiques, It's the fourteenth Guernica we've had this week.' There are lyrical layers of meaning. The fall-out from the multiple Guernicas, the effect of ariel bombardment of civilians, is an art sale of looted treasures from ancient civilization. The subject of Pablo Picasso's most famous painting is copied; it and its effects are reduced to 'stuff you can buy'. Guernica is a metaphor for the illegality of war and the commodification of culture. The deceptively simple repeating refrain, 'Babylon back to Babylon', swings from the ancient city to contemporary Iraq, past to present, then back again. Chumbawamba tracks shifting Babylons: a site of a classical civilization where the US army built a military base on its ruins and a biblical Babylon, a culture of envy without restraint from the pleasures of earthly goods that created a city of decadence tall enough to cheat a way into heaven. This Babylon was adopted and adapted as the summary of the corruption of capitalism protected by the state's police in the music of reggae then punk.

The tuneful phrasing of *On eBay* captures the rhythm of discarded things into purchased objects that now circles around the globe with every click of a computer key. Each tap becomes a digital code on an internet auction site that instigates the movement of money and objects, between bank accounts and houses: a cycle of commodity exchanges in the global market of second-hand goods.[2] Chumbawamba's wry analysis of how artefacts of historical significance 'ends up as stuff you can buy' can be applied to the sale of the material culture of the H Blocks.

Keys to the H Blocks: stuff you can buy

On 21 September 2010 an eBay seller, 'big_balls_from_the_falls1888', listed a collection of keys to the H Blocks of Long Kesh/Maze and one of its security cameras.[3] He (and I am assuming the seller is male from his chosen macho avatar) presented himself as a representative of the catholic nationalist community of West Belfast through which the Falls Road is the main route. He priced the key collection, comprising 23 keys and 57 key tags to cells, catwalks, grilles, switch and control rooms for blocks H1, H2, H4 and H6, at £3,499.99. The security camera was sold for £375 just two days after it was put up for auction. The listing of the keys to the H Block ended early, on 30

September, which typically indicates an offline deal and an offer of more money than either the reserve or the starting price.

This chapter is an attempt to understand the act of selling the H Block keys and their meaning. They are just bits of metal, keys to disused and demolished buildings, without any association to a particular building would be scrapped without a second thought. However, their past appears in their material form; they are, at least to the people who spent so much money on them, agents of history. They are not much to look at but have the kind of indexical properties that Alfred Gell has attributed to artworks: they make connections (Figure 6.1). Works of art, Gell argues, have the ability to reinstate the person who created them; an index to, or even of, the artist: art is their substitute and exerts a form of their agency.[4] The H Block keys are not, however, works of art defined by the artistic status of their maker; the anonymous industrial locksmith who created the moulds for the lock barrels of prison doors and those that pressed out the grooves of keys to slot into their mechanisms is entirely bypassed.

FIGURE 6.1 'H Block keys'. Whyte's (23 April 2010), '1971–2000 HM Prison The Maze-Long Kesh "H Blocks" – keys and key tags'. Reproduced with the permission of Whyte's, Dublin.

They are indexes and understood as such without any need of a theory of art and agency. All keys have a simple semiotics. Their forms are metonyms for doors and the building into which the doors open. But these clever chains of reference, the imaginative devices of representation, have a real force, a material agency. The forms of the keys of the H Blocks have the power to reconstitute a place, its past and its relationships.

On eBay

The sale of the keys of H Blocks on eBay seems exceptional and ordinary, unique and mundane at the very same time. The material culture of Long Kesh/Maze is bought and sold on a weekly basis on eBay. Indeed, every day on eBay it is possible to bid on a hundred or so things related to the history of Long Kesh/Maze: prison art, the images and objects made by its prisoners; cards, postcards and letters sent by them, pamphlets and books written about them; badges worn by prison officers; photographs of the prison and the protests over it and, occasionally, part of the prison itself, such as its keys. All these things will be presented as singular artefacts, all of them a lucky find, serendipitous objects and an opportunity to own a unique item if a buyer uses eBay searches astutely and has the patient determination to wait until the last hour of the auction to place the winning bid. But the unique is endlessly repeated in every sale every day. An internet auction is monitored within the routines of housework, washing the dishes or sweeping the floor then opening a laptop or swiping a mobile to look at the figures rising on a screen; the pre-sale bidding is also followed during hours of paid labour, taking a short break from office work to open a tab on the same computer screen or reach for a mobile phone to see how many other people are watching those rising figures. The matter of history is an everyday affair on eBay.

The material culture of the conflict in and about Northern Ireland is extensive, an effect of a long low-intensity war that attempted 'normalization' as a political strategy of pretence that meant that its commodity economy never entirely ceased to function and the institutions that preserved objects did not shut.[5] Forms of conflict could be collected almost as soon as they were created. The *Artefacts Audit*, a Healing Through Remembering project, and publication collated and written by Kris Brown, maps 420,000 items in 79 public and private collections.[6] Although I was aware of this vast sea of things through my involvement with Healing Through Remembering, the explosion of objects on eBay still took me by surprise for two reasons. First, I am a little stuck on the idea that historical objects are too important to circulate in commercial spaces and ought to reside in publicly accessible archives or museums and, secondly, since much of my academic life has been spent using my art historical training to understand the materiality of life, it is difficult to shake off the assumption that the digital is only a pixelated reflection of real things always elsewhere. eBay was not where I would have expected, or wanted, to find a history of the H Blocks or, indeed, parts of the prison itself.

A colleague who knew I was documenting the H Blocks alerted me to the sale at a Penzance auction house of an artefact from the period of internment in Long Kesh, a handkerchief decorated with a pencil drawing of Cage 19.[7] We shared some discomfort about the commodification of conflict and the profiting from the incarceration of others. Then, someone, and I don't recall who, said: 'You should take a look on eBay.' So, I spent a year, 2010 to 2011, using the eBay tools of commercial traders, dedicated collectors and occasional buyers to research, without ever attempting to purchase, the objects auctioned for their relationship to Long Kesh or Maze Prison.[8] These tools were my search terms and the words used to generate alerts sent straight to my personal email address. I received a daily delivery of a indiscriminate array of objects that once belonged to prisoners and prison officers, to republicans and loyalists, or the families of all. The things that arrived in my inbox were ordered only by the date and time of their listing, reappearing with reminders of their closing sale. Most were second-hand goods sold by individuals consistent with eBay's inception as a peer-to-peer internet platform for used objects. Now a multinational e-commerce corporation, eBay may be closer to an online transnational high street than virtual global car boot sale, but its collections of second-hand artefacts remain accessible for sellers as buyers and has thus levelled the once exclusive antique trade.[9] 'That stuff inside your houses' as the song goes, 'all ends up as stuff you can buy'.

Algorithms write alternatives: division into juxtaposition

Not only is there a vast quantity of objects relating to the history of the H Blocks on eBay, but they are unsorted, or at least not sorted according to the political categories of the conflict in and about Northern Ireland. The absence of a political order, an unintentional algorithm effect, offers an alternative way of 'dealing with the past'.[10] Throughout the Northern Ireland peace process much of the material culture of conflict has remained within its community of origin: republicans archive republican artefacts, loyalist preserve loyalist objects and prison officers have their own museum. Remembering conflict is often a single identity community affair. However, my year-long survey of 2010 and my random searches since continue to return an array of artefacts that are not categorized according to community affiliation.

The algorithm of an opening search on eBay using the term 'Maze Prison' brings artefacts associated with the experience of prison officers and prisoners onto the same first page: unionist and republican imagery lined up together; the eBay buyer and browser can scroll up and down over both. The prediction of preferences delivered by internet shopping, the balance of things across screens, jumbles the lines of political separations into juxtapositions. One bright spring Sunday morning, 11 April 2021, I typed 'Maze Prison' into eBay's search engine and these things were delivered to my screen:

Original Christmas Card from Long Kesh Prison (Maze) 1974, Cost 5p, £14.99

Maze Dirty Protest, Hunger Strike Northern Ireland Prison, NIPS ira HM pin badge £5.95

HMP Maze H Blocks: the facts Northern Ireland Office 1980 £40.61

N.I. P.S. Northern Ireland Maze Prison Transport Pin Badge £5.00

Northern Ireland H.M. Prison Service Crest Maze UK NIPS HM Map Ulster Pin Badge £4.75

N.I. P.S. Northern Ireland Maze Prison Transport Pin Badge £3.00

Large Vintage Aluminium Metal Canteen Food Serving Tray Military Prison HMP Maze £22.79

1980 Press Photo March Supporting Hunger Strike H Block Maze Prison Belfast 1980 £17.47

A few days after my Sunday morning eBay search, on a colder Tuesday afternoon of 13 April, I tapped 'Long Kesh' into the eBay box that invites a potential buyer to 'Search for anything'. The first name of the internment camp that republicans and loyalists continued to use for HMP Maze to assert its origins in administrative detention without trial, 'Long Kesh' set in motion another algorithm and spread across my screen a slightly different set of objects. The 'Original Christmas Card from Long Kesh Prison (Maze)' came up again. With both the prison's names in the title line, perhaps it was bound to be high on the bill of things once more, but it was followed by:

Irish Republican Postcard Long Kesh H-Block Martyr 1981 Bobby Sands MP Sinn Fein £2.50

Three Envelopes from Inmates of Long Kesh with Censor Marks £10.00

Envelope addressed to internee of HMP Maze, Long Kesh, of 3 May 1974 £5.75

Irish Republican Postcard Long Kesh Victory to the Blanket-Men Dirty Protest IRA £2.50

Irish Republican Postcard Bobby Sands Long Kesh Hunger Strike Commemoration 1981 £2.50

Loyalist Republican Historical POW Leather Bag RUTH Long Kesh Prison
    Art Deer £64.99

Long Kesh Sinn Fein Irish Republican IRA Derry Donegal Belfast RUC Irish
    Ulster £7.99

Irish Republican Postcard Set Long Kesh Hunger Strikers Bobby Sands Sinn
    Fein £20.00

The different names, Long Kesh or Maze, for the same jail pull up through the morass of all eBay's 'stuff you can buy' similar material forms. There are the paper objects that seduce collectors of ephemera: cards, postcards, envelopes, pamphlets, photographs. They jostle with commemorative material of metal: the badges of devotion and service. The flimsy fabric of a document, a paper object, is likely to be found in an archive, acknowledged as historically valuable and available to view rather than own. In fact, the third item to appear on my Sunday morning Maze Prison search on 11 April, 'HMP Maze H Blocks: the facts Northern Ireland Office 1980' at £40.61, I had read many years ago in University of Sussex Library that then had a political documents collection on its first floor. I still have a faint and fading photocopy in a cabinet in my office (Figure 6.2). Its correct title, *H Blocks: The Facts* has been augmented to broaden its appeal to eBay browsers.[11] The badges, on the other hand, tend to circulate in the spheres of commercial collecting. The

FIGURE 6.2 *'Fading photocopy of* H Block: The Facts *(1980)'*, *Northern Ireland Office*, H Blocks: The Facts *(London: Northern Ireland Office, 1980). Photograph: Louise Purbrick.*

one called 'Maze Dirty Protest' in its eBay entry is another act of naming to encourage sales. The only text on the badge itself is NIPS, the acronym for the Northern Ireland Prison Service, beneath a depiction of a prison officer. In simple metallic lines a small figure is distinguished by a peaked cap, shirt collar and tie tucked behind the large jacket lapels but the official blue uniform colour altered to shit brown and covered in the arrows of cartoon-strip convict clothing. An ironic evocation of the hardships for prison officers during the no-wash campaign, the badge is one of hundreds from a large collection of Northern Ireland security force badges. Northern Ireland Prison Service is represented alongside the British Army, Royal Ulster Constabulary, Ulster Defence Regiment as well as loyalist groups, indicative of the political affiliations of the seller and the military culture of metal badges. 'columbo-999' offers free postage when additional badges are bought at the same time as the selected purchase.[12]

The mix of metal and paper, the balance of the type of artefact, varies with the search term: more paper is thrown up by Long Kesh and more metal by Maze Prison. eBay's algorithm intersects with historical materiality, to some extent at least. Three of the nine objects rounded up on the Tuesday afternoon Long Kesh search were postcards produced by and for the movement in support of the H Block struggles. Paper was an essential tool of their campaign, as for others of the 1980s, communicating their cause as well as distributing information about events. The material culture of prison officers, of which the enamelled badge of service is a small but important part, asserts attachment to the institution under its official name. eBay search terms have historical tendencies, yet neither of the two prison titles arranges objects exclusive to any one group that occupied its architecture. Occasionally, the desire to sell squeezes every name for the jail and as many of its known historical associations into the small space of the 80-character title box. The search term strategy is evident in the wildly misleading title of a text about the Easter Rising of 1916 titled 'Long Kesh Sinn Fein Irish Republican IRA Derry Donegal Belfast RUC Irish Ulster' that turned up on my screen that Tuesday afternoon. Such selling strategies have unexpected effects. The spatial divisions of the H Blocks, which reproduced the sectarian geography of Northern Ireland, where republicans and loyalists live next to each other on either side of solidly symbolic walls, is flattened out across a computer screen: on eBay, their objects share the same page. Another sporadic search that I started as my editing skills began to fail me after a weekday morning's work on 22 April drew loyalist and republican prisoner artefacts into alignment, at least in the commercial digital domain of an internet auction. Two paintings of loyalist emblems Union Jacks, Ulster and Scottish Flags attributed to both the Ulster Defence Association (UDA) and the Ulster Volunteer Force (UVF) landed above a copy of *An Phoblacht* marking the death of Hunger Strikers Martin

Hurson and Joe McDonnell and a framed Irish tricolour decorated with the names of 'Ireland's Patriot Dead'.

Thus, the divisive debate about the place of Long Kesh/Maze in the process of transformation from conflict to peace has been accompanied by a bustling trade in its material culture. While public entry to H Blocks is not permitted, cycles of exchanges of objects associated with them occur and recur. Restricted access to these listed buildings on a demolished site now abandoned to nature has not deterred interest in purchasing a piece of their past. This contradiction can be explained through differences between political position and commercial desire, between state history and collective memory, official and unofficial heritage practices. The fear of the history and the future of the H Blocks seems to be limited to political discourse rather than widely shared. Certainly, the proliferation of the sale of artefacts of the H Blocks on eBay indicates an easy acceptance of parts of the prison in everyday life. While fraught and faltering political debate about the preservation of Long Kesh/Maze has tended to end in silence and stalemate in the Northern Ireland Executive, an alternative register of interest in the past of the prison is to be found on eBay and in the material transactions of its artefacts.

The politics of the last atrocity and the work of an art historian

In a 2012 *Independent* article about the war in Syria, Patrick Coburn reminded his readers about the politics of the last atrocity, which occurs 'when the latest act of violence and the retaliation it provokes dictates the direction of day to day policies'.[13] A politics of the last atrocity defined 'The Troubles': every bomb and each shooting were separated from the conditions that caused them and any attempt to understand those conditions ran the risk of the accusation of refusing to condemn. Patrick Coburn made a plea to understand the longer history and wider context of war rather than only ever to react to violence and thus allow it to be repeated for the neglect of its underlying cause. His is an urgent appeal, ignored by those with the political power to conduct wars, that is answered by the established practice of historians of art, design and architecture, who often are too late and usually too far removed from politics and power to intervene in any immediate way. But they, and I am one of them, have the antidote to the politics of the last atrocity. Placing things in their wider context and longer history is the stock-in-trade empirical endeavour of historians of the material world. Attention to the form of objects permits the most important question: how did these things happen? Examining the details of images, the precise forms of objects, the composition of structures, tracing their symbols, styles and shapes that circulate through economies, in cultures and for politics broadens the view of the historical relationships in which acts of creativity and destruction occur. We can ask who held the gun, who carried the bomb, but it explains very little. Better to know the mechanisms through which a specific weapon design eventually arrived in someone's hand or the burden of significance of a structure that has been blown up. It is not possible to isolate an individual or organization for blame. Attention to materiality that is so characteristic of the work of art, design and architectural historians, unfolds the largest historical questions: What are the conditions of existence? How did this come to be here? My question runs along the same lines but is less expansive: Why were the keys of the H Blocks on sale on eBay?

The material culture of imprisonment

The listing of the keys to the H Blocks on eBay occurred because big_balls_from_the_falls uploaded an image of objects in his possession. This individual act, seemingly so full of intention, is actually no more than an historical effect. The decision to auction these artefacts is premised on historical conditions that lie beyond any such proprietorial gesture: the existence of H Blocks and the duration of their structures. A note in the 'Description' space allocated on eBay for sellers to give details of their items for sale claimed 'they were acquired along with other items by a consortium of historians and collectors from the demolition people'. But again, this is another effect, no matter how much agency big_balls asserts for himself. Demolition at the site of Long Kesh/Maze, around some of its listed structures, was one of the political compromises of the peace process that followed some six years after the final release of prisoners, some under the Good Friday Agreement. The H Block keys had served their function as tools of penal architecture; they were no longer needed, left behind until the buildings were knocked down.

In a University of Ulster seminar series organized by Elizabeth Crooke, shortly after the signing of the Good Friday Agreement and devoted to understanding heritages in a period of post-conflict,[14] I recall a then-curator of the Ulster Museum arguing that the material culture of conflict was more objective in its account of difficult legacies of division and violence than textual descriptions, printed or spoken. Material culture was arbitrary, not intentional. I did not entirely agree then, and do not now, with this traditional notion of objects as evidence, but the remark has stayed with me because it indicates how materiality is an embodiment of its own making, just there as a record of its event, a happening of history. The keys of H Blocks are parts of their existence, essential to the operation of the architecture of Long Kesh/Maze. Their sing-song journey towards eBay ending up as 'stuff you can buy' has started.

The vast amount of material culture of Long Kesh/Maze, of which the keys to the H Blocks are just a few pieces, that sell on eBay or indeed anywhere else, relates to the scale of imprisonment in Northern Ireland. Imprisonment was a key strategy through which the conflict was both conducted and contained by the British government.[15] Over the thirty years of the conflict in and about Northern Ireland, imprisonment affected a large proportion of its population, families of prisoners as well as prisoners themselves: one in eight people, estimates former republican prisoner organization Coiste na nIarchimí.[16] Thus a large proportion of the material culture during the conflict is one of imprisonment: it relates to the scale of incarceration. Much of it is generated 'in and about' Long Kesh/Maze, the conflict's largest jail with the 'strongest community links of any prison in the world', according to the International Red Cross.[17]

The artefacts of the H Blocks, as objects in other prisons, do not circulate in the same way as commodities in a capitalist system in which most of the world lives: the selection for purchase of products delivered to markets that then serve domestic consumption. The removal from everyday life that is the punishment of a prison is also a forced withdrawal from exchange relationships of the market. In prison, objects are imposed and distributed, given and smuggled, shared, borrowed or bartered, crafted and created. Permitted and prohibited objects are pushed through prison in different ways; they have separate circuits; prisoners circumvent the restricted exchanges of the prison regime. But whatever the differences between prison control over possessions and the market circulation of things, material culture performs the same function in jail as it does in everyday life everywhere: it is the means through which relationships are made and maintained.

The power relationships between prison officers and prisoners were upheld through the possession of objects. Wielding weapons and keeping keys are acute exercises in power; the limitation of freedom of movement, the sentence itself, is enforced through their possession and use. The regime of H Blocks, as we know, was shaped by the oppressions of the soft forms of fabric. Prison clothing continuously expresses adherence to the prison. This is the function of wearing a uniform: an expression of agreement to an institution, an individual affirmation of its collective identity. Uniforms worn by prison officers demonstrate a unity of purpose that institutionalizes their power over prisoners who must appear differently to them. The hierarchical embrace of a prison uniform is made most starkly clear by the republican refusal to wear it: a rejection of the conformity to authority embodied in the arrangements of cloth. All prison regimes prescribe the types of things that can be held within them; they restrict access to objects: the passage and possession of them through their systems is a matter of prison rules. The greater or lesser presence of forms of material culture defines the extent of autonomy within prison spaces. It is all a matter of who is allowed what where.

In environments where material culture is restricted it becomes of heightened significance. The right to weekly rather than monthly parcels was one of the five demands of the H Block struggle; the amount of things a prisoner could receive from their visitors was more than a matter of their comfort in their cells but a sign of status; the higher the number of material artefacts held by a prisoner the higher his political status and amount of personal agency he exercised within the prison. The architecture of Long Kesh/Maze was crossed with gift after gift, usually from mothers to sons, wives to husbands, sisters to brothers. Smuggling contraband, tobacco wrapped in cling film, the inside of biros, tiny radios and messages or 'comms' are the types of material transfers for which the Long Kesh/Maze is so famous, but there was also a high volume of traffic in many more mundane permitted goods over the whole period of its operation: fruit and biscuits, vitamins and chocolate, shampoo and shaving cream, socks, pants and T-shirts, birthday cards, love letters, children's drawings and family photographs. Familial relationships sustained by material exchanges extended into the spaces of the prison. The gift economy of the family was enlarged to include the occupants of the H Blocks and its asymmetrical exchange relationships, wherein female relatives offer and male relatives receive, intersected with the inequalities of imprisonment.[18]

Prisoners also contributed to the gift economy of the family through the production of prison art. These artefacts created from within Long Kesh/Maze are regularly auctioned on eBay and relatively highly valued. Images and texts drawn and written within cells, such as the 'Original Christmas Card' on eBay for almost £15, were posted out to relatives to mark special occasions; the objects produced in craft workshops and art classes taken home, such as Ruth's bag, which turned up on my laptop screen on that chilly Tuesday afternoon, 13 April, priced at £64.99. The direction of travel of prison art, the journey from inside the prison to prisoners' homes outside, ensures it is available for eBay auctions. It is found in the same place, someone's home, from which online sales are initiated and where the internet is accessed. It may have remained in a domestic setting since the closure of the prison or sometime before when the prisoner had served his sentence and returned home. Since prison art is always a gift, it is usually kept, an acknowledgment of the presence of the maker in its materials and, if not proudly displayed, then usually safely stored away.[19]

Prisoners' political communities were also the recipients of their art. Writings and drawings were sent out for publication and artefacts included in auctions at social events to raise funds for their and other prisoners' families. Each of the republican and loyalist groups in Long Kesh/Maze had their own prisoner support groups that also generated artworks: commemorative objects, campaigning images and political texts. A material culture of solidarity that accompanied imprisonment throughout the conflict has found its way, like the postcards of the Hunger Strikers at £2.50 a piece, onto eBay. Much of the material culture of Long Kesh/Maze was produced and distributed by supporters of prisoners rather than the prisoners themselves. Objects of solidarity are dominant in the second-hand internet sales. The imperative to provide financial and political support for prisoners demanded the design and distribution of artefacts, posters, badges and T shirts, more often associated with music fandom, and the production of publications, pamphlets and books, similar to a political party. The 'stuff you can buy on eBay' is both the stuff of the H Blocks and the stuff about them.

It is possible to write, as I am doing here, about the material culture of H Blocks as an entity, a body of artefacts deployed in routines of repression and resistance. Its function across the different groups inside the jail, republican prisoners, loyalist prisoners, unionist prisoner officers, the families and communities on its outside who supported each, can be generalized to all. However, the historical condition of imprisonment in Long Kesh/Maze was separation. Life in the H Blocks was defined by the isolation of republican and loyalist groups from each other and the adaptation of their routines to ensure they did not meet. Separation was integral to its regime. A failed attempt to integrate republican and loyalist prisoners after the Hunger Strikes, in 1982, entrenched the practice of devoting blocks and wings to the internal control of prisoners' own organizations.[20] Proscribed outside the jail, IRA, INLA, UDA, UVF and LVF operated openly and easily inside it, housed in their groups. The recognition of the collective identity of prisoners through the allocation of separate organizational spaces, their own H Blocks or, at least, their own wings, cultivated the production of a prolific quantity of prison art but in just two styles: the iconography of Ireland or of Ulster.

Republican prison art is distinguished by its Celtic interlacing, harps, Easter lilies, St Bernadette crosses, the colours of the Irish tricolour and the starry plough. Red hands, Ulster flags and Union Jacks define that of loyalist.[21] Artefacts were made from the same materials, the leather or wood of the taught prison craft practice or the textiles and paper of the independent political art in the cell, but different decorative schemes were worked out upon their surfaces. The acquisition of skills for individual expression and self-reflection associated with creativity and therapeutic rehabilitation were appropriated in the H Blocks to advocate the politics for which its practitioners were sentenced. These forms of material culture were then inserted into the family and community economies that supported them and their organizations. Objects of the same type of materials created through some of the same kinds of prison routines and exchanged for the same kinds of reasons carried the signs of opposing identities. The political symbols of prison art attest to a continued adherence to a proscribed group. Thus, the material culture of the H Blocks produced over prolonged periods of imprisonment reproduced a limited visual repertoire of opposing symbolic schemes of republicanism and loyalism that became increasingly fixed, almost unchanging.

Dismantling and debris, closure and circulation

All the H Block 'stuff' on eBay, seen across a digital flatscape then posted off in its solid shapes, exists because of the scale of imprisonment in Long Kesh/Maze and the entrenched divisions of its architecture. The forms of material culture of imprisonment in Northern Ireland derive, of course, from their formation: created inside a structure of British occupation that perpetuated sectarian separations. However, their circulation is an effect of their demolition. The sale of the keys to the H Blocks is directly related to the end of the operation of the jail, its de-commissioning as part of the Home Office prison estate. Indeed, the eBay seller, big_balls_from_the_falls, authenticates these bits of metal with an account of a negotiation with the 'demolition people'. There is a hint of the financial dealing in material history that is often obscured, disguised in the standard phrases of second-hand markets.

The dinner tray that arrived on my laptop on that sunny Sunday morning of 11 April was misleadingly described as 'pre-owned' like a party dress from a high street store that was only worn once or twice, not quite the right kind of things for its current owner but fine for someone else. In the long eBay title, 'Large Vintage Aluminium Metal Canteen Food Serving Tray Military Prison HMP Maze' I could also take issue with the insertion of 'vintage' to suggest the trendy authenticity of a second-hand commodity, but the matter of ownership is a more important issue. The 'pre-owned' label barely captures the historical layers of stewardship and shared use, rather than ownership, of prison objects. In the period before the marketization of the security industry, prison spaces, such as kitchens, were stocked through the direct provisioning of the British government. The use of these forms of state property were highly regulated; they were not owned by the prison officers who were nevertheless responsible for their care and the supervision of the prisoners that used them. Catering equipment, such as my sunny Sunday morning dinner tray, was stacked, filled, served, collected, cleaned and stacked again by prisoners who worked in the kitchens. Although H Block prisoners refused to work, it would be wrong to assume that state property was never handled by them. To ensure the least interference in the running of their wings, some prison work, cleaning collective spaces, for example, or dishing up food, was undertaken by autonomously organized political prisoners.[22] Food would arrive at the top of the wing to be distributed according to the work rotas of prisoners' own groups. The dinner tray turns out to be a complex historical artefact for which concepts of ownership that control the circulation of commodities do not readily, should not really, apply. And its price of £22.79 seems far too cheap. It was the slow processes of the closure of Long Kesh/Maze that allowed a prison object that was never owned by an individual nor held in a commodified condition to be fixed with a price. The material culture of the H Blocks has been dispersed into commercial markets where some uncertainty about origin or ownership of an historical object matters less than the money it may fetch. Were parts of the prison, its structures, the objects through which it operated, salvaged or stolen, purchased or plundered?

Before the site of Long Kesh/Maze was passed from the Northern Ireland Office to the Northern Ireland Executive, from the British government to the consociational arrangements that followed the Good Friday Agreement, it fell into limbo: a jail empty of prisoners but still standing. For three years, from 2000 to 2003, the fabrics of incarceration were collected and stored for redistribution and reuse. The decommissioning of the whole prison, its twenty-two compounds, its eight H Blocks, its paraphernalia of containment within its perimeter wall, was a process of removing remaining state property, shifting piles of prison artefacts. The clearing out of cells, a regular practice during the lifetime of Long Kesh/Maze as prisoners finished their sentences and their cell spaces were made ready for others still detained by theirs, was extended with the implementation of the Good Friday Agreement. When entire wings and blocks became unoccupied, the interiors of the cells were dismantled: standard cell furniture, furnishings and fittings, the beds, the shelves, the curtains, the lights were removed and stored. Then, the archivists, collectors and looters arrived. They have come and gone. They took what they fancied or thought might be of historical or financial value or both. I know this happened because after asking question upon question about the design of the prison to its prison officer maintenance crew, I was handed rolls of architectural plans. 'Take them, no-one else needs them', I was told. Some of the objects had already made their way into Billy's Museum, an extraordinary act of stewardship of the material culture of imprisonment in Long Kesh/Maze recorded by artist Amanda Dunsmore then accessioned by The Ulster Museum.[23] Collecting objects for the Northern Ireland Prison Service's teaching college in Millisle, known as their museum, accelerated and included digging out a marble memorial to prison officers killed during the conflict. The Public Record Office of Northern Ireland (PRONI) arrived to begin the work of officially archiving. And there were auctions. Inside the jail. '[T]here has been anger that the prison service has been auctioning off chunks of Maze history, including snooker tables for £80', reported the *Guardian*'s Ireland correspondent Angelique Chrisafis in an 18 February 2004 article. 'A former governor told the *Guardian* £10,500 had been made at auction, but mostly from kitchen equipment and staff lockers – "nothing of historical importance"'.[24] Except, perhaps, for a dinner tray.

Prison art and the personhood of the prisoner

The dismantling at Long Kesh/Maze and dispersal of the artefacts present at its end is immediately and obviously connected to the auctions on eBay. It is where parts of the prison have ended up, as Chumbawamba predicted. But the proliferation of sales of all kinds of H Block artefacts is also associated with its absence. Since the jail is gone, its material culture in its entirety has been accessioned into history. Things sent out from the prison, such as prison art, as well as that which remained within it until the end, are now pieces of the past.

'Prison art is ubiquitous', observed Kris Brown in a Healing Through Remembering workshop following the publication of the *Artefacts Audit* in 2008. 'Jail artworks and crafts' are important artefact types that contribute to the 'abundant' material 'relating to the Prison experience'.[25] The amount of prison art is an effect of the scale of imprisonment. Its recurring forms in leather and wood, the materials of the workshop curriculum at Long Kesh/Maze prison as it was in many other British jails of the same period, are always found on eBay. Those emblazoned with political symbols vaunt their makers' continued defiance to either the force or failings of the British state and demonstrate collective resistance to the individualizing, normalizing work of rehabilitation through prison crafting. Nevertheless, artefacts made by prisoners were expressions of their personal achievement, demonstrations of the perseverance required both to serve a prison sentence and to become sufficiently dexterous to create meaningful shapes from stubborn materials. The connection to the prisoner as a person is visible and tangible in the carved or stitched forms. Prison art is evidence of the intentions and actions of the prisoner who created it, a material manifestation of the extent of his agency expressed in the selection of shapes and the manipulation of surfaces. Such an artefact embodies the person and carries their moment of imprisonment from the past into the present. Alfred Gell argues that an artefact refers, even returns, to its maker and the person for whom the artefact was made:

> the personhood of the artist, the prototype, or the recipient can fully invest the index in artefactual form, so that to all intents and purposes it becomes a person, or at least a partial person. It is a congealed residue of performance and agency in object-form, through which access to other persons can be attained, and via which their agency can be communicated.[26]

Prison art, to use another of Gell's terms, can 'substitute'[27] the person who made it; the leather or wood that holds their intentions, their actions, their existence in the past can reinstate it in the present. The application of paint on wood, the staining of dye on leather is an index of an individual person that is also coded into an expression of collective identity. This is the particularity of the crafted artefacts of the H Blocks. It appropriated techniques and materials of its penal workshops to produce artefacts that were simultaneously personal and political. Personhood does not disappear into political symbol in the handmade artefact: the prisoner who pressed out the curving forms of Celtic interlacing on leather shapes or painted Red Hands in the centre of the Ulster flag on a wooden plaque persists in their marked surfaces. Indeed, prison art functioned as a marker of presence within the domestic economy of prisoners' households; an object offered and accepted as a gift indicated the inclusion of the absent person in the space of the family.

The circulation of prison art while Long Kesh/Maze was operational was limited to the domains defined by gift relationships: a family's social life shaped in the Northern Ireland context by political affiliation. Prison art was not an object of market transactions; only on eBay does it appear in a commodified condition. Only as pieces of the past has prison art acquired a market price. Despite its prevalence, ubiquity, as Kris Brown observed, prison art is a relatively expensive eBay object and has over the years since the closure of Long Kesh/Maze increased in price. On 5 September 2010, a '1970s ULSTER VOLUNTEERS POW LEATHER WALLET LONG KESH' sold for £46,[28] whereas Ruth's bag was listed on 13 April 2021 at a penny short of £65 (Figure 6.3).

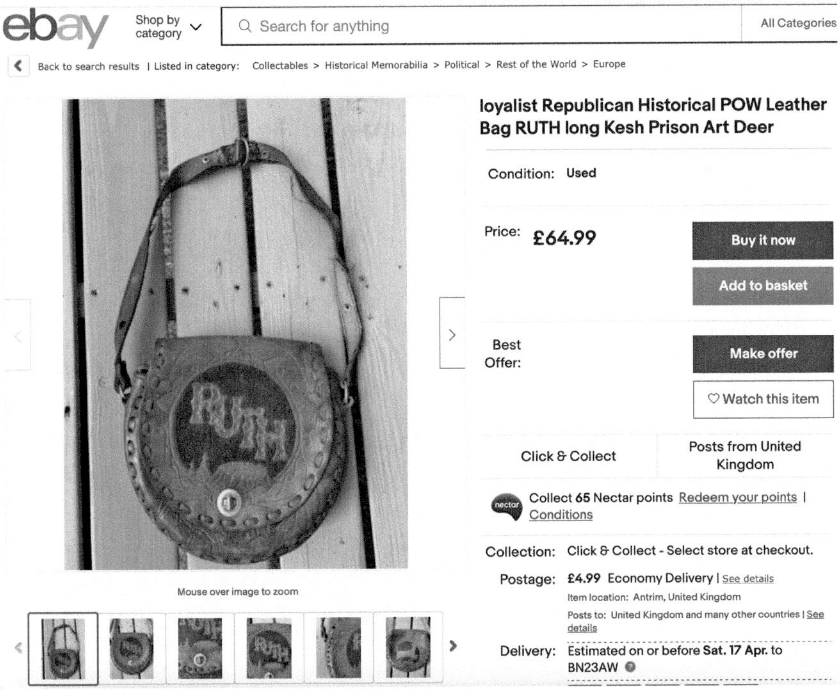

FIGURE 6.3 *'Ruth's Bag', 13 April 2021, eBay.co.uk. Reproduced with thanks to Cate Hann.*

Individually crafted objects do command higher prices. eBay auctions exploit human relationships to material culture. Flea markets and craft fairs, car boots and gallery shops, all and any second-hand stalls, do the same. A desire to own an object with a human connection, marks of the maker visible on its surface, signs of the brush or blade and the hand that held them, raise their value. Unique and rare are the market terms applied to handmade. Both words are used by sellers so often on eBay that most buyers must have learnt to read past them but they still lever up an urgency to bid and buy: not to miss this one and the only opportunity to own a special thing. A competitive discourse of scarcity leads to the market explanation of value registered by price. But scarcity, rarity and uniqueness do not fully account for the particularity of prison art. It is enchanted. 'Technical virtuosity is intrinsic to the efficacy of works of art in their social context', argues Alfred Gell. Whoever views or holds or even owns a piece of art becomes involved in 'reconstructing the processes' that brought it 'into existence'. Skill embedded in the work of art is its enchantment: pencil lines and brushstrokes, stitches and carvings, create lines for the beholder to trace back to the maker opening up a 'channel' between them for 'further social relations'.[29] Prison art is empowered to present the prisoner and the context of his creativity while imprisoned.

Ruth's bag is a round purse with a long strap in tan leather (see Figure 6.3). A 1970s hippy style, it has natural colours, shapes and motifs. Wave forms encircle tree forms with the embossed capitalized female name as its centrepiece, The bag is edged with large leather stitches.. Clicking on the supporting images supplied by the seller reveal a leaping deer in the place of RUTH on the reverse side. Zooming in on these photographs reveal scuff marks where the bag had been placed on or had brushed past or collided with other surfaces; it has been well used. 'Vintage prison made leather shoulder bag with strap' in 'Overall good condition', claimed the eBay seller. Postage at £4.99 was not included in the £64.99 price but it would be 'Dispatched with Royal Mail 2nd Class signed for'.

Vintage is the label for the things of the past. A hook. There are others for those in the market for the history of the H Blocks. The eBay title of Ruth's bag that surround her name with search terms to entice the collectors of prison art may have little to do with her: 'loyalist Republican Historical POW Leather Bag RUTH long Kesh Prison Art Deer'. The scope of its title stacked it up, digitally speaking, with Hunger Strike postcards and badges. This is, of course, the coding work of an algorithm. My interest in the intersection of the personal and political in the material culture of Long Kesh and in this bag, the shape and colour of which reminds me of those that belonged to fashionable female relatives as I was growing up, entices me to click to its own page. Then, my next search using 'Long Kesh' brings more loyalist and republican goods into the same digital space. I should expect no less from the predictable profiling of commercial coding. However, the dual attribution of loyalist and republican to Ruth's bag that pressed the algorithm into action is unusual and inaccurate. All the more interesting for that. The seller cannot be the owner, cannot be Ruth, not the wife, not the partner or the girlfriend, neither the mother, nor the sister or nor the daughter of the H Block prisoner who carried her personal possessions in the bag for long enough that it bore the marks of use. She would have known his political identity. Her bag would have been part of the gift economy of imprisonment that sustains social relationship over periods of separation. Her biblical name, fulsome on the front, does not position her as a republican or loyalist, catholic or protestant, but speaks of an unnamed attachment to the prisoner whose hands worked upon the surface of leather, enchanting it with affectionate skill. The deer on the reverse, may be a version of a Celtic stag, one of the national images of Ireland that featured on its 'Free State' currency, the punt. The noble wild animal might indicate that the bag was made by a republican prisoner, but its lack of nationalistic stylization does not fix this attribution. This guess is not a 'good one'.[30] Rather than either loyalist and republican, as the seller claims, I would suggest that Ruth's bag is neither; it is part of a prison material culture of personal attachment that cannot be reduced to political affiliation. And, it is also not necessarily from Long Kesh/Maze. It could have been made in HMP Magilligan, the far less famous prison seventy miles away towards Limavady. On eBay, there is often only the sellers' words, the 'Long Kesh' of the title line, as provenance. An appeal to buyers, it is a narrative of authenticity rather than evidence of origin. The inclusive attributions of Ruth's bag, 'Historical POW' as well as 'loyalist Republican' is certainly a cynical sell that attempts to encompass the political differences of the collectors of the material culture of imprisonment. It is also an alternative intervention into the heritage of the H Blocks: it foregrounds the historical importance of the prison itself: association with the prison alone is more important than adherence to its divisions. This is a small detail, soon to disappear from the digital space of an internet auction, but worthy of note.

Small batch commodity production of the histories of repression: paper and metal

Regardless of the type of object or the search term that uploads it, eBay defines the material culture of the H Blocks as 'collectable'. 'Collectables & art' is one of eBay's ten categories that correspond to different kinds of shopping practices, from buying new clothes to collecting antique treasures. A collecting culture of the artefacts of conflict evident on eBay is an established business within the antique trade that occurs in different domains: at auctions of expensive medals of nineteen-century colonial wars, in junk shops that sell damaged First World War shell cases or on the street stalls sought out by tourists searching for souvenirs, such as Zippo lighters from the Vietnam war.[31] eBay's 'Collectables & art' category, which contains so many unexpected political juxtapositions, also jumbles up the old and the new, the historical and its reproduction; it mixes the categories that are usually separated by dealers of antiques. The lists of things that slip up and down a scrolling screen include artefacts with a physical connection to the prison, such as the keys that turned the H Block doors, or the art that was made inside them or which has an historical association to them; they float above or below objects that have neither of these relationships.

Some H Blocks artefacts are historical reproductions, created long after the prison's closure and are part of its commemorative culture. Two types of reproductions in the materials of metal and paper were pulled up with the search term 'Maze Prison' on my 11 April Sunday morning exploration on eBay: four shiny metal badges and one glossy paper photograph. Documentary images often occur on eBay. Photographs of the prison's history that took place outside it, particularly protests and funerals, have been pulled up with every search of mine, systematically undertaken in 2010 and sporadically since. Most derive from press coverage of the height of the H Blocks struggle from the late 1970s to the early 1980s, a period of intense international media interest in the conflict and the generation of wealth of photographic documentation. Only very occasionally can I find images taken inside its architecture. Sunday morning's photographic find, with key search terms 'Hunger Strike H Block Maze Prison Belfast' squeezed into its title, is a photograph of an 8 December 1980 London demonstration, protestors crossing its wide south-west avenues surrounded by police officers, carrying banners and placards in support of the first, lesser known, political fast of the H Blocks. It is typical eBay photographic fare, an example of a 'found' print culture sustained by out-of-business press agencies selling off their analogue back catalogue to dealers who use eBay as one of their outlets. The picture of marchers on their way from Hyde Park to Kilburn in the winter of 1980 was priced at $24 or a little over £17 excluding almost equally expensive postage and packing from California, where the internet store of late-twentieth-century ephemera, gregsfunshop, is based (Figure 6.4).

Photography is a technology of reproduction. Nevertheless, this Hyde Park image appears as a real thing. The sale and resale of the original prints taken by photojournalists who made their living capturing the 'decisive moment' that defined newsworthiness are archival objects.[32] They do have a material relationship to Long Kesh/Maze as historical objects that circulated at the time of H Blocks and because of the conflict within them. But photography is also used to create a new commemorative culture that is distant in time and place from the prison. My 2010 eBay survey showed how eBay trader, 'sham1916',

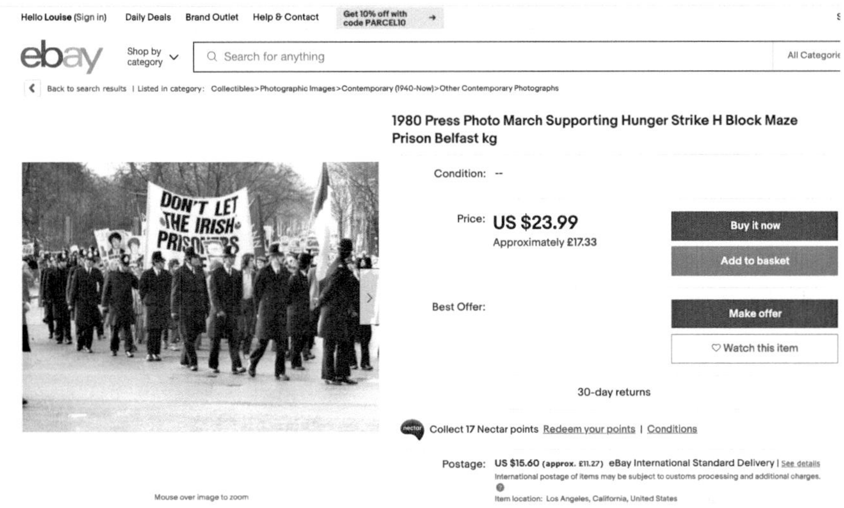

FIGURE 6.4 *London H Block demonstration 8 December 1980 titled with search terms 'Hunger Strike H Block Maze Prison Belfast', 11 April 2012, eBay.co.uk. Reproduced with permission of Greg Rivera.*

listed and re-listed 'PICTURES OF IRA HUNGER STRIKE FUNERALS, LONG KESH, EIRE'.[33] He used his description box to present details of the bundle of photos he promised to post to his bidding customer. 'YOU WILL RECEIVE 8 PICTURES (6X4) OF THERE FUNERALS INCLUDING THE FINAL SALUTE OF ANY OF THEM. (JUST LET ME KNOW WHAT U PREFER OR LEAVE IT UP TO ME!)' He does not pretend he is auctioning archival prints. 'THESE PICTURES ARE COPIES OF ORIGINAL'S TAKEN IN 1981 BUT GOOD HISTORIC PHOTOS'.[34] sham1916 is selling snapshot-sized digitally reproduced images of photographs of the large local gatherings of people who publicly mourned and protested the deaths of the Hunger Strikers. His work of re-issuing is not new. Funeral photographs have been re-published many times to mark each anniversary of the deaths of Hunger Strikers. Personal admiration and political veneration for republican martyrs explains an eBay buyer's interest in sham1916's copies with his promise of always including a shot of the final salute. The entwined emotions held in that moment, loss and defiance, love and violence, recorded in one photograph is imitated in another. A sheen slides over an original to create a poor copy and a commodity. Digital cameras coupled with personal computers attached to printers, all purchased in high street stores, facilitate image reproduction at home. Workshops or workspaces within houses supply eBay with all kinds of copies, commodity production on a domestic scale but a commodity production, nevertheless. A condition of a commodity is its separation from lived experience,[35] an eviction of the real thing from time and place. The eBay sales of photographic copies may be best understood as one of the lines in the small batch commodity production of histories of repression.

Metal held sway over paper in the Sunday morning 'Maze prison' search. Four of the eight objects, half of them, were the same: enamelled metal badges of prison officers, the solid materials of their culture. Since the official name of the jail was always used and upheld by the Northern Ireland Prison Service, it is no surprise that their badges are high up on the page, their frequency following the Maze search term. These adornments of a suited man, lapel badges and tie pins, also called tie tacs, are another regular across eBay's webpages. Badges of uniformed service are typical fare of military memorabilia that circulate through spheres of commercial collecting; they have been sold by the security forces who owned them or the family members who inherited them to dealers and collectors who displayed them in antique showrooms, flea markets, vintage fairs or junk shops for many decades before much of their trade gravitated online. The eBay sellers of Northern Ireland Prison Service badges have extensive lists of all the emblems of British and unionist groups involved in the security economy of the conflict: they are dealers in the right-wing military culture of the British state.

Badges worn by prison officers who worked in Long Kesh/Maze are discreet announcements of their affiliation to the Northern Ireland Prison Service during a conflict in which the jail was a frontline. Their discretion rests, in part, on their size. Small, they are readable only at an intimate distance. They are also coded. The acronyms of the protagonists in the conflict abound and are reproduced in the lapel and tie badge culture of commemoration. The badges mark, in the abbreviated codes characteristic of emblems that are intended to limit recognition, belonging and affiliation. The NIPS acronym on the badges of my April searches, which refers to Northern Ireland Prison Service, might be obvious enough but historical knowledge of, if not political allegiance to, particular protagonists is necessary to decipher many of the badges on sale on eBay. Acronyms abound. Their reading is restricted to the political circle and the personal space of the wearer: their exclusivity is understood by the buyer who seeks to display his acquired knowledge and desire to belong.

Deliberately obscure objects are always intentionally partially visible. Their power to exclude is based on their being seen. Although discreet, badges are assertive. They are pinned through the fabric placed upon a body, attached to the respectable attire of a jacket or a tie. They announce a connection between the person and an organization. All the NIPS badges for lapels or ties auctioned on eBay perform a politics of institutional allegiance. Many are merely descriptive and awarded after a period of service in a sector of work. Capitalized text, such as 'TRANSPORT' or 'DOGS' confirm simple visual depictions. Others reproduce in raised metal or enamel paint a sectarian play on words that celebrate the violence of prison officers against prisoners. A tie pin put up for sale on eBay in the year I spent surveying its sales commemorates 'HMP MAZE PEST CONTROL UNIT' with a version of a Jolly Roger, batons crossed like bones beneath the skull. In 'mint unworn condition' and listed several times by sellers 'dogrlamppost' and 'pimp-my-dogtags', the badge is obviously one of multiples.[36] All are inexpensive, varying from £2 to £4, and frequently sold through the 'Buy it Now' function that mimics the high street way of shopping for the ever present rather than the bidding for a unique object in an auction. Indeed, many are newly made; the Sunday morning Maze search contained duplicates, one 'pre-owned' and another 'brand new'. NIPS badges of service at Long Kesh/Maze must have a market beyond the limited number of prison officers who once worked in the jail. Their trade is another line of batch production which commemorates a history of repression and is another example of the domestic workshop economy of eBay commodification. None of this means, of course, that the glossy paper of photographs or the shiny metal of badges cannot be considered part of the material culture of Long Kesh/Maze. Commodity culture is a material culture.

The keys to the H Blocks and the price of history

On eBay, as everywhere else, the mechanically or digitally reproduced is ranked below the artefact worked by hand. 'Aura' is exploited on eBay; the hand-made is more expensive.[37] But the very highest prices for H Block artefacts are reserved for parts of the prison structure. Price is a brutal financial indicator of value. Take that of the keys to the H Blocks (see Figure 6.1). At £3,500, give or take a penny, they are, for an eBay object, very expensive. big_balls_from_the_falls attempts to explain their value, using capitals, bolded, enlarged and centred for extra emphasis throughout his entry. His title is full of key search terms, 'The Long Kesh/Maze Prison Key Collection Irish Troubles' while his seller's 'Description' is something of a lesson in 'Modern Irish History' and the place of this 'Unique Collection' within it:

> THE PRISON WAS PARAMOUNT IN POLITICAL STRIFE IN THE NORTH OF IRELAND THROUGHOUT THE LATE TWENTIETH CENTURY. IT WILL BE FOREVER REMEMBERED FOR SUCH THINGS AS THE 1981 HUNGER STRIKES LED BY BOBBY SANDS IN WHICH 10 REPUBLICAN PRISONERS DIED, THE 1983 BREAKOUT IN WHICH 38 REPUBLICANS BROKE FREE.[38]

Since so many eBay sellers claim a connection between their wares and the Hunger Strikers, and especially with Bobby Sands, the use of his name in this sensationalist account of the significance of the H Blocks is not especially convincing. Objects that assert an association with the Hunger Strikes are ever present in eBay's array of H Block artefacts. Always in stock. Listing, selling, bidding and buying them dominates its trade in the material culture of Long Kesh/Maze. Hunger Strike historical material is abundant. A mass print culture was generated through the solidarity movement that extended across the globe. Commemorative items continually circulate around the cycle of anniversaries of Hunger Strikers' deaths. Practices of collecting and cultures of commemoration are shaped by an understanding of historical importance, such as the H Block struggles as a pivotal historical event, hammered home by big_balls in the capitalized 'Impact' font he chose for his description of the prison's keys. He need not have worried. Media narratives have secured the Hunger Strikes in the collective memory. Indeed, their media record of is now an historical record, of which even a right-wing British tabloid's coverage has been listed for sale on eBay. But the constant repetition of Bobby Sands's name, its reproduction across so many screens because so many sellers believe it will increase the price of their item for sale, begins to accumulate, act as attrition, against the aura of artefacts with either a political or personal connection to him. Sadly, something of Sands's personhood also wears away into an historical sign.

But this seller does not exclusively rely upon Bobby Sands's sacrifice for his sale. He deploys an additional marketing strategy. He draws on the narrative of notoriety of infamous jails, in which Long Kesh/Maze is included in a spectrum from the Tower of London to Alcatraz, to sell the keys of the H Blocks. The 1983 prison escape begins an account of infamy.

> THE PRISON HOUSED BOTH REPUBLICAN AND LOYALIST
> PRISONERS FROM MANY DIFFERENT ORGANISATIONS. IT WAS
> KNOWN TO HOUSE THE HIGHEST CONCENTRATION OF PEOPLE
> CONVICTED OF MURDER ANYWHERE IN THE WORLD AT ONE
> STAGE MAKING IT A SOMEWHAT UNIQUE PRISON.[39]

Since the prison has closed, the H Block keys offer the proximity of danger from a position of safety, a similar kind of seduction to that of dark tourism. For Malcolm Foley and John Lennon, dark tourism is 'the presentation and consumption (by visitors) of real and commodified death and disaster sites'.[40] It is akin to A.V. Seaton's definition of thanatourism as 'the desire for actual or symbolic encounters with death, particularly, but not exclusively, violent death'. Travel to sites of death, their memorials, their 'symbolic representations' or 're-enactments' fulfils a 'fascination' that, I would suggest, can also be achieved by seeking possession of an object from such sites.[41] The seller's description of the keys attempts to thrill the eBay audience by evoking the dangerous prisoners locked up by them. That the collection of keys includes three 'Red Book' ones is listed twice and the date of the republican prisoners' escape repeated:

THE COLLECTION I HAVE ON OFFER COMPRISES OF 80 DIFFERENT ITEMS FOR 4 OF THE BLOCKS H1,H2,H4 AND H6 IT INCLUDES 55 KEYS PLATES 20 KEYS 3 RED BOOK SPECIAL STATUS KEYS AND 2 RED BOOK STATUS KEY TAGS THE PLATES ARE INGRAVED WITH THERE PURPOSES, GUARDROOMS, OPERATIONS AREAS, WASH ROOMS AND OTHER PARTS OF THE PRISON . . . IN THE COLLECTION THE RAREST ITEMS HAVE TO BE THE 3 KEYS AND 2 KEY TAGS FROM THE RED BOOK STATUS PRISONERS AREA. THIS WAS INTRODUCED AFTER 1983 TO HOUSE THE SO CALLED HIGH RISK PRISONERS.[42]

The high-risk category was disputed by prisoners who argued that inclusion in a 'Red Book' was a punishment applied to those in leadership positions, the IRA's OCs. It was an attempt unsettle them and their command structure, a personal disruption of daily life for political effect. Red Book prisoners were frequently moved from wing to wing and block to block, limiting their capacity to socialize and organize. But high-risk is repeated on eBay for its thrilling effect. big_balls casts the keys of the H Blocks as republican objects; they are inserted into the republican narrative of Long Kesh/Maze, from the 1971 British army swoops that interned only catholics, to the heroism of the 1981 Hunger Strikes and the republican confrontation of prison authorities through the 1983 escape to the authorities' subsequent attempts to repress the leading republican figures. But to whom do the keys to the H Block really belong? Skilful shoppers in all second-hand markets ask this question about the objects they are interested in buying; the uncertainty about ever receiving an accurate or honest answer is part of the risky pleasure of an auction. Some eBay sellers of H Blocks artefacts will be family members of prisoners looking for a way to divest themselves of their inheritances. Certainly, many sellers in the years immediately following the prison's closure were relatives, often daughters or nieces, female guardians of material culture. Their ownership of an auctioned object and its authenticity validated by well-worn phrases: 'in the family' but now 'letting it go'.[43] Easy access to the eBay market, open at any time in any place to anyone able to set up an internet account, has flat-lined different kinds of relationships between people and their things into indistinguishable screen identities, different forms of ownership collapse into one another. Everyone trades under avatars. Those turning 'stuff inside your houses' into 'stuff you can buy' may be prisoners' relatives or established auctioneers whose stock of items happen to include a purchased prison artefact; they could be accomplished dealers in military memorabilia or just someone who makes ends meet by selling a family history no long meaningful enough to keep. Some are certainly both, commercial dealers in their own stuff; their auctions are small businesses in a shed economy of the self-employed, an ongoing attempt to supplement income in the market for commemorative items because they need extra cash in a tight household budget. Types of sellers are superficially indistinguishable along the flatscape of an internet sale.

Some eBay buyers of the H Block material culture will be gift shoppers; a person looking for that ever-so-special thing for someone that they love. But many more will be collectors of republican or loyalist artefacts or military memorabilia more generally. big_balls shows he knows his market in his closing appeal:

> THIS COLLECTION HAS TO BE UNDOUBTEDLY THE BGGEST TO COME TO LIGHT SINCE ITS CLOSURE. THEY WHERE OBTAINED ALONG WITH OTHER ITEMS BY A CONSORTIUM OF HISTORIANS AND COLLECTORS FROM THE DEMOLITION PEOPLE. THIS IS A ONE OFF CHANCE TO BUY SUCH A UNIQUE COLLECTION AND IT WILL SURELY BECOME MORE COLLECTABLE AND VALUEABLE THROUGH TIME.[44]

Here is the authentication of the objects; big_balls implied that the keys are in his possession because he was one of 'the consortium of historians and collectors' who retrieved them from the site of the prison as it was about to be demolished. Here, too, is the contradiction in all auctions, or indeed all sales of once owned things: the object being disposed of has at the same time to be deemed worthy of keeping. The 'one off chance for a unique collection' must raise the question of why such a precious set is for sale. But, as Annette Weiner has argued, some things are exchanged to preserve others from the same fate,[45] which explains, at least in part, the blurred lines between collectors and dealers found in all second-hand markets, including eBay: selling one artefact to fund the acquisition of another regarded more highly.

The questions that play on the mind of second-hand shopper, as they decide to bid in an auction, circle around this contradiction. Why is an owner, who says this thing is so important, selling it? If they are the owner, for how long did they have it? Do I believe their story about the thing being in the family or are they making a profit from a previous purchase? These are questions of cultural property and definition of heritage. For whom is the object of exchange a precious possession and for whom can its meaning be reduced to its price? Who has an historical and cultural attachment to the artefacts of the H Blocks and who is merely dealing in e material culture of its past? Who has inherited the material culture of Long Kesh/Maze?

The geographical, political and patriarchal assertations of big_balls_from_ the_falls's avatar position him as a republican nationalist man from West Belfast: he is selling parts of his own history. Maybe. And maybe, he was one the 'consortium of historians and collectors' that did a deal with 'the demolition people'. Maybe not. The 'Long Kesh/Maze Prison Key Collection' uploaded to eBay on 21 September 2010 for £3,499 had been listed at €3,000 and sold for €2,900 in Whyte's auction house in Dublin five months earlier, 23 April 2010. They were lot 291 (Figure 6.5).

The tone of the Whyte's description is more muted, less sensationalist, but some of the phrases are the same:

1971–2000 HM Prison The Maze-Long Kesh "H Blocks" – keys and key tags. A unique collection

Steel, each 8 by 4cm, 3 by 1.5in.

Each key is stamped, eg. "H6 D WING CATWALK", "H6 MOVEMENT CONTROL GRILLE", "H2 INNER GRILLE", "H2 CELL DOORS & LOCK BACK C WING", "H2 YARD A WING", "HG HALL GUARD", "IRF HUNT", "ABF MASTER", and a bunch of individual cell numbers – "H4/1" to "H4/30". Also two circular brass tags with cabinet keys inscribed "Red Book H6" ("Red Book prisoners were "high security risks", usually escapees or those considered dangerous to prison staff and security forces.) Also some paper tagged keys including "H6 (B) Shower and Bath" and "FAB Search Hut" etc. A fascinating and unique collection of artefacts from a challenging chapter in Ireland's history. (50 + items)[46]

These are certainly the same keys sold by big_balls. Moreover, the security camera that he listed at the same time on eBay, which was sold for £375, was lot 302 in Whyte's auction and described in words repeated on eBay: 'a rare piece of Modern Irish History'.[47] Historical significance, provenance and sales pitch become blurred in the commercial spaces of an auction, its rooms or its screens. Since such textual descriptions are so loaded with financial gain, I would like to leave them behind and consider the only materiality of the H Block keys.

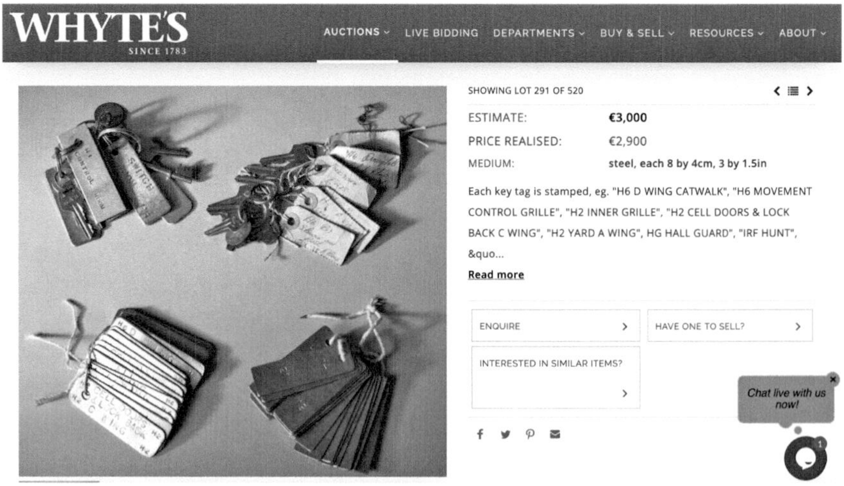

FIGURE 6.5 *'H Block keys'. Whyte's (23 April 2010), '1971–2000 HM Prison The Maze-Long Kesh "H Blocks" – keys and key tags/'. Reproduced with permission of Whyte's, Dublin.*

Keys

Bits of metal and pieces of paper. Not particularly precious. But the grey steel tags and beige parcel labels bear the names of the spaces that comprise an H Block: wings, cells yards and the divisions between them, huts and grilles. The keys are components of the structure of the prison, essential to its functioning, one of its forms, part of its fabric. They are archaeological fragments that function in the same way as flint tool or a shard of ceramic: they are from the time and the space of a site, a settlement, a building, a monument. But they exist, persist, into the present and carry their time and space with them. The H Block keys do have the indexical properties found in a semiotic sign or one of Alfred Gell's artefacts; they perform a powerful act of reference that brings to the fore the H Block cell doors that line an H Block wing and then draws into view the cells behind the doors opened and shut by the keys. The repeating shape of the cells creates the stems of the H shape; its keys make the prison, always removed from view and now mostly demolished, visible.

An artefact, according to Gell, has the material force to reach back to its 'recipient';[48] the H Blocks keys remain connected to the person who held them. On eBay they are positioned in a republican history, yet they are hardly, let alone exclusively, republican objects. Prison officers held the keys; they were their tools. The keys were pieces of a structure designed to contain and control those it imprisoned. The daily routine of the prison regime and the regime itself, one of restricted movement within an enclosed architecture, hung upon the keys. The action of turning a key in a lock finalizes the denial of free movement and facilitates its limited range. Locked in a cell overnight. Locked in a wing during the day except for two hours in the afternoon. Locked back in a cell. Locked in an H Block unless accompanied by a prison officer with his keys on a chain on his belt to visit relatives or to attend worship. Locked in a jail.

The work of keys has been already carefully theorized. I would like to give the last word, almost the last, to their theorist, Bruno Latour. Latour has written eloquently about the agency of a key.[49] A Berliner key is quite particular: it has no head but notched bits at both ends. It was designed for the external door of a multiple occupancy, a shared door of an apartment building that opens directly onto a street. The key itself ensures that this door is always locked as tenants come and go; the people who live in the building never have to remember to leave it secure. Once a Berliner key is put in the lock and turned to open, it can only be taken out from the door's other side; it must be pushed through the barrel mechanism, locking the door behind the person who has stepped onto the street. Such a key can reassure a worried or defensive landlord against a forgetful or lazy tenant. Latour suggests 'social relations' between 'tenants and owners, inhabitants and thieves' are 'mediated by the key'.[50] It is 'an intermediary' that carries, expresses, reflects or even objectifies 'the class struggle' between 'tenants and owners, rich people and thieves, right-wing Berliners and left-wing Berliners'. He is not, however, satisfied with this account of the power of the key, for the notched metal not only absorbs what is going on around it, such as an absent landlord making those who pay his rent responsible for the security of his property, it acts within this battle of control. If the key is a mediator or intermediary then the word, and work, of mediation must also, 'designate the actions of mediators'.[51] Berliner keys do not 'express' or 'objectify' or even 'symbolise' the 'disciplinary relations' of a locking door. Latour argues, 'they make them, form them'.[52]

The H Block keys can no longer act as formative mediators; the relationship of control of prison officers over prisoners constituted through the keys has gone with the building. But the keys still contain the 'script'[53] of imprisonment at Long Kesh/Maze. The repeating circular motions of the metal teeth of keys inside the cylinder of a lock that align with its pins are connected to twisting hands, reaching arms and footsteps across the door sills of cells and blocks. Compressed in their metal is the charge of power that accrued to the prison officer but challenged by prisoners in the solace of their cells and then in the widening range of movement through the H Blocks that ultimately made the keys redundant. The experience of imprisonment in Long Kesh/Maze cannot be separated from the materiality of the keys. A human experience was uploaded for sale on eBay. No wonder it had a high price.

In the market for difficult heritage

The material culture of the H Blocks has not reproduced the entrenched oppositions of the conflict in and about Northern Ireland that have been structured into the peace process. Every agreement about the development of the site of Long Kesh/Maze has been re-negotiated then never entirely fulfilled; the preservation of prison structures for future use turned into an argument about its past.[54] The prison is empty; most of its structures levelled and left to nature; those that remain are abandoned and unvisited. The hesitant and halting debate about the demolished prison site, acrimonious and unforgiving at times, has been, however, accompanied by the click and ker-ching of the trade in its material culture. The silence and fear that surrounds the prison site within political discourse has an internal logic that has not entirely pervaded the commercial marketplace. Avoidance and remembering, denial and attachment, articulated in the political dialogue about 'dealing with the past' and the attempts to 'make peace' with it[55] are still at play in the swirling mass of objects auctioned on eBay. Here, the separations of sectarianism, violence and conflict do not simply disappear in the act of consumption over the internet but their force is flattened by the accessibility of eBay: a peer-to-peer shared global platform. The single identity politics that defines Northern Ireland is presented as preference for a purchase in a digital space where objects associated with all protagonists of the conflict coexist. An alternative understanding of the past of the H Blocks is found on eBay; it is always available to the highest bidder and can be shared as far as the inequalities of market capitalism allows.

Furthermore, an interpretation of the conflict in and about Northern Ireland is manifested in internet exchanges of its material culture. I must argue, rather reluctantly but unavoidably, that the digitized commercial space of buying and selling is where the heritage of the H Blocks is practised.[56] Participation in heritage usually turns upon access and attendance: visiting a destination that has been designated as historically significant or standing still to mark an important historical event in a relevant public place. Long Kesh/Maze has not been made public nor turned into a destination in the aftermath of conflict despite its importance as one of its sites. Heritage cannot be practised through the participation in its spaces. The Maze Long Kesh Corporation, appointed by the Northern Ireland Executive to manage the 347-acre site on which the H Blocks were built, have overseen their remains slowly falling back to earth as other attractions developed by the Ulster Aviation Society and the Royal Ulster

Agricultural Society have become permanent features. In the absence of official intervention to open the spaces of the H Blocks to visitors, to stabilize its structures to ensure the safety of people who want to step inside and view, to offer information about its architectural and historical record, those interested in its past have simply made it their own business. They have not patiently waited for official permission to participate in the heritage of the H Blocks but have taken possession of pieces of it. They have bought it on eBay.

The searching for, identifying, bidding for and buying of second-hand goods is a treasure hunt and quest of knowledge. The skilled manoeuvres through the commercial landscape of collectors and dealers in historical artefacts or commemorative objects is motivated by a desire to own a material form of the past; finding that form, discovering it amongst the mountain of irrelevant matter always for sale, displays the owner's understanding of its history. H Block artefacts sold on eBay demonstrate the historical evaluation of the buyers of material culture. The acquisition of objects is always a sign of success and that of second-hand goods a particular achievement: they confer historical knowledge; they are cultural capital. Heritage that has been called contested or dissonant, dark or difficult, is not avoided on eBay but sought after for its high status; new owners can demonstrate their accomplishments in the interpretation of the complexities of conflict. Furthermore, the destination of such difficult heritage is a domestic setting: the material culture of conflict is mounted on the walls, displayed on mantlepieces, kept in the cabinets and cupboards of a home. From the humdrum rhythms of buying and selling that punctuate the internet auctions of an online economy, artefacts of the H Blocks are incorporated into everyday life. People like to live with the past.

Purchasing the past is always problematic; it asserts individual ownership of cultural property and can only be described as an act of appropriation. Why should one person and not another be able to hold the material compressions of historical relationships that are the H Block keys? Auctions do not recognize historical rights or concepts of collective stewardship, just the power to outbid. The equanimity and tolerance for the oppositional forms of the conflict in and about Northern Ireland sliding across the digital space of second-hand commodity exchange, which I reluctantly suggest can be considered an alternative heritage practice, is ended after objects are sold. Artefacts of imprisonment are once more out of sight in private collections. High prices for hidden treasures makes any market in heritage, internet or otherwise, a poor substitute for public access. Material culture of the H Blocks, the spoils of conflict, are hopelessly entangled in commodity culture, as Chumbawamba so sweetly argued in their song. Babylon back to Babylon.

Conclusion

In the end, Joe Strummer was not the iconoclast of the H Blocks. My best guess is that he would have wanted to see their solid structures. To see them again, to make a return journey of a kind. Global witnesses, of which he was just one, do seek out sites they have already seen through an image, then step in. But the monumental H Blocks were brought down by others. All, except one, smashed to pieces after their meaning had been irrevocably altered by the prisoners who inhabited them and those who supported them. The work of iconoclasm was completed by the demolition teams employed by the Northern Ireland Executive (Figure 7.1). Not directly, of course.

FIGURE 7.1 *The demolition of the H Blocks. Photograph: Louise Purbrick.*

Nothing is ever done directly in a neoliberal state, consociational or otherwise. The architecture of Long Kesh/Maze was brought down through the Reinvestment and Reform Initiative that create a Maze Regeneration Site.[1]

Historical loss

Demolition is a common enough occurrence in almost every urban area, a decisive moment in the land grab of global financial capitalism that is always an attack upon history. The removal of old buildings, an architecture placed in the past by the very decision to remove it, begins what is called 'regeneration', a biological metaphor for planned alterations to a particular space and to the relationships that have occurred in and about it. Destruction creates as great a material change as construction, if not more so. It breaks with the past rather than adding another layer in the architectural and historical record. But erasure is never entirely effective, for the structures leave their marks where they were built: a site still contains what has happened at its surface. People and their processes occur within a malleable material world. Our fabrics bear the signs of our life; they show how long we have inhabited them where they thin to holes: the weight of a body over time in a particular place. We no more float free from the architecture in which we live than our clothes that may be a little closer to our skin. Always in touch with both. Always making impressions that eventually appear as absences. Walter Benjamin warned us that to live is to leave traces.[2] There are precious few pristine places.

At sites of conflict that have been designated heritage destinations, authorized as places where the material record of past resides, an atmosphere of the presence of absent others surrounds them. The gentle pace of walking, the directed looking followed by distant gazing then quiet reflection is a ritual of remembrance that bears similarities to funerals for, and anniversaries of, the dead. Concentrated attention within the space of the past calls up its presences and pulls them into a shared moment in time.[3] When I first visited the H Blocks, less than two years after they had been emptied, my study of its spaces was rather like an extended heritage journey. A return of a global witness. The strangeness of walking inside an icon never left me; I was a person inside an image with a perspective that veered from the safety of viewing the past from the present to being so close up that it enclosed me.

My strongest feeling was the terrible loss of separation. The scale of that loss was suggested, but not quite fully materialized, in the size of the space and in the repetition of its spatial composition. All the H Blocks and the structures that surrounded them were still standing. Loss multiplied. How many cells were occupied by how many people over how long? And how could this calculation, only possible if someone collated the records of every prisoner who lived in every cell over the prison's lifetime, equal all the feelings of separation? On that first visit, I walked around every day for a week. How many previous prisoners' and prisoner visitors' journeys did I stumble over? How many hours were wasted by how many prisoners and those who waited for their release? I cannot wait for a bus. I walk on to the next stop and then the next when the bus I should have waited for overtakes me. I am most restless in the last hours of train journeys home and spend much of my time trying to hide the physical discomfort of separation from my family and friends from other passengers and to halt it from intruding too far into myself.

Unresolved differences of the conflict in and about Northern Ireland had been allowed to settle upon the abandoned architecture of the H Blocks but the empty prison buildings did not sustain the simple symmetry of sectarianism. They evoked an experience of imprisonment as isolation and offered an impression of the historical loss of time. From reading personal accounts of prisoners and political analysis of imprisonment, I already had some understanding of another experience in the H Blocks: the collective life of political prisoners through which communities were reconstituted in he H Blocks, which may have overcome some of the separation from those outside. But this also appeared as a loss: the spaces actively appropriated by prisoners were now utterly abandoned. They were cold and damp: their paint peeling, walls rotting, ceilings falling.

I made further visits to the H Blocks over the next four years. Then I watched their demolition. I spent two days observing a process that took two years. The hydraulic booms operating breakers, crushers and excavators cracked the prison walls then crashed them to the ground but only served to open out the interiors of the cells to view; it was possible, momentarily, to see the shapes of incarceration (Figure 7.2). Once all the 96 single cells numbered 2 to 25 across four wings A to D were reduced to ground level and the rubble mechanically shovelled away to be sorted into its different material types, the entire footprint of each H Block was exposed; the stems and crossbar of its letterform precisely delineated by the straight dusty edge along the rusty reinforcements, the steels (Figure 7.3). More marks of absence. Demolition left its own trace on broken surfaces of the former prison site.

Loss in the landscape of Long Kesh/Maze was visible and tangible: it is seen and still felt. Loss appears to a person, or at least has appeared to me, as loneliness. But this sensation cannot be in the atmosphere of absent presence around the material record of the past because most of the prison buildings are gone. Loss belonged to the land before it got to me. The architecture is absent but the land itself holds an experience of imprisonment and the attempt to erase it. Much is missing, of course. The remains of all but one of the H Blocks were reduced to fragmentary foundations but these are resilient material forms that still held their symbolic force.

FIGURE 7.2 *Internal cell view of an H Block cell. Photograph: Louise Purbrick.*

FIGURE 7.3 *H Block footprint. Photograph: Louise Purbrick.*

Managing history

The Maze Long Kesh Development Corporation opened a new footpath and cycleway to serve Halftown Road residents who live on the edge of the former prison site. The smooth surfaces of new lanes are easy underfoot for pedestrians and offer no friction to a cyclists' tyres. The way for both cleared and wide enough for share. This is no narrow verge. Wet grasses do not dampen the trousers of walkers, trailing branches will not slap their faces or interfere with the wheels of bicycles spinning safely away from the roar of traffic. Halftown Road is now connected to the 24-kilometre Blaris Greenway to Belfast that runs along the Lagan Towpath. One of the 'traffic-free paths for everyone' promoted by the 'custodians' of the National Cycle Network, Sustrans, it provides the tick box triumvirate of sustainability, accessibility and inclusivity.[4] The Halftown Road section delivers Maze Long Kesh Development Corporation's community engagement agenda that is also a form of control over the former prison site. The new path along the old road is a small channel in the zoning of Long Kesh/Maze, designing the movement in and about it, determining the activities that occur within. Landscaping is an attempt to manage the past that lies in the land.

Maze Long Kesh Development Corporation, an ALB (Arm's-Length Body) of the Executive Office of Northern Ireland, do not deny the past of imprisonment at its site; it is included in its 'compelling and varied history' and is positioned about halfway down its 'timeline' which starts in 1941 when the RAF air base opened.[5] Agriculture precedes its military, political and economic history. 'Agricultural use' is listed before the timeline begins and is presented as a pre-historical state, the natural condition of the land. Indeed, a return to agriculture, if that is what is meant by an Enterprise Zone for 'agri-food business' as outlined in the West Lisburn Development Framework,[6] is planned for the former prison spaces where there are no structures subject to the statutory protection of heritage listing. The organic origins of agriculture allow an awful omission in the online information provided by both Northern Ireland's public governmental bodies and the private organizations constituted to carry out their work, such as the Maze Long Kesh Development Corporation that followed the Reinvestment and Reform Initiative. The earthy surface of the lands on which the H Blocks were built was a political terrain before it became a prison site. The deep cultivation or ridge system of growing vegetables, especially potatoes, was 'ground to dust' by rack-renting of landlords in mid-nineteenth-century Ireland.[7] Whatever was planted when Long Kesh was a field or a meadow, it grew under the historical conditions of colonization. Agricultural systems are embedded in land ownership, the unequal property relationships that exhaust the earth and the labourers whose lives depend upon it, leaving both hungry. Plans locating the agri-food zone at

Long Kesh may seem a proper ending to a problematic past, back to business as usual as if the H Blocks were a state of exception. Yet, both agriculture and imprisonment in Ireland are historical formations of the same colonial order that the Hunger Strikers understood so well. They knew their place in the history of starvation in Ireland.

There is natural process at work across and under the surfaces of the site of Long Kesh/Maze. The long years in which its listed buildings, the last H Block, the hospital, the chapel, the administration centre, the watchtower outside a section of the perimeter wall have been left unattended has paved the way for a return to nature.[8] Bushes spread out across the walls, grass grows tall along the borders of roads, trees reach above the wire fences, greening over the grey metal. Weeds grow. The weeds are natural evidence of political neglect. They perform its work. Their relentless land reclamation will eventually turn concrete into soil and bury the past of imprisonment. Meanwhile, the slow seasonal process of their growth is opening out the fibres of a British fortress to the air. In the decomposition of the H Blocks, different substances become entangled together to create natural and historical formations. The bark of a tree pushes through Portland cement shedding sand particles around its base, the chlorophyll of leaves lies over oxidizing metal. A ruin is forming and the past, ever more fragmentary, appears again. The passing of time can be seen in the slow drama of decay in a ruin. A reminder of what was there, of what has gone. Loss has another material form.

The absent architecture of the demolished H Blocks is altered by the weeds. The irregular organic patterns of weed growth disrupt the straight hard lines of the architecture of imprisonment. Their long, strong roots are prising apart stony environments in preparation for more plants; their long, spindly stems raising seed heads in preparation for wide dispersal across an environment made less hostile by their roots. Another colonialization has begun. The ruins of Long Kesh/Maze, the lines of rubble that form the stem and cross bar of the H shaped cell units that held such symbolic power in the print culture of protest across the globe, are being covered up by an army of wild flowers. The H becoming hidden, gradually pushed down into the ground. Their lifetime as a space of incarceration falling into a layer of the lifetime of the land. An act of erasure obscured.

Notes

Introduction

1 The phrase 'in and about' Northern Ireland, which is also used in the subtitle of this book, is the much debated description of the conflict by conflict-resolution group Healing Through Remembering (http://www.healingthroughremembering.org. It acknowledges that the status of Northern Ireland itself is contested.

2 Jonathan Watkins, 'Back to the Black Country', in *Rita Donagh*, Rita Donagh (Birmingham: Ikon Gallery, 2005), 18.

3 See, for example, Tom Murtagh, *The Maze Prison: A Hidden Story of Chaos, Anarchy and Politics* (Hook: Waterside Press, 2018).

4 Laura McAtackney, *An Archaeology of the Troubles: The Dark Heritage of Long Kesh/Maze Prison* (Oxford: Oxford University Press, 2014).

5 Ibid., 40.

6 Marcia Pointon, *Brilliant Effects: A Cultural History of Gem Stones and Jewellery* (Yale: Yale University Press, 2009), 51–2.

7 Alongside many other Brighton-based activists, I was part of the Save Omar campaign for the release from Guantánamo Bay of Omar Deghayes, whose family had lived in the city for many years. On his return, he talked about some of his experiences. For an account of the campaign see Pollyanna Ruiz, *Articulating Dissent: Protest and the Public Sphere* (London: Pluto Press, 2014).

8 ASBO, *Bang-Up and Smash* (London: Active Distribution, 2017), 7.

9 Lucy Robinson, 'Things are Messy: Be Careful What You Wish For', in *Now That's What I Call History*, https://proflrobinson.com/2015/07/04/things-are-messy-be-careful-what-you-wish-for/#comments (accessed 11 June 2022).

10 Susheila Nasta, '"Messy Solidarities": Reflections on the Politics of the Present', *South Asian Review* 43, no. 1–2 (2022), 137.

11 Peg Fraser, 'Messy History', *Cultural Studies Review* 25, no. 2 (2019), 264.

12 Murtagh, *The Maze Prison; Maze* (2017), [Film] Dir. Stephen Burke, Ireland: Filmgate Films.

13 Louise Purbrick, 'The History Block', *Museums Journal*, July 2001, 26–7.

14 Brian Graham and Sara McDowell, 'Meaning in the Maze: The Heritage of Long Kesh', *Cultural Geographies* 14, no. 3 (July 2007): 343.

15 Maze Long Kesh Development Corporation, 'Welcome', http://mazelongkesh.com/ (accessed 7 January 2021).

16 Laurjane Smith, *The Uses of Heritage* (Abingdon: Routledge, 2006).

17 Kris Brown, 'Political Commemoration and Peacebuilding in Ethno-national Settings: The Risk and Utility of Partisan Memory', *Peacebuilding* 7, no. 1 (2019): 51–70.

18 Eikon Exhibition Centre, 'It's All in the Show', https://www.eikonexhibitioncentre.co.uk/events/balmoral-show (accessed 7 January 2021); Maze Long Kesh Development Corporation, 'The Balmoral Show'.

19 Lisburn and Castlereagh City Council, *West Lisburn Development Framework* (Lisburn: Lisburn and Castlereagh City Council, 2015), 44.

20 The clearest articulation of this was by Margaret Thatcher at a press conference on 21 April 1981, during the hunger strike. She stated: 'Crime is crime is crime, it is not political', *Conflict Archive on the Internet* (hereafter CAIN) Web service, 'The Hunger Strike of 1981 – A Chronology of Main Events' http://cain.ulst.ac.uk/events/hstrike/chronology.htm (accessed 7 November 2009).

21 *Northern Ireland (Emergency Provisions) Act 1973*, The General Public Acts (London: HMSO, 1974).

22 John McGarry and Brendan O'Leary, *Broken Images: Explaining Northern Ireland* (Oxford: Blackwell, 1995), 1–2.

23 Ibid.

24 John Tonge, *Northern Ireland* (Cambridge: Polity, 2006), 13.

25 John McGarry and Brendan O'Leary, *The Northern Ireland Conflict: Consociational Engagements* (Oxford: Oxford University Press, 2004).

26 For an architecture of separation, division and opposition between the two communities, see Krieder-O'Leary, *Peacewall Archive*, http://www.peacewall-archive.net/ (accessed 23 January 2022).

27 Louise Purbrick, 'British Watchtowers', in *British Watchtowers*, ed. Donovan Wylie (Göttingen: Steidl, 2007), 57–71.

Chapter one

1 Henry McDonald, 'No Ordinary Joe', *The Guardian*, 29 Dec 2002, https://www.theguardian.com/music/2002/dec/29/artsfeatures.popandrock2 (accessed 17 December 2021).

2 Ed Dorrell, 'Problems and Opposition Dog Maze Stadium Plans', *Architects' Journal*, 12 August (2005), http://www.architectsjournal.co.uk/news/problems-and-opposition-dog-maze-stadium-plans/583950.article (accessed 14 January 2010).

3 Sites of Conscience, 'Reconciliation Report Triggers Controversy in Northern Ireland', *Matters of Conscience*, January to March (2009), http://www.sitesofconscience.org/resources/newsletters/2009-03-31/en/ (accessed 14 January 2010).

4 Dan Keenan, 'History of Prison Stands as Microcosm of Northern Conflict', *Irish Times*, 30 October 2006, http://www.irishtimes.com/news/history-of-prison-stands-as-a-microcosm-of-northern-conflict-1.1022676 (accessed 5 August 2015); Peter Foster, 'Inside Story of the Maze, A Jail Like No Other', *The Telegraph*, 28 July 2000, http://www.telegraph.co.uk/news/uknews/1350686/Inside-story-of-the-Maze-a-jail-like-no-other.html (accessed 5 August 2015); John O'Farrell, 'The Maze Slams Shut at Last', *The Guardian*, 23 July 2000, http://www.theguardian.com/uk/2000/jul/23/northernireland.johnofarrell (accessed 5 August 2015).

5 Michel Foucault, *Discipline and Punish: The Birth of the Prison* (Harmondsworth: Penguin, 1979), 200.

6 Ibid., 201.

7 Ibid., 200.

8 Ibid., 205.

9 Ibid., 202.

10 Stanley Cohen, *Visions of Social Control: Crime, Punishment and Classification* (Cambridge: Polity, 1985), 10.

11 Foucault, *Discipline and Punish*, 211.

12 Ibid., 205.

13 John Dinwiddy, *Bentham* (Oxford: Oxford University Press, 1989), 7.

14 Jeremy Bentham, *The Works of Jeremy Bentham Published Under the Superintendence of his Executor John Bowring*, Volume 4, (1838–1843, New York, Russell and Russell, 1962), 37, https://oll.libertyfund.org/title/bowring-the-works-of-jeremy-bentham-vol-4 (accessed 27 September 2021).

15 Ibid., 40.

16 Ibid.

17 Ibid., 41.

18 Ibid., 66.

19 Foucault, *Discipline and Punish*, 200.

20 Jeremy Bentham, *The Works of Jeremy Bentham*, 43.

21 Ibid., 41.

22 Ibid., 42.

23 David Lyons, *In the Interest of the Governed: A Study in Bentham's Philosophy and Utility of Law* (Oxford: Clarendon Press, 1973), 50.

24 Mary Mack, *Jeremy Bentham: An Odyssey of Ideas, 1748–1792* (London: Heinemann, 1963), 50.

25 John Dinwiddy, *Bentham*, 17.

26 C.K. Ogden, *Jeremy Bentham* (London: Kegan Paul, 1932), 115.

27 Ibid., 114.

28 Foucault, *Discipline and Punish*, 206.

29 Ibid., 205.

30 C.K. Ogden, *Jeremy Bentham*, 116.

31 Quoted in ibid.

32 This conversation took place at Long Kesh/Maze on my first visit in January 2002.

33 Ibid.

34 *Report of a Committee to Consider, in the Context of Civil Liberties and Human Rights, Measures to Deal with Terrorism in Northern Ireland* (hereafter The Gardiner Report), Cmnd. 5847 (HMSO, January, 1975), 36. See also *Committee of Inquiry into the United Kingdom Prison Services*, Cmnd. 7676 (London: HMSO, October 1979).

35 Allan Brodie, Jane Croom and James O. Davies, *English Prisons: An Architectural History* (Swindon: English Heritage, 2002), 207–11; See Norman Johnston, *Forms of Constraint: A History of Prison Architecture* (Urbana: University of Illinois Press, 2000), 149.

36 *Report of the Work of the Prison Department 1974*, Cmnd. 6148 (London: HMSO, July 1975).

37 Merlyn Rees, *Northern Ireland: A Personal Perspective* (London: Methuen, 1985), 141.

38 Merlyn Rees, personal correspondence (7 July 2003).

39 Andrew Saint, *Towards a Social Architecture: The Role of School-building in Post-war England* (New Haven, CT: Yale University Press), 1987.

40 A.W. Peterson, 'The Prison Building Programme', *The British Journal of Criminology* 1, no. 4 (1961): 307; Allan Brodie, Jane Croom and James O. Davies, *English Prisons*, 196.

41 Ibid., 213.

42 Norman Johnston, *The Human Cage: A Brief History of Prison Architecture* (New York: The American Foundation, 1973), 51.

43 Leslie Fairweather, 'The Evolution of the Prison', in *Prison Architecture*, ed. United Nations Social Defence Research Institute (London: Architectural Press, 1975): 13–40.

44 Ibid., 149. Other H Blocks, but with three storeys, were built in Portugal and Portuguese territory: Linho (1954) outside Lisbon, Porto (1957), Bie in Angola (1956). See also: Jim Challis, *The Northern Ireland Prison Service 1920–1990. A History* (Belfast: Northern Ireland Prison Service, 1999), 66–79 for references to Magilligan, which also consisted of H blocks.

45 *Report of an Inquiry by HM Chief Inspector of Prisons into the Security Arrangements at HM Prison, Maze*, Cmnd. 203 (London: HMSO, January 1984), hereafter The Hennessy Report.

46 National Army Museum, 'The Troubles', https://www.nam.ac.uk/explore/troubles-1969-2007 (accessed 25 January 2022).

47 Lord Gardiner, 26 June 1975, *Parliamentary Debates (Hansard)*, Fifth Series, Volume CCCLI (London: HMSO), 1646. He also implies in this speech that in practice the interim custody orders lasted longer than 28 days, ibid., 1647.

48 Michael Farrell, *Northern Ireland: The Orange State* (1976; London: Pluto Press, 1992), 281–84; J. Bowyer Bell, *The Irish Troubles: A Generation of Violence 1967–1992* (Dublin: Gill and Macmillan, 1993), 212–48.

49 Brian Gormally, Kieran McEvoy and David Wall, 'Criminal Justice in a Divided Society: Northern Ireland Prisons', in *Crime and Justice: A Review of Research* 17, ed. M. Tonry (Chicago: Chicago University Press, 1993), 72; Chris Ryder, *Inside the Maze: The Untold Story of the Northern Ireland Prison Service* (London: Methuen, 2000), 152; J. Bowyer Bell, *The Irish Troubles*, 212.

50 Brian Gormally, Kieran McEvoy and David Wall, 'Criminal Justice in a Divided Society', 73.

51 Lord Gardiner, *Parliamentary Debates*, 1646.

52 Brian Gormally, Kieran McEvoy and David Wall, 'Criminal Justice in a Divided Society', 74.

53 Northern Ireland (Emergency Provisions) Act 1973, *The General Public Acts* (London: HMSO, 1974)

54 John McGuffin, *Internment* (Tralee, Ireland: Anvil Books, 1973), 90–1.

55 The Gardiner Report, 67.

56 The Gardiner Report, 66.

57 The Hennessy Report, 1.

58 Max Arthur, *Northern Ireland Soldiers Talking, 1969 to Today* (London: Sidgwick and Jackson, 1981), 64.

59 Jim Challis, *The Northern Ireland Prison Service*, 59.

60 Chris Ryder, *Inside the Maze*, 152.

61 Quoted in Peter Taylor, *Loyalists* (London: Bloomsbury, 2000), 141.

62 Colin Crawford, 'The Compound System: An Alternative Penal Strategy', *The Howard Journal of Criminal Justice* 21, no. 3 (1982): 155–8. This article was based on the author's 1979 Cranfield Institute of Technology M.Sc.

63 Quoted in Laurence McKeown, *Out of Time: Irish Republican Prisoners Long Kesh, 1972–2000* (Belfast: Beyond the Pale Publications, 2001), 35.

64 Quoted in ibid.

65 Jim Challis, *The Northern Ireland Prison Service*, 63.

66 Quoted in Laurence McKeown *Out of Time*, 35.

67 Gerry Adams, *Cage 11* (Dingle: Brandon Books, 1990), 45.

68 *The Gardiner Report*, 33.

69 Ibid., 54.

70 *Parliamentary Debates (Hansard)* 885, HMSO,1975.

71 Merlyn Rees, *Northern Ireland: A Personal Perspective*, 140.

72 'A New Kind of Prison', *Architectural Forum*, December (1954): 149.

73 For more on lift-slab techniques see: C.H. Goodchild, *Hybrid Concrete Construction* (Crowthorne: British Cement Association, 1995), 43; J.G. Richardson, 'Precast concrete: Its production, transport and erection', in *Handbook of Structural Concrete*, ed. F.K. Kong, R.H. Evans, E. Cohen, F. Roll (London: Pitman, 1983), 18–10 to 18–19; George Winter and A.H. Wilson, *Design of Concrete Structures* (New York: McGraw-Hill Book Company, 1972) 413–30.

74 The modernism of Nathaniel Curtis of Curtis and Davis is also evident in their other buildings: Teaching Hospital for the Free University of Berlin; Louisiana Superdome; Rivergate, Port of New Orleans Exhibition Center.

75 'A New Kind of Prison', 150. See also: Nathaniel C. Curtis, 'Medium Security Institution: Programming and Design', *Architectural Record*, September (1959): 221–25.

76 Norman Johnston, 'Recent Trends in Correctional Architecture', *The British Journal of Criminology* 1, no. 4 (April 1961): 331.

77 *Recent Prison Construction. Supplement to the Handbook of Correctional Institutional Design and Construction* (United States Bureau of Prisons, 1960).

78 A.E.J. Morris, *Precast Concrete in Architecture* (London: George Goodwin, 1978), 269.

79 Norman Johnston, *The Human Cage*, 51.

80 A.M. Haas, *Precast Concrete: Design and Applications*, (London: Applied Science Publishers, 1983), 47–9.

81 Stefan Aust, *The Baader-Meinhof Group* (London: Bodley Head, 1985).

82 Lord Donaldson, 26 June 1975, in *Parliamentary Debates (Hansard)*, Fifth Series, Volume CCCLI (London: HMSO): 1650.

83 Allan Brodie, Jane Croom and James O. Davies, *English Prisons*, 232.

84 Jeremy Bentham, *The Works of Jeremy Bentham*, 97.

85 Ibid., 105.

Chapter two

1 Peter Shirlow and Kieran McEvoy, *Beyond the Wire: Former Prisoners and Conflict Transformation in Northern Ireland* (London: Pluto, 2008), 26–7.

2 Brain Gormally, Kieran McEvoy and David Wall, 'Criminal Justice in a Divided Society: Northern Ireland Prisons', in *Crime and Justice: A Review of Research*, vol. 17, ed. M. Tonry (Chicago: 1993), 77–85.

3 John Ditchfield, *Control in Prisons: A Review of the Literature* (London: HMSO, 1980) 77.

4 See Stanley Cohen, 'Prisons and the Future of Control Systems: From Concentration to Dispersal', in *Welfare in Action*, ed. Mike Fitzgerald (London: Open University/Routledge, 1977), 220–1, and Sean McConville, 'The Architectural Realisation of Penal Ideas', in *Prison Architecture. Policy, Design and Experience*, ed. Leslie Fairweather and Sean McConville (Oxford: Architectural Press, 2000), 1–15.

5 Laurence McKeown, *Out of Time: Irish Republican Prisoners Long Kesh 1972–2000* (Belfast: Beyond the Pale, 2001), 51.

6 Brian Campbell, Laurence McKeown and Felim O'Hagan (eds), *Nor Meekly Serve My Time: The H-Block Struggle 1976–1981* (Belfast: Beyond the Pale, 1994), 4. All testimony from participants in the H Block struggle cited in this chapter are drawn from two oral history works, the jointly authored text by Campbell, McKeown and O'Hagan (ibid.) and McKeown, *Out of Time*, as well as 'in-depth' interviews undertaken in 2005 by Brandon Hamber for Cúnamh, a Derry-based community organization. Brandon Hamber, *Blocks to the Future: A Pilot Study of the Long-term Psychological Impact of the 'No Wash/ Blanket Protest* (Belfast: Action and Research International/Cúnamh, 2005). Hamber, *Blocks to the Future*, 37.

7 Campbell et al., *Nor Meekly Serve My Time*, 4.

8 Hamber, *Blocks to the Future*, 37–9.

9 Ibid., 37.

10 Campbell et al., *Nor Meekly Serve My Time*, 8–9.

11 Tim Ingold, *The Perception of the Environment: Essays on Livelihood, Dwelling and Skill* (London: Routledge, 2000), 172.

12 Ibid., 173.

13 Tim Ingold, 'Building, Dwelling, Living: How Animals and People Make Themselves at Home in the World', in *Shifting Contexts: Transformations in Anthropological Knowledge*, ed. Marilyn Strathern (London and New York: Routledge, 1995), 77.

14 See Leslie Fairweather, 'The Evolution of the Prison' in *Prison Architecture*, ed. United Nations Social Defence Research Institute (London: Architectural Press, 1975), 13–40; Norman Johnston, *Forms of Constraint* (Urbana: University of Illinois Press, 2000); Norman Johnston, *The Human Cage*: *A Brief History of Prison Architecture* (New York: The American Foundation, 1973).

15 Tim Ingold, 'Building, Dwelling, Living', 76.

16 Antonio Gramsci in *Selections from the Prison Notebooks of Antonio Gramsci*, ed. Quintin Hoare and Geoffrey Nowell Smith (London: Lawrence and Wishart, 1973), 242 and 262–3; Giuseppe Fiori, *Antonio Gramsci: Life of a Revolutionary* (1965; London: Verso: 1990), 235–87.

17 *The Prison Rules 1964, Statutory Instruments*, no. 388 (London: HMSO, 1964), 8; See Juliet Ash, *Dress Behind Bars: Prison Clothing as Criminality* (London: I.B. Tauris, 2009); Juliet Ash, 'Prison Dress', in *The Encyclopaedia of Clothing and Fashion*, ed. Valerie Steele and Christopher Breward (New York: Charles Scribner's Sons, 2005).

18 Archbishop Tomas O'Fiaich's description following a visit to Maze/Long Kesh in August 1978, quoted in David Beresford, *Ten Men Dead* (London: Harper Collins, 1987), 184.

19 Campbell et al., *Nor Meekly Serve My Time*, 70.

20 Claude Leroy, 'Space in Prison', in *Prison Architecture*, ed. United Nations Social Defence Research Institute (London: Architectural Press, 1975).

21 By early 1978, 250 republicans were protesting, which rose to 300 by the end of the year. Numbers rose to 500 at the end of the protest in 1981. See Gormally et al., 'Criminal Justice in a Divided Society', 82.

22 Laurence McKeown, *Out of Time*, 55.

23 Campbell et al., *Nor Meekly Serve My Time*, 72.

24 Ibid., 35 and 54.

25 Ibid., ix.

26 Ibid., 21.

27 Ibid., 22.

28 Ibid., 31; Laurence McKeown, *Out of Time*, 56.

29 Campbell et al., *Nor Meekly Serve My Time*, 32–3.

30 Ibid., 33.

31 Chris Ryder, *Inside the Maze: The Untold Story of the Northern Ireland Prison Service* (London: Methuen, 2000), 195.

32 Hamber, *Blocks to the Future*, 40.

33 Campbell et al., *Nor Meekly Serve My Time*, 72.

34 Hamber, *Blocks to the Future,* 8.

35 Campbell et al., *Nor Meekly Serve My Time*, 9–11.

36 Laurence McKeown, *Out of Time*, 50.

37 Campbell et al., *Nor Meekly Serve My Time*, 51.

38 Ibid., 55.

39 Ibid., 42 and 57; Hamber, *Blocks to the Future*, 40.

40 Campbell et al., *Nor Meekly Serve My Time*, 47.

41 See Mary Douglas, *Purity and Danger: An Analysis of Concepts of Pollution and Taboo* (London: Routledge, 1966).

42 Campbell et al., *Nor Meekly Serve My Time*, 57.

43 Ibid., 22.

44 Ibid., 53.

45 Ibid., 51.

46 Hamber, *Blocks to the Future*, 43.

47 Campbell et al., *Nor Meekly Serve My Time*, 47.

48 'Sin é' translates as 'that's it' and was a call to order, see Campbell et al., *Nor Meekly Serve My Time*, 35 and x. 'Bear in the air' was prison slang for prison officer on the wing, see ibid., vii.

49 Ibid., 52.

50 Ibid., 75.

51 Ibid., 74.

52 Ibid., 73–4.

53 Ibid., 73.

54 Ibid., 75.

55 A good example of this is the song 'Back Home from Derry' recorded by Christy Moore in *Ride On*, 1984, written by Bobby Sands. Sands adapted words and music of Canadian folk musician Gordon Lightfoot and his 'The Wreck of the Edmund Fitzgerald' 1976.

56 Campbell et al., *Nor Meekly Serve My Time*, 81.

57 Feargal Mac Ionnrachtaigh, *Language, Resistance and Revival* (London: Pluto, 2013).

58 T.G. Ashplant, Graham Dawson and Michael Roper, *The Politics of War Memory and Commemoration* (London: Routledge, 2000).

59 Campbell et al., *Nor Meekly Serve My Time*, 71.

60 Richard English, *Armed Struggle: The History of the IRA* (London: Pan Macmillan, 2003). See also, Kirsty Scott, 'Men of Letters, Men of Arms', *The Guardian*, Saturday Review 2 December, 2000, 1.

61 David Held et al., eds., *States and Societies* (Oxford: Martin Robinson/Open University, 1983).

62 Georgio Agamben, *Homo Sacer: Sovereign Power and Bare Life* (Stanford, CA: Stanford University Press, 1998).

Chapter three

1 'Thousands of Protestors in New York Stand with Hunger Strikers', *Irish People*, 8 August, 1981, 2.

2 William Borders, 'An Ocean of Union Jacks and Chanting Throngs Along Procession Route', *New York Times*, 30 July, 1981, 10.

3 Simon Faulkner, Farida Vis and F. d'Orazio, 'Analysing Social Media Images', in *The Sage Handbook of Social Media*, ed. J. Burgess, A. Marwick and T. Poell (London: Sage, 2018), 160–78.

4 Edward Said, *Humanism and Democratic Criticism* (Basingstoke: Palgrave Macmillan, 2004), 142. 'The Public Role of Writers and Intellectuals' reproduced here was first published in *The Nation*, 2001.

5 *The Prison Rules 1964* Statutory Instruments, no. 388 (London: HMSO). Juliet Ash, *Dress Behind Bars: Prison Clothing as Criminality* (London: I.B. Tauris, 2010).

6 Imogen Tyler, *Revolting Subjects: Social Abjection and Resistance in Neoliberal Britain* (London: Zed Books, 2013), 10. Imogen Tyler is interpreting the work of Judith Butler here.

7 Quoted in F. Stuart Ross, *Smashing H Block: The Rise and Fall of the Campaign Against Criminalization, 1976–1982* (Liverpool: Liverpool University Press, 2011), 3.

8 See Peter Catterall and Sean McDougall, *The Northern Ireland Question in British Politics* (London: Macmillan, 1996) for consideration of the BBC position as independent from that of government.

9 Liz Curtis, *Ireland, The Propaganda War: The British Media and the 'Battle for Hearts and Minds'* (London: Pluto Press, 1984); Walter Laqueur, 'Is Britain losing the propaganda war?' *Sunday Times*, 31 May 1981, 17; David Miller, *Don't Mention the War: Northern Ireland, Propaganda, and the Media* (London: Pluto Press, 1994).

10 'Hunger Strikes 1980–1981' Bitesize, *BBC*, https://www.bbc.co.uk/bitesize/guides/zx49cj6/revision/3 (accessed 11 October 2021).

11 Robert Savage, *The BBC's Irish Troubles: Television, Conflict and Northern Ireland* (Manchester: Manchester University Press, 2015). See chapter 5.

12 F. Stuart Ross, *Smashing H Block*, 5.

13 Quoted in ibid., 22.

14 Ibid., 23.

15 Ibid., 22.

16 Jacqueline Hogge, 'Behind the Men Stood a Group of Gallant Women who Opened and Maintained a Vital Line of Communication to and from Long Kesh' *Nuachtáin Commemoration Special*, May 2011, 8–9.

17 Begoña Aretxaga, *Shattering Silence: Women, Nationalism and Political Subjectivity in Northern Ireland* (Princeton, NJ: Princeton University Press, 1997), see Chapter 5, 105–21.

18 Katherine Side, 'Mairéad Farrell in Armagh Jail', in *The Carceral Network in Ireland: History, Agency and Resistance*, ed. Fiona McCann (London: Palgrave Macmillan, 2020), 162 [155–77]. See also: *Armagh Stories* (2015) [Film] dir. Cahal McLaughlin, Belfast: Prisons Memory Archive, https://www.prisonsmemoryarchive.com/feature_films/armagh-stories (accessed 11 June 2022) and the director's reflections upon the film's making in McLaughlin, 'Memory, Place and Gender: Armagh Stories: Voices from the Gaol', *Memory Studies* 13, no. 4 (2017): 677–90;

19 Nell McCafferty, "It is my belief that Armagh is a feminist issue", *The Irish Times*, 22 August 1980. F. Stuart Ross, *Smashing H Block*, 5. Azrini Wahidin, 'Menstruation as a Weapon of War: The Politics of the Bleeding Body of Women on Political Protest at Armagh Jail, Northern Ireland', *The Prison Journal*, 99, no. 1 (2019): 121–31.

20 Kevin Meagher, 'If Jeremy Corbyn was wrong on Northern Ireland, so was Nelson Mandela', *The New Statesman*, 7 September 2015, https://www.newstatesman.com/politics/2015/09/if-jeremy-corbyn-was-wrong-northern-ireland-so-was-nelson-mandela (accessed 12 October 2021); Graham Spencer, *From Armed Struggle to Political Struggle: Republican Tradition and Transformation in Northern Ireland* (London: Bloomsbury, 2015); Peter Taylor, 'The Hunger Strikes', Archive on 4, *BBC* https://www.bbc.co.uk/programmes/m000vpyd (accessed 11 October 2021); '1981 was the Major Turning Point in the History of the Six Counties, *Nuachtáin Commemoration Special* May 2001, 3.

21 Éamon Phoenix quoted in Sean Murray, '"It doesn't diminish": The Legacy of the 1981 Hunger Strikes, 40 Years On', *The Journal*, 27 February 2021, https://www.thejournal.ie/bobby-sands-40th-anniversary-5358326-Feb2021/ (accessed 11 October 2021); Peter Taylor, 'The Hunger Strikes'.

22 Ibid., 62, 80 93.

23 Brian Hanley, 'The Politics of Noraid', *Irish Political Studies* 19, no. 1, (2004): 3.

24 F. Stuart Ross, *Smashing H Block*, 60.

25 John Dumbrell, 'The United States and the Northern Irish Conflict 1969–94: From Indifference to Intervention', *Irish Studies in International Affairs* 6 (1995): 107–25.

26 Mark Malony, 'Bernie Sanders Letter to Margaret Thatcher over the 1981 H-Blocks Hunger Strikes', *Anphoblacht*, 19 February 2016, https://www.anphoblacht.com/contents/25744 (accessed 12 October 2021).

27 'Members of US Congress to MT', Prime Ministerial Office Files, *Margaret Thatcher Foundation,* https://www.margaretthatcher.org/document/125265 (accessed 12 October 2021).

28 Brian Hanley, 'The Politics of Noraid', 10–11.

29 Judith Butler and Athena Athanasiou, *Dispossession: The Performative in the Political* (Cambridge: Polity, 2013), 197.

30 R.W. Apple 'Mrs Thatcher says Death of Sands Won't Alter London's Ulster Policy', *New York Times*, 30 July 1981, 14.

31 Chris Raleigh, 'Support from Afar – Australian Support for the Hunger Strikers' *An Phoblacht/Republican News*, Thursday 7 June 2001, 15.

32 I am grateful to my anonymous peer reviewer for pointing out the longer tradition of funeral procession as protest march and drawing attention to its Irish studies scholarship: See, for example, Gabriel Doherty and Dermot Keogh, '"Sorrow but No Despair – The Road is Marked": the Politics of Funerals in post-1916 Ireland', in *Michael Collins and the Making of the Irish State*, ed. Gabriel Doherty and Dermot Keogh (Cork: Mercier, 2006), and Owen McGee, '"God Save Ireland": Manchester-Martyr Demonstrations in Dublin, 1867–1916', *Éire-Ireland* 36, no. 3–4 (2001): 39–66.

33 Padraig O'Malley, *Biting at the Grave: The Irish Hunger Strikes and the Politics of Despair* (Boston: Beacon Press, 1991).

34 Manhattan Unit Publicity Committee, Irish Northern Aid, 'An Open Letter to the American People', 17 June 1981, Archives of Irish America, NYU Library, https://digitaltamiment.hosting.nyu.edu/s/irish-america/item/5227 (accessed 13 October 2021).

35 Emma Clancy, 'Irish Hunger Strike Remembered', *Green Left*, Issue 710, 18 May 2001, https://www.greenleft.org.au/content/irish-hunger-strike-remembered (accessed 19 April 2021).

36 Chris Raleigh, 'Support from Afar', 15.

37 Ibid.

38 Pollyanna Ruiz, *Articulating Dissent: Protest and the Public Sphere* (London: Pluto Press, 2014), 87.

39 Ibid.

40 Chris Raleigh, 'Support from Afar', 15.

41 Walter Vandereycken and Ron van Deth, *From Fasting Saints to Anorexic Girls: The History of Self-Starvation* (London: Athlone Press, 1994).

42 Emilie Pine, *The Politics of Irish Memory: Performing Remembrance in Contemporary Irish Culture* (Basingstoke: Palgrave Macmillan, 2011).

43 Padraig O'Malley, *Biting at the Grave*, 109.

44 Bobby Sands, *Writings from Prison* (Cork: Mercier Press, 1998), 64.

45 Anthony Phalen, 'Bolivian Tin Miners' Wives Fast, Win Amnesty, Jobs, Freedom, 1977–1978', *Global Nonviolent Action Database*, 11 November

2009, https://nvdatabase.swarthmore.edu/content/bolivian-tin-miners-wives-fast-win-amnesty-jobs-freedom-1977-1978 (accessed 30 October 2021)

46 Charlotte England, 'Yarl's Wood Hunger Strike: 120 Detainees Refuse Food in Protest Against Home Office', 23 February 2018, *Novara Media* https://novaramedia.com/2018/02/23/yarls-wood-hunger-strike-120-detainees-refuse-food-in-protest-against-home-office/ (accessed 30 October 2021).

47 Imogen Tyler, *Revolting Subjects*, 9.

48 Achille Mbembe, 'Necropolitics', *Public Culture* 15, no. 1 (2003), 11.

49 Ibid.

50 Ibid., 12.

51 Ibid., 40.

52 Ibid., 39. See Paul Gilroy, *Black Atlantic: Modernity and Double Consciousness* (London and Boston: Verso and Harvard University Press, 1993), 63.

53 Pierre Bourdieu, 'The Forms of Capital', in *Handbook of Theory and Research for the Sociology of Education*, ed. J. Richardson (Westport, CT: Greenwood, 1986), 15–29; Pierre Bourdieu, 'Symbolic Capital and Social Classes', *The Journal of Classical Sociology* 13, no. 2 (2013): 292–302.

54 Michael Taussig, 'I'm so Angry I Made a Sign', *Critical Inquiry* 39, no. 1 (Autumn 2012): 76.

55 Ibid., 75.

56 Ibid.

57 Ibid.

58 F. Stuart Ross, *Smashing H Block*, 2.

59 Miller, *Don't Mention the War*, 20.

60 Richard Rogers, 'Brian Anson Obituary', *The Guardian*, Thursday 17 December, 2009 https://www.theguardian.com/artanddesign/2009/dec/17/brian-anson-obituary (accessed 25 October 2021).

61 Brian Anson, 'Hunger Strike Memories', *An Phoblacht/Republican News*, Thursday 23 November 2000, 8.

62 Bernadette McAliskey, 'Foreward' in *Nor Meekly Serve My Time: The H Block Struggle 1976–1981*, ed. Brian Campbell, Laurence McKeown and Felim O'Hagan (Belfast: Beyond the Pale, 1994), xiv.

63 Roisin de Rosa, 'A Mother's Loyalty: Mary Nelis and the Relatives Action Committees, Strikers', *An Phoblacht/Republican News*, Thursday 9 November 2000, 9.

64 Quoted in F. Stuart Ross, *Smashing H Block*, 42.

65 Hebe Bonafini, 'The Madres de la Plaza de Mayo', *Index on Censorship* 19, no. 9 (October 1990), 26–27.

66 Chris Raleigh, 'Support from Afar', 15.

67 Judith Butler and Athena Athanasiou, *Dispossession*, 197.

68 Ibid.

69 Annette Weiner and Jane Schneider 'Introduction', in *Cloth and the Human Experience*, ed. Annette Weiner and Jane Schneider (Washington, DC: Smithsonian Institution Press, 1989), 1–29. I develop Weiner and Schneider's argument in relation to political imprisonment in Louise Purbrick, 'Cloth, Gender, Politics: The Armagh Handkerchief, 1976', *Clio: Femmes, Genre, Histoire*, 40, (2014), 105–23.

70 Paul Gilroy, *After Empire: Melancholia or Convivial Culture* (Abingdon: Routledge, 2004), 89–90.

71 Ibid.

72 Ibid.

73 'Hunger Strike Monument Unveiled', *An Phoblacht/Republican News*, Thursday 23 May 2002, 16; Rosaleen Walsh, *Prelude to '81*, (2002); *Hunger* (2008), [Film] Dir. Steve McQueen, UK: Film 4.

74 Melanie McFadyean, 'The Legacy of the Hunger Strikers', *The Guardian Weekend*, 4 March 2006, 48–51 and 77–79.

75 Bill Rolston, *Drawing Support: Murals in the North of Ireland* (Belfast: Beyond the Pale Publications, 1992).

76 'The first TV pictures of the "dirty protest" in the Maze prison', Newsnight, *BBC*, https://www.bbc.co.uk/programmes/p00lx397 (accessed 1 October 2019).

77 Walter Benjamin, 'A Small History of Photography', in *One Way Street and Other Writings*, (London: Verso, 1979), 243.

78 *Acquisition Priorities: Aspects of Postwar Painting in Europe*, Solomon R. Guggenheim Museum, New York, May to September 1983; *A Cellular Maze: Rita Donagh, Richard Hamilton*, Orchard Gallery, Londonderry, November 1983; ICA, April to May 1984; *The Hard-Won Image*, Tate Gallery, July to September 1984; *Falls the Shadow: Recent British and European Art*, Hayward Gallery, April to June 1986; *Richard Hamilton*, Fruitmarket Gallery, Edinburgh, March to May 1988 and Museum of Modern Art, Oxford, May to July 1988. This list has been compiled from Terry Riggs, 'Richard Hamilton, The citizen 1981-3', July 1998, *The Tate*, https://www.tate.org.uk/art/artworks/hamilton-the-citizen-t03980 (accessed 1 October 2019). See the following review: Belinda Loftus, 'Rita Donagh and Richard Hamilton, a Cellular Maze Orchard Gallery, Derry 9 December 1983 – 7 January 1984', *Circa*, 14, (1984): 41–2.

79 Terry Riggs, 'Richard Hamilton'.

80 Ibid.

81 Ibid.

82 Ibid.

Chapter four

1 Sarah Irving, *Leila Khaled: Icon of Palestinian Liberation* (London: Pluto Press, 2012), 49.

2 Ibid., 39.

3 The first women, all republican and often young, were interned from the end of 1972 and their numbers rose to 236 in six months. Begoña Aretxaga, *Shattering Silence: Women, Nationalism, and Political Subjectivity in Northern Ireland* (Princeton, NJ: Princeton University Press, 1997), 75–6.

4 Linda Edgerton, 'Public Protest, Domestic Acquiescence: Women in Northern Ireland', in *Caught up in Conflict: Women's Responses to Political Strife*, ed. Rosemary Rudd and Helen Callaway (London: Palgrave, 1986); Lynda Walker, *Living in an Armed Patriarchy* (Belfast: Unity Press, 2019).

5 Doreen Massey, *Space, Place and Gender* (Minneapolis: University of Minnesota Press, 1994), 80.

6 War journalist Kate Adie's words quoted by Laura Aguiar, 'Back to Those Walls: The Women's Memory of the Maze and Long Kesh Prison in Northern Ireland', *Memory Studies* 8, no. 2 (2015): 230.

7 Bernadette O'Hagan, 'Last Visit: Bernadette O'Hagan and Siobhan Maginn', *Prisons Memory Archive,* https://www.prisonsmemoryarchive.com/films/extracts/ (accessed 14 December 2021).

8 Eileen Fairweather, Roisin McDonough, Melanie McFadyean, eds. *Only the Rivers Run Free: Northern Ireland: The Women's War* (London: Pluto, 1984); Sandra McEvoy, 'Loyalist Women Paramilitaries in Northern Ireland: Beginning a Feminist Conversation about Conflict Resolution', *Security Studies* 18, no. 2 (2009): 262–86. Eilish Rooney, 'Women in Political Conflict', *Race and Class* 37, no. 1 (1995): 51–6; Rosemary Sales, *Women Divided: Gender, Religion and Politics in Northern Ireland* (London: Routledge, 1997); Rachel Ward, 'Invisible Women: The Political Roles of Loyalist and Unionist Women in Contemporary Northern Ireland, *Parliamentary Affairs*, 55 (2002): 167–78.

9 Hester Dunn, 'A Woman's Place in the Loyalist Community', *Fortnight*, no. 220 (27 May–9 June 1985): 7.

10 Ibid.

11 Ward, 'Invisible Women', 167.

12 McEvoy, 'Loyalist Women Paramilitaries', 262.

13 Laura Aguiar, 'Back to Those Walls', 239.

14 Ibid., 227.

15 The reading of Sara Ahmed's *Living a Feminist Life* (Durham, NC: Duke University Press, 2017) by my colleague and friend Charlotte Nicklas inspired the writing of this chapter and informed the way in which it is written. Jane Rendall's 'site-writing' has also helped think about how to write a spatial politics. Jane Rendall, *Site-Writing: The Architecture of Art Criticism* (London: I.B. Tauris, 2006), https://www.janerendell.co.uk/books/site-writing (accessed 11 June 2022).

16 *We Were Here* (2014) Dir. Laura Aguiar and Cahal McLaughlin, Belfast: Prisons Memory Archive https://www.prisonsmemoryarchive.com/feature_films/we-were-there/; 'Extracts' https://www.prisonsmemoryarchive.com/films/extracts/; 'Full Recordings' https://www.prisonsmemoryarchive.com/films/full-length-recordings/ (accessed 12 December 2021).

17 Breda Gray, 'Becoming Non-Migrant: Lives Worth Waiting For', *Gender, Place and Culture* 18, no. 3 (2011): 421.

18 Melanie Friend, *Border Country* (Belfast: Belfast Exposed and Winchester Gallery, 2007), 58.

19 Alex Hall, 'Border Country', in Melanie Friend, *Border Country*, 56.

20 Deirdre Conlon, 'Waiting: Feminist Perspectives on the Spacings/Timings of Migrant (Im)Mobility', *Gender, Place and Culture* 18, no. 3 (2011): 356.

21 Ibid., 353.

22 Gray, 'Becoming Non-Migrant', 420.

Chapter five

1 Belfast Exposed is 'Northern Ireland's leading photography organisation'. It was established in the wake of the Hunger Strikes, in 1983, 'by a group of local photographers as a challenge to media representation of Belfast's experience of conflict.' https://www.belfastexposed.org (accessed 17 December 2021).

2 Donovan Wylie, *The Maze* (London: Granta, 2004).

3 Michel Foucault, *Discipline and Punish: The Birth of the Prison* (Harmondsworth: Penguin, 1979), 205.

4 For more on the responses to the exhibition, *The Maze*, see Louise Purbrick, 'Disturbing Memories: Photography and the Architecture of the H Blocks, Northern Ireland', in *The Politics of Cultural Memory*, ed. Lucy Burke, Simon Faulkner and Jim Aulich (Newcastle-Upon-Tyne: Cambridge Scholars Publishing, 2010), 115–31.

5 *Inside Story Special: The Maze Enemies Within* [TV programme], BBC1, 20 January 1990.

6 Humphrey Atkins, *House of Commons Debates (Hansard)* 1000, 3 March 1981, https://api.parliament.uk/historic-hansard/commons/1981/mar/03/northern-ireland-prisons#S5CV1000P0_19810303_HOC_185 (accessed 18 December 2021).

7 Humphrey Atkins, *House of Commons Debates (Hansard)* 1000, 5 February 1981, https://api.parliament.uk/historic-hansard/written-answers/1981/feb/05/maze-prison#S5CV0998P0_19810205_CWA_10 (accessed 18 December 2021).

8 James Prior, *Parliamentary Debates (Hansard)*, 10, 29 October 1981 (London: HMSO): 980.

9 James Hennessy, *Report of an Inquiry by HM Chief Inspector of Prisons into the Security Arrangements at HM Prison, Maze*, Cmnd. 203 (London: HMSO, 1984), 56.

10 Lord Gardiner, *Report of a Committee to Consider, in the Context of Civil Liberties and Human Rights, Measures to Deal with Terrorism in Northern Ireland*, Cmnd. 5847 (London: HMSO, January, 1975), 35.

11 Hennessy, *Security Arrangements at HM Prison, Maze*, 65.

12 Northern Ireland Prison Service, *Corporate and Business Plan 1998–2000* (Belfast: Northern Ireland Prison Service, 1998).

13 Quoted in *Inside Story Special: The Maze Enemies Within*.

14 Quoted in Chris Ryder, *Inside the Maze: the Untold Story of the Northern Ireland Prison Service* (London: Methuen, 2000), 337.

15 Bill Rolston, 'Prison as a Liberated Zone: The Murals of Long Kesh, Northern Ireland', *State Crime Journal* 2, no. 2 (Autumn 2013): 149–72. http://statecrime.org/journal/prison-as-a-liberated-zone-the-murals-of-long-kesh-northern-ireland/ (accessed 19 December 2021).

16 For examples of public and private collections of this form of material culture of the H Blocks. See the prison art category in Kris Brown, *Artefacts Audit: A Report of the Material Culture of the Conflict in and about Northern Ireland* (Belfast: Healing Through Remembering, 2008). The following chapter of this book offers an account of prison art.

17 Dominic Bryan, *Orange Parades: The Politics of Ritual, Tradition and Control* (London: Pluto Press, 2000), 6.

18 Parades Commission https://www.paradescommission.org/About-Us/Commission.aspx (accessed 20 December 2021).

19 Bryan, *Orange Parades*, 9.

20 Judith Butler and Athena Athanasiou, *Dispossession: the Performative in the Political* (Cambridge: Polity, 2013), 197.

21 Bryan, *Orange Parades*, 9–10.

22 Ibid., 19.

23 Ibid., 8.

24 Judith Butler, *Gender Trouble: Feminism and the Subversion of Identity* (New York: Routledge, 1999), 175.

25 Ibid., 179.

26 Ibid., 178.

27 Ibid., 179

28 Ibid.

29 Bill Rolston, *Drawing Support 1: Murals in the North of Ireland* (Belfast: Beyond the Pale Publications, 1992); Bill Rolston, *Drawing Support 2: Murals of War and Peace* (Belfast: Beyond the Pale Publications, 1995); Bill Rolston, *Drawing Support 3: Murals and Transition in the North of Ireland* (Belfast: Beyond the Pale Publications, 2003); Bill Rolston, *Drawing Support 4: Murals and Conflict Transformation in Northern Ireland* (Belfast: Beyond the Pale Publications, 2013).

30 Rolston, 'Prison as a Liberated Zone', 157.

31 Ibid., 155–6.

32 Ibid., 150.

33 Ibid., 165.

34 David Beresford, *Ten Men Dead* (London: Grafton, 1987).

35 Rolston, 'Prison as a Liberated Zone', 161.

36 Jonathan McCormick and Neil Jarman, 'Death of a Mural', *Journal of Material Culture* 10, no. 1 (2005): 50.

37 Neil Jarman, *Material Conflicts: Parades and Visual Displays in Northern Ireland* (Oxford: Berg, 1997), 210.

38 McCormick and Jarman, 'Death of a Mural', 50.

39 For a colour version taken while the H blocks were still occupied, see *The Guardian's* Maze Prison picture gallery http://www.guardian.co.uk/world/gallery/2008/apr/29/northernireland?picture=333820433 (accessed 20 December 2021).

40 One is listed at Ebrington Street, Waterside, Derry in Album 10 of Dr Jonathan McCormick's 'A Directory of Murals' hosted on the CAIN Archive (Conflict and Politics in Northern Ireland) https://cain.ulster.ac.uk/mccormick/album10 (accessed 20 December 2021) and another at Bonds Street, Derry, photographed and interpreted by Bill Rolston, 'Contemporary Murals in Northern Ireland – Loyalist Tradition', CAIN Archive http://cain.ulst.ac.uk/bibdbs/murals/slide4.htm (accessed 20 December 2021).

41 Rolston, 'Prison as a Liberated Zone', 165.

42 Jarman, *Material Conflicts*, 210.

43 Susan McKay, *Northern Protestants: An Unsettled People* (Belfast: Blackstaff Press, 2000), 24; Peter Taylor, *Loyalists* (London: Bloomsbury, 2000); Martin Melaugh, Brendan Lynn and Fionnuala McKenna, 'Abstracts on Organisations', CAIN Archive http://cain.ulst.ac.uk/othelem/organ/uorgan.htm (accessed 20 December 2021).

44 Malcolm Sutton, *An Index of Deaths from the Conflict in Ireland* (The Sutton Index of Deaths), http://cain.ulst.ac.uk/sutton/index.html (accessed 7 November 2009).

45 Harding Smith quoted in Taylor, *Loyalists*, 115.

46 Sutton, *An Index of Deaths*. Since I have cited the numbers of the killings by UDA/UFF as part of the reading of the H7 mural series, I should note that numbers of people killed over the period of conflict, itself differently delimited, have been differently calculated. CAIN, importantly, introduces the various statistical sources and provides links: https://cain.ulster.ac.uk/issues/violence/counting.htm (accessed 19 July 2022). See also, Jonathan Tonge, *Northern Ireland* (Cambridge: Polity, 2006), 1. Rolston indicates an asymmetry in the representation of killings in his analysis of the H Block murals. Since the opponent of republicanism is obviously the British state, this enemy does not have to be specified in a mural: Rolston, 'Prison as a Liberated Zone', 167.

47 Taylor, *Loyalists*, 206–10.

48 Harding Smith quotes in Taylor, *Loyalists*, 206–10.

49 Paul Williams, *Memorial Museums: The Global Rush to Commemorate Atrocities* (Oxford: Berg, 2007).

50 Rolston, 'Prison as a Liberated Zone', 167.

51 Taylor, *Loyalists*, 225.

52 The names and biographical details of those killed in these three incidents can be found in David McKittrick, Seamus Kelters, Brian Feeney and Chris Thornton, *Lost Lives: The Stories of the Men, Women and Children who Died as a Result of the Northern Ireland Troubles* (Edinburgh: Mainstream Publishing, 1999), 1277–80; 1328–33; 1335–7.

53 Ian S. Wood, *Crimes of Loyalty: A History of the UDA* (Edinburgh: Edinburgh University Press, 2006), 181.

54 Ibid., 182.

55 McKay, *Northern Protestants*, 95.

56 McCormick and Jarman, 'Death of a Mural', 50.

57 Pierce Kehoe and Luke Dunne, '"Muralling" and Reconciliation in Northern Ireland: The Complex Role of Public Art in Peace Processes', A Contested Histories Occasional Paper, March (2021), Contested Histories in Public Spaces, *Institute of Historical Justice*, https://ihjr.org/ (accessed 20 December 2021).

58 One important and often cited example of such a disappearance are the murals that covered the Lower Shankilll area of West Belfast in the latter years (2000–2002) of Johnny Adair's dominance within UFF. The names, mottos, slogans and portraiture of the UFF and the UDA were repeatedly painted. Defacement of these murals accompanied feuding within the UFF with the end of Adair's regime declared when many were painted over in magnolia; McCormick and Jarman, 'Death of a Mural,' 63–4.

59 Rolston, 'Prison as a Liberated Zone', 167.

60 Ibid., 150.

61 'Peter Taylor', Full Recordings', *Prisons Memory Archive*, https://www.prisonsmemoryarchive.com/films/full-length-recordings/ (accessed 20 December 2021).

Chapter six

1 *On eBay*, written and produced by Jude Abbott, Dunstan Bruce, Neil Ferguson, Darren Hamer, Nigel Hunter, Alice Nutter, Louise Watts, and Allan Whalley, was released on the album *Un* in 2004 and as a single in the same year.

2 Ken Hillis, Michael Petit and Nathan Scott Epley, eds, *Everyday Ebay: Culture, Collecting and Desire* (New York: Routledge, 2006).

3 big_balls_from_the_falls1888, 'Long Kesh/Maze Prison Key Collection Irish Troubles', *eBay.co.uk*, http://cgi.ebay.co.uk/ws/eBayISAPI.dll?ViewItem&Item=16048389761&ssPageName+ADME:B:SSGB:1123 #ht_1240wt_902 (accessed 17 November 2010) and big_balls_from_the_falls1888, 'Long Kesh/Maze Prison Security Camera', *eBay.co.uk*, http://cgi.ebay.co.uk/ws/eBayISAPI.dll?ViewItem&Item=16048389761&ssPageName+ADME:B:SSGB:1123 #ht_500wt-917 (accessed 17 November 2010).

4 Alfred Gell, *Art and Agency: An Anthropological Theory* (Oxford: Clarendon Press, 1998), 20.

5 The making of the Northern Ireland Political Collection at the Linen Hall Library is an important example of collecting through conflict, see: https://linenhall.com/. An early account of the material culture of conflict is found in Neil Jarman, *Material Conflicts: Parades and Visual Displays in Northern Ireland* (Oxford: Berg, 1997).

6 Kris Brown, *Artefacts Audit: A Report of the Material Culture of the Conflict in and about Northern Ireland* (Belfast: Healing Through Remembering, 2008).

7 This was Deborah Sugg-Ryan and I am indebted to her for sharing this find and the conversation that followed.

8 For an overall and textual analysis of the findings, see Louise Purbrick, 'Trading the Past: Material Culture of Long Kesh/Maze, Northern Ireland', *Journal of War and Culture Studies* 6, no. 1 (2012): 58–74.

9 Nicky Gregson and Louise Crewe, *Second-Hand Cultures* (Oxford: Berg, 2003).

10 Brandon Hamber, *Past Imperfect: Dealing with the Past in Northern Ireland and Societies in Transition* (Derry: INCORE, 1998).

11 Northern Ireland Office, *H Blocks: The Facts* (London: Northern Ireland Office, 1980).

12 ccolumbo999, *eBay* (2011) https://www.ebay.co.uk/usr/columbo-999?_trksid=p2047675.l2559 (accessed 27 November 2021).

13 Patrick Coburn, 'Syria is Too Far Steeped in Blood for Resolution by Negotiation', *The Independent*, 10 April 2012 https://www.independent.co.uk/voices/commentators/patrick-cockburn-syria-is-too-far-steeped-in-blood-for-resolution-by-negotiation-7628096.html (accessed 1 May 2016).

14 The following article represents Elizabeth's Crooke early intervention into debates about the uses of the material culture of conflict: Elizabeth Crooke, 'Confronting a Troubled History: Which Past in Northern Ireland's Museums?' *International Journal of Heritage Studies*, 7, no. 2 (2001): 119–36.

15 Kieran McEvoy, *Paramilitary Imprisonment in Northern Ireland: Resistance, Management, and Release* (Oxford: Oxford University Press 2001).

16 Mike Ritchie, 'Coiste Proposals' in *Museum of Long Kesh or the Maze? Report of Conference Proceedings* 14 June 2003 (Belfast, Coiste na nIarchimí, 2003), 27.

17 Ibid.

18 Aafke Komter, 'Women, Gifts and Power', in *The Gift: An Interdisciplinary Perspective*, ed. Aafke Komter (Amsterdam: Amsterdam University Press, 1996), 119–31.

19 Annette Weiner, 'Inalienable Wealth', *American Ethnologist* 12, no. 2 (1985): 210–27

20 Chris Ryder, *Inside the Maze: The Untold Story of Northern Ireland Prison Service* (London: Methuen, 2000), 176.

21 For a comprehensive account of loyalist prison art see, Erin Hinson, 'Compounding Identities: The Production of Artefacts within the UVF/RHC Prison Experience' (Ph.D diss., Queens University Belfast, 2016), and her subsequent article, Erin Hinson, 'Crafting Identities: Prison Artefacts and

Place-Making in Pre- and Post-Ceasefire Northern Ireland', in *Ethnographies of Movement, Sociality and Space: Place-Making in the New Northern Ireland*, ed. Milena Komarova and Maruška Svašek (New York: Berghahn Books. 2018): 60–84.

22 Brian Campbell, Laurence McKeown and Felim O'Hagan, eds. *Nor Meekly Serve My Time: The H-Block Struggle* (Belfast: Beyond the Pale Publications, 1994).

23 *Billy's Museum* [Film] Dir. Amanda Dunsmore (2004), *Amanda Dunsmore*, 'Billy', http://amandadunsmore.com/billy.html (accessed 30 November 2021).

24 Angelique Chrisafis, 'Maze Keeps Ulster Divided', *The Guardian* 18 February 2004, 7.

25 Brown, *Artefacts Audit*, 28.

26 Gell, *Art and Agency*, 68.

27 Ibid., 5.

28 earp1001, '1970s Ulster Volunteers POW Leather Wallet Long Kesh' *eBay. co.uk*, http://cgi.ebay.co.uk/ws/eBayISAPI.dll?ViewItem&Item=20051372672 8&ssPageName+ADME:B:SSGB:1123 #ht_500wt_917 (accessed 17 November 2010).

29 Alfred Gell, 'The Technology of Enchantment and the Enchantment of Technology', in *Anthropology, Art and Aesthetics*, ed. Jeremy Coote and Anthony Shelton (Oxford: Clarendon, 1992), 52 [40–66].

30 Clifford Gertz, *The Predicament of Culture: Twentieth-century Ethnography, Literature and Art* (Cambridge, MA: Harvard University Press, 1988).

31 Ian Walters, 'Vietnam Zippos', *Journal of Material Culture* 2, no. 1 (1997): 61–97.

32 Henri Cartier-Bresson, *The Decisive Moment* (1952; Göttingen: Steidl, 2014).

33 sham1916, 'Pictures of IRA Hunger Strike Funerals, Long Kesh, Eire' *eBay. co.uk*, http://cgi.ebay.co.uk/ws/eBayISAPI.dll?ViewItem&Item=17054020389 5&ssPageName+ADME:B:SSGB:1123 #ht_538wt_891 (accessed 17 November 2010).

34 Ibid.

35 Guy Debord, *The Society of the Spectacle* (1967; Detriot: Black and Red, 1983).

36 Dogrlamppost, 'Maze Prison 1978–2000 Hospital Tie Tac', *eBay.co.uk*, http:// cgi.ebay.co.uk/ws/eBayISAPI.dll?ViewItem&Item=370453819028&ssPageNa me+ADME:B:SSGB:1123 #ht_500wt_906 (accessed 17 November 2010) and pimp-my-dogtags, 'Rare Pest Control Unit Tie Pin HMP Maze Riot Prison', *eBay.co.uk*, http://cgi.ebay.co.uk/ws/eBayISAPI.dll?ViewItem&Item=2805829 88970370453819028&ssPageName+ADME:B:SSGB:1123 #ht_706wt_891 (accessed 17 November 2010).

37 Walter Benjamin, 'The Work of Art in the Age of Mechanical Reproduction', in *Illuminations*, ed. Hannah Arendt (London: Fontana, 1992), 211–44.

38 big_balls_from_the_falls1888, 'Long Kesh/Maze Prison Key Collection'. For an account of the political and historical contest of the 1983 escape, see: Campbell, McKeown and O'Hagan, eds., *Nor Meekly Serve My Time*.

39 Ibid.

40 Malcolm Foley and J. John Lennon, 'JFK and Dark Tourism: A Fascination with Assassination', *International Journal of Heritage Studies* 2, no. 4 (1996): 198. See also Michael Welch, 'Political Imprisonment and the Sanctity of Death: Performing Heritage in "Troubled" Ireland', *International Journal of Heritage Studies* 22, no. 9 (2016): 664–78.

41 A.V. Seaton, 'Guided by the Dark: From Thanatopsis to Thanatourism, *International Journal of Heritage Studies* 2, no. 4 (1996): 240–42.

42 big_balls_from_the_falls1888, 'Long Kesh/Maze Prison Key Collection'.

43 Purbrick, 'Trading the Past'.

44 big_balls_from_the_falls1888, 'Long Kesh/Maze Prison Key Collection'.

45 Annette Weiner, *Inalienable Possessions: The Paradox of Keeping-While-Giving* (Berkeley: University of California Press, 1992).

46 Whyte's, *History and Literature*, 23 April 2010 (Dublin: Whyte's, 2010). See also: https://www.whytes.ie/auction/history-literature/739/ (accessed 30 November 2021) and https://www.whytes.ie/art/1971-2000-hm-prison-the-maze-long-kesh-quoth-blocksquot-keys-and-key-tags-a-unique-collection/1325 06/?SearchString=&LotNumSearch=&GuidePrice=&OrderBy=&ArtistID=&Ar rangeBy=list&NumPerPage=15&offset=290 (accessed 30 November 2021).

47 Ibid. and see https://www.whytes.ie/art/1971-2000-hm-prison-the-maze-long-kesh-quoth-blacksquot-two-security-cameras/132508/?SearchString=&LotNu mSearch=&GuidePrice=&OrderBy=&ArtistID=&ArrangeBy=list&NumPerPag e=15&offset=292 (accessed 30 November 2021).

48 Gell, *Art and Agency*, 68.

49 Bruno Latour, 'The Berlin Key or How to Do Words with Things'. In *Matter, Materiality and Modern Culture*, ed. Paul Graves Brown (London: Routledge, 1991), 10–21.

50 Ibid., 18.

51 Ibid., 19.

52 Ibid.

53 Ibid., 17.

54 Brian Graham and Sara McDowell, 'Meaning in the Maze: The heritage of Long Kesh', *Cultural Geographies* 14, no. 3 (2007): 343–68. M.K. Flynn, 'Decision-making and Contested Heritage in Northern Ireland: The Former Maze Prison/Long Kesh', *Irish Political Studies* 26, no. 3 (2011): 383–401; Kate Keane, 'Stories from the Cells: The Role of Maze/Long Kesh in Peacetime Northern Ireland', in *The Carceral Network in Ireland: History, Agency and Resistance*, ed. Fiona McCann (Basingstoke: Palgrave Macmillan, 2020): 179–205; Louise Purbrick, 'Long Kesh/Maze: A Case for Participation in Post-Conflict Heritage', in *Heritage After Conflict: Northern* Ireland, ed. Elizabeth Crooke and Tom Maguire (Abingdon: Routledge, 2018): 84–102; For the constructive role of prisoners in conflict transformation, most of whom served sentences at Long Kesh/Maze, see: Peter Shirlow, and Kevin McEvoy, *Beyond the Wire: Former Prisoners and Conflict Transformation in Northern Ireland* (London: Pluto, 2008).

55 Graham Dawson, *Making Peace with the Past?: Memories, Trauma and the Irish Troubles* (Manchester: Manchester University Press, 2010); Neil Jarman, 'Troubling Remnants: Dealing with the Remains of Conflict in Northern Ireland', in *Matériel Culture: The Archaeology of Twentieth Century Conflict*, ed. John Schofield, William Gray and Colleen M. Beck (London: Routledge: 2002): 281–95; Kieran McEvoy, *Making Peace with the Past: Options for Truth Recovery Regarding the Conflict in and about Northern Ireland*, (Belfast: Healing Through Remembering, 2006); Kieran McEvoy and Brian Gormally, *Dealing with the Past in Northern Ireland 'From Below'* (Belfast: Community Foundation for Northern Ireland, 2009).

56 This could be considered unauthorized heritage in Laurajane Smith's terms; Laurajane Smith, *Uses of Heritage* (Abingdon: Routledge, 2006).

Chapter seven

1 The Executive Office, 'Regeneration Sites Team', https://www.executiveoffice-ni.gov.uk/articles/regeneration-sites-team (accessed 20 January 2022).

2 Walter Benjamin, *Charles Baudelaire: A Lyric Poet in the Era of High Capitalism* (London: Verso, 1997).

3 Avril Maddrell, 'Living with the Deceased: Absence, Presence and Absence-Presence', *Cultural Geographies* 20, no. 4 (2013): 501–22.

4 Sustrans, 'Paths for Everybody', https://www.sustrans.org.uk/about-us/paths-for-everyone (accessed 20 January 2022).

5 Maze Long Kesh Development Corporation, 'Site History', http://mazelongkesh.com/site-history/ (accessed 20 January 2022).

6 Lisburn and Castlereagh City Council, *West Lisburn Development Framework* (Lisburn: Lisburn and Castlereagh City Council), 44.

7 Karl Marx and Frederick Engels, *Ireland and the Irish Question* (New York: International Publishers, 1972), quoted in John Bellamy Foster and Brett Clark, *The Robbery of Nature: Capitalism and the Ecological Rift* (New York: Monthly Review Press, 2020), 74.

8 Caitlin DeSilvey, 'Observed Decay: Telling Stories with Mutable Things', *Journal of Material Culture* 11, no. 3 (2006): 318–38.

Bibliography

Adams, Gerry. *Cage 11*. Dingle: Brandon Books, 1990.

Agamben, Georgio. *Homo Sacer: Sovereign Power and Bare Life*. Stanford, CA: Stanford University Press, 1998.

Aguiar, Laura. 'Back to Those Walls: The Women's Memory of the Maze and Long Kesh prison in Northern Ireland'. *Memory Studies* 8, no. 2 (2015): 227–241.

Ahmed, Sara. *Living a Feminist Life*. Durham, NC: Duke University Press, 2017.

Aretxaga, Begoña. *Shattering Silence: Women, Nationalism and Political Subjectivity in Northern Ireland*. Princeton, NJ: Princeton University Press, 1997.

Arthur, Max. *Northern Ireland Soldiers Talking, 1969 to Today*. London: Sidgwick and Jackson, 1981.

ASBO. *Bang-Up and Smash*. London: Active Distribution, 2017.

Ash, Juliet. *Dress Behind Bars: Prison Clothing as Criminality*. London: I.B. Tauris, 2009.

Ash, Juliet. 'Prison Dress'. In *The Encyclopaedia of Clothing and Fashion*, ed. Valerie Steele and Christopher Breward. New York: Charles Scribner's Sons, 2005.

Ashplant, T.G., Graham Dawson and Michael Roper. *The Politics of War Memory and Commemoration*. London: Routledge, 2000.

Aust, Stefan. *The Baader-Meinhof Group*. London: Bodley Head, 1985.

Benjamin, Walter. 'A Small History of Photography'. In *One Way Street and Other Writings*, 240–257. London: Verso, 1979.

Benjamin, Walter. *Charles Baudelaire: A Lyric Poet in the Era of High Capitalism*. London: Verso, 1997.

Benjamin, Walter. 'The Work of Art in the Age of Mechanical Reproduction.' In *Illuminations*, ed. Hannah Arendt, 211–244. London: Fontana, 1992.

Bentham, Jeremy. *The Works of Jeremy Bentham Published Under the Superintendence of his Executor John Bowring*, Volume 4. New York: Russell and Russell, 1838–1843/1962.

Beresford, David. *Ten Men Dead*. London: Harper Collins, 1987.

Bourdieu, Pierre. 'Symbolic Capital and Social Classes'. *The Journal of Classical Sociology* 13, no. 2 (2013): 292–302.

Bourdieu, Pierre. 'The Forms of Capital'. In *Handbook of Theory and Research for the Sociology of Education*, ed. J. Richardson, 15–29. Westport, CT: Greenwood, 1986.

Bowyer Bell, J. *The Irish Troubles. A Generation of Violence 1967–1992*. Dublin: Gill and Macmillan, 1993.

Brodie, Allan, Jane Croom and James O. Davies, *English Prisons: An Architectural History*. Swindon: English Heritage, 2002.

Brown, Kris. *Artefacts Audit: A Report of the Material Culture of the Conflict in and about Northern Ireland*. Belfast: Healing Through Remembering, 2008.

Brown, Kris. 'Political Commemoration and Peacebuilding in Ethno-national Settings: The Risk and Utility of Partisan Memory'. *Peacebuilding* 7 no. 1 (2019): 51–70.

Bryan, Dominic. *Orange Parades: The Politics of Ritual, Tradition and Control*. London: Pluto Press, 2000.

Butler, Judith and Athena Athanasiou. *Dispossession: The Performative in the Political*. Cambridge: Polity, 2013.

Butler, Judith. *Gender Trouble: Feminism and the Subversion of Identity*. New York: Routledge, 1999).

Campbell, Brian and Laurence McKeown, Felim O'Hagan, eds *Nor Meekly Serve My Time: The H-Block Struggle 1976–1981*. Belfast: Beyond the Pale, 1994.

Cartier-Bresson, Henri. *The Decisive Moment*. 1952. Göttingen: Steidl, 2014.

Catterall, Peter and Sean McDougall. *The Northern Ireland Question in British Politics*. London: Macmillan, 1996.

Challis, Jim. *The Northern Ireland Prison Service 1920–1990. A History*. Belfast: Northern Ireland Prison Service, 1999.

Cohen, Stanley. *Visions of Social Control: Crime, Punishment and Classification*. Cambridge: Polity, 1985.

Cohen, Stanley. 'Prisons and the Future of Control Systems: From Concentration to Dispersal'. In *Welfare in Action*, ed. Mike Fiztgerald, 220–221. London: Open University/Routledge, 1977.

Conlon, Deirdre. 'Waiting: Feminist Perspectives on the Spacings/Timings of Migrant (Im)Mobility, *Gender, Place and Culture* 18, no. 3 (2011): 353–360.

Crawford, Colin. 'The Compound System: An Alternative Penal Strategy'. *The Howard Journal of Criminal Justice* 21 no. 3 (1982): 155–158.

Crooke, Elizabeth. 'Confronting a Troubled History: Which Past in Northern Ireland's Museums?' *International Journal of Heritage Studies* 7, no. 2 (2001): 119–136.

Curtis, Liz. *Ireland, The Propaganda War: The British Media and the 'Battle for Hearts and Minds'*. London: Pluto Press, 1984.

Curtis, Nathaniel, C. 'Medium Security Institution: Programming and Design'. *Architectural Record*, September 1959.

Dawson, Graham. *Making Peace with the Past?: Memories, Trauma and the Irish Troubles*. Manchester: Manchester University Press, 2010.

Debord, Guy. *The Society of the Spectacle*. Detriot: Black and Red, 1967/1983.

DeSilvey, Caitlin. 'Observed Decay: Telling Stories with Mutable Things'. *Journal of Material Culture* 11 no. 3 (2006): 318–338.

Dinwiddy, John. *Bentham*, Oxford: Oxford University Press, 1989.

Ditchfield, John. *Control in Prisons: A Review of the Literature*. London: HMSO, 1980.

Doherty, Gabriel and Dermot Keogh. '"Sorrow but No Despair – The Road is Marked": The Politics of Funerals in post-1916 Ireland'. In *Michael Collins and the Making of the Irish State*, ed. Gabriel Doherty and Dermot Keogh. Cork: Mercier, 2006.

Douglas, Mary. *Purity and Danger: An Analysis of Concepts of Pollution and Taboo*. London: Routledge, 1966.

Dumbrell, John. 'The United States and the Northern Irish Conflict 1969–94: From Indifference to Intervention'. *Irish Studies in International Affairs* 6 (1995): 107–125.

Dunn, Hester. 'A Woman's Place in the Loyalist Community'. *Fortnight*, no. 220, May 27–June 9 (1985): 7.

Edgerton, Linda. 'Public Protest, Domestic Acquiescence: Women in Northern Ireland'. In *Caught up in Conflict: Women's Responses to Political Strife*, ed. Rosemary Rudd and Helen Callaway. London: Palgrave, 1986.

English, Richard. *Armed Struggle: The History of the IRA*. London: Pan Macmillan, 2003.

Fairweather, Eileen, Roisin McDonough, and Melanie McFadyean, eds. *Only the Rivers Run Free: Northern Ireland: the Women's War*. London: Pluto, 1984.

Fairweather, Leslie. 'The Evolution of the Prison'. In *Prison Architecture*, ed. United Nations Social Defence Research Institute, London: Architectural Press, 1975.

Farrell, Michael. *Northern Ireland: The Orange State*. London: Pluto Press, 1976/1992.

Faulkner, Simon, Farida Vis and F. d'Orazio, 'Analysing Social Media Images'. In *The Sage Handbook of Social Media*, ed. J. Burgess, A. Marwick and T. Poell, 160–178. London: Sage, 2018.

Fiori, Giuseppe. *Antonio Gramsci: Life of a Revolutionary*. London: Verso, 1965/1990.

Flynn, M. K. 'Decision-making and Contested Heritage in Northern Ireland: The Former Maze Prison/Long Kesh'. *Irish Political Studies* 26, no. 3 (2011): 383–401.

Foley Malcolm and J. John Lennon. 'JFK and Dark Tourism: A Fascination with Assassination'. *International Journal of Heritage Studies* 2, no. 4 (1996): 198–211.

Foster, John Bellamy and Brett Clark, *The Robbery of Nature: Capitalism and the Ecological Rift*. New York: Monthly Review Press, 2020.

Foucault, Michel. *Discipline and Punish: The Birth of the Prison*. Harmondsworth: Penguin, 1979.

Fraser, Peg. 'Messy History', *Cultural Studies Review* 25, no. 2 (2019): 262–264.

Friend, Melanie. *Border Country*. Belfast: Belfast Exposed and Winchester Gallery, 2007.

Gell, Alfred. *Art and Agency: An Anthropological Theory*. Oxford: Clarendon Press, 1998.

Gell, Alfred. 'The Technology of Enchantment and the Enchantment of Technology'. In *Anthropology, Art and Aesthetics*, ed. Jeremy Coote and Anthony Shelton, 40–66. Oxford: Clarendon, 1992.

Gertz, Clifford. *The Predicament of Culture: Twentieth-century Ethnography, Literature and Art*. Cambridge, MA: Harvard University Press, 1988.

Gilroy, Paul. *Black Atlantic: Modernity and Double Consciousness*. London and Boston: Verso and Harvard University Press, 1993.

Gilroy, Paul. *After Empire: Melancholia or Convivial Culture*. Abingdon: Routledge, 2004.

Goodchild, C.H. *Hybrid Concrete Construction*. Crowthorne: British Cement Association, 1995.

Gormally, Brian, Kieran McEvoy and David Wall. 'Criminal Justice in a Divided Society: Northern Ireland Prisons'. In *Crime and Justice: A Review of Research* 17, ed. M. Tonry. Chicago: Chicago University Press, 1993.

Graham, Brian and Sara McDowell. 'Meaning in the Maze: The Heritage of Long Kesh'. *Cultural Geographies* 14, no. 3 (July 2007): 343–368.

Gramsci, Antonio. *Selections from the Prison Notebooks of Antonio Gramsci*, ed. Quintin Hoare and Geoffrey Nowell Smith. London: Lawrence and Wishart, 1973.

Gray, Breda. 'Becoming Non-Migrant: Lives Worth Waiting For', *Gender, Place and Culture* 18, no. 3 (2011): 417–432.

Gregson, Nicky and Louise Crewe *Second-Hand Cultures*. Oxford: Berg, 2003.

Haas, A.M. *Precast Concrete: Design and Applications*. London: Applied Science Publishers, 1983.

Hamber, Brandon, *Blocks to the Future: A Pilot Study of the Long-term Psychological Impact of the 'No Wash/Blanket Protest*. Belfast: Action and Research International/Cúnamh, 2005.

Hamber, Brandon. *Past Imperfect: Dealing with the Past in Northern Ireland and Societies in Transition*. Derry: INCORE, 1998.

Hanley, Brian. 'The Politics of Noraid'. *Irish Political Studies* 19, no. 1 (2004): 1–17.

Held, David et al., eds. *States and Societies*. Oxford: Martin Robinson/Open University, 1983.

Hillis, Ken, Michael Petit and Nathan Scott Epley, eds. *Everyday Ebay: Culture, Collecting and Desire*. New York: Routledge, 2006.

Hinson, Erin. 'Crafting Identities: Prison Artefacts and Place-Making in Pre- and Post-Ceasefire Northern Ireland'. In *Ethnographies of Movement, Sociality and Space: Place-Making in the New Northern Ireland*, ed. Milena Komarova and Maruška Svašek, 60–84. New York: Berghahn Books, 2018.

Ingold, Tim. 'Building, Dwelling, Living: How Animals and People Make Themselves at Home in the World'. In *Shifting Contexts: Transformations in Anthropological Knowledge*, ed. Marilyn Strathern. London: Routledge, 1995.

Ingold, Tim. *The Perception of the Environment: Essays on Livelihood, Dwelling and Skill*. London: Routledge, 2000.

Irving, Sarah. *Leila Khaled: Icon of Palestinian Liberation*. London: Pluto Press, 2012.

Jarman, Neil. *Material Conflicts: Parades and Visual Displays in Northern Ireland*. Oxford: Berg, 1997.

Jarman, Neil. 'Troubling Remnants: Dealing with the Remains of Conflict in Northern Ireland'. In *Matériel Culture: The Archaeology of Twentieth Century Conflict*, ed. John Schofield, William Gray and Colleen M. Beck, 281–295. London: Routledge, 2002.

Johnston, Norman. *Forms of Constraint: A History of Prison Architecture*. Urbana: University of Illinois Press, 2000.

Johnston, Norman. 'Recent Trends in Correctional Architecture'. *The British Journal of Criminology* 1, no. 4, 1961: 307–316.

Johnston, Norman. *The Human Cage: A Brief History of Prison Architecture*. New York: The American Foundation, 1973.

Keane, Kate. 'Stories from the Cells: The Role of Maze/Long Kesh in Peacetime Northern Ireland'. In *The Carceral Network in Ireland: History, Agency and*

Resistance, ed. Fiona McCann, 179–205. Basingstoke: Palgrave Macmillan, 2020.

Komter, Aafke. 'Women, Gifts and Power'. In *The Gift: An Interdisciplinary Perspective*, ed. Aafke Komter, 119–131. Amsterdam: Amsterdam University Press, 1996.

Latour, Bruno. 'The Berlin Key or How to Do Words with Things'. In *Matter, Materiality and Modern Culture*, ed. Paul Graves Brown, 10–21. London: Routledge, 1991.

Leroy, Claude. 'Space in Prison'. In *Prison Architecture*, ed. United Nations Social Defence Research Institute. London: Architectural Press, 1975.

Lyons, David. *In the Interest of the Governed: A Study in Bentham's Philosophy and Utility of Law*. Oxford: Clarendon Press, 1973.

Maddrell, Avril. 'Living with the Deceased: Absence, Presence and Absence-Presence'. *Cultural Geographies* 20, no. 4 (2013): 501–522.

Mac Ionnrachtaigh, Feargal. *Language, Resistance and Revival*. London: Pluto, 2013.

Mack, Mary. *Jeremy Bentham: An Odyssey of Ideas, 1748–1792*. London: Heinemann, 1963.

Massey, Doreen. *Space, Place and Gender*. Minneapolis: University of Minnesota Press, 1994.

Mbembe, Achille. 'Necropolitics'. *Public Culture* 15, no. 1 (2003): 11–40.

McAliskey, Bernadette. 'Foreward'. In *Nor Meekly Serve My Time: The H Block Struggle 1976–1981*, ed. Brian Campbell, Laurence McKeown and Felim O'Hagan. Belfast: Beyond the Pale, 1994.

McAtackney, Laura. *An Archaeology of the Troubles: The Dark Heritage of Long Kesh/Maze Prison*. Oxford: Oxford University Press, 2014.

McConville, Sean. 'The Architectural Realisation of Penal Ideas'. In *Prison Architecture. Policy, Design and Experience*, ed. Leslie Fairweather and Sean McConville, 1–15. Oxford: Architectural Press, 2000.

McCormick Jonathan and Neil Jarman, 'Death of a Mural'. *Journal of Material Culture* 10, no. 1 (2005): 49–71.

McEvoy, Kieran and Brian Gormally, *Dealing with the Past in Northern Ireland 'From Below'*. Belfast: Community Foundation for Northern Ireland, 2009.

McEvoy, Kieran. *Making Peace with the Past: Options for Truth Recovery Regarding the Conflict in and about Northern Ireland*. Belfast: Healing Through Remembering, 2006.

McEvoy, Kieran. *Paramilitary Imprisonment in Northern Ireland: Resistance, Management, and Release*. Oxford: Oxford University Press, 2001.

McEvoy, Sandra. 'Loyalist Women Paramilitaries in Northern Ireland: Beginning a Feminist Conversation about Conflict Resolution'. *Security Studies* 18, no. 2. (2009): 262–286.

McGarry, John and Brendan O'Leary. *Broken Images: Explaining Northern Ireland*. Oxford: Blackwell, 1995.

McGarry, John and Brendan O'Leary. *The Northern Ireland Conflict: Consociational Engagements*. Oxford: Oxford University Press, 2004.

McGee, Owen. '"God Save Ireland": Manchester-Martyr Demonstrations in Dublin, 1867–1916', *Éire-Ireland* 36, no. 3–4 (2001): 39–66.

McGuffin, John. *Internment*. Tralee, Ireland: Anvil Books, 1973.

McKay, Susan. *Northern Protestants: An Unsettled People*. Belfast: Blackstaff Press, 2000.

McKeown, Laurence. *Out of Time: Irish Republican Prisoners Long Kesh, 1972–2000*. Belfast: Beyond the Pale Publications, 2001.

McKittrick, David, Seamus Kelters, Brian Feeney and Chris Thornton. *Lost Lives: The Stories of the Men, Women and Children who Died as a Result of the Northern Ireland Troubles*. Edinburgh: Mainstream Publishing, 1999.

McLaughlin, Cahal. 'Memory, Place and Gender: Armagh Stories: Voices from the Gaol', *Memory Studies* 13, no. 4 (2017): 677–690.

Miller, David. *Don't Mention the War: Northern Ireland, Propaganda, and the Media*. London: Pluto Press, 1994.

Morris, A.E.J. *Precast Concrete in Architecture*. London: George Goodwin, 1978.

Murtagh, Tom. *The Maze Prison: A Hidden Story of Chaos, Anarchy and Politics*. Hook: Waterside Press, 2018.

Nasta, Susheila. '"Messy Solidarities": Reflections on the Politics of the Present', *South Asian Review* 43, no. 1–2 (2022): 136–143.

Ogden, C.K. *Jeremy Bentham*. London: Kegan Paul, 1932.

O'Malley, Padraig. *Biting at the Grave: The Irish Hunger Strikes and the Politics of Despair*. Boston: Beacon Press, 1991.

Peterson, A.W. 'The Prison Building Programme'. *The British Journal of Criminology* 1, no. 4 (1961): 307–316.

Pine, Emilie. *The Politics of Irish Memory: Performing Remembrance in Contemporary Irish Culture*. Basingstoke: Palgrave Macmillan, 2011.

Pointon, Marcia. *Brilliant Effects: A Cultural History of Gem Stones and Jewellery*. New Haven, CT: Yale University Press, 2009.

Purbrick, Louise. 'The History Block', *Museums Journal*, July 2001, 26–27.

Purbrick, Louise. 'Trading the Past: Material Culture of Long Kesh/Maze, Northern Ireland'. *Journal of War and Culture Studies* 6, no. 1 (2012): 58–74.

Purbrick, Louise. 'Cloth, Gender, Politics: the Armagh Handkerchief, 1976', *Clio: Femmes, Genre, Histoire*, 40, (2014): 105–12.

Purbrick, Louise. 'British Watchtowers'. In *British Watchtowers*, ed. Donovan Wylie, 57–71. Gottingen: Steidl, 2007.

Purbrick, Louise. 'Disturbing Memories: Photography and the Architecture of the H Blocks, Northern Ireland' in *The Politics of Cultural Memory*, ed. Lucy Burke, Simon Faulkner and Jim Aulich, 115–131. Newcastle-Upon-Tyne: Cambridge Scholars Publishing, 2010.

Purbrick, Louise. 'Long Kesh/Maze: A Case for Participation in Post-Conflict Heritage'. In *Heritage After Conflict: Northern Ireland*, ed. Elizabeth Crooke and Tom Maguire. 84–102, Abingdon: Routledge, 2018.

Rees, Merlyn. *Northern Ireland: A Personal Perspective*. London: Methuen, 1985.

Rendall, Jane. *Site-Writing: The Architecture of Art Criticism*. London: I.B. Tauris, 2006.

Richardson, J. G. 'Precast Concrete: Its Production, Transport and Erection'. In *Handbook of Structural Concrete*, ed. F.K. Kong, R.H. Evans, E. Cohen, F. Roll. London: Pitman, 1983.

Rolston, Bill. *Drawing Support: Murals in the North of Ireland*. Belfast: Beyond the Pale Publications, 1992.

Rolston, Bill. *Drawing Support 2: Murals of War and Peace*. Belfast: Beyond the Pale Publications, 1995.

Rolston, Bill. *Drawing Support 3: Murals and Transition in the North of Ireland*. Belfast: Beyond the Pale Publications, 2003.

Rolston, Bill. *Drawing Support 4: Murals and Conflict Transformation in Northern Ireland*. Belfast: Beyond the Pale Publications, 2013.

Rolston, Bill. 'Prison as a Liberated Zone: The Murals of Long Kesh, Northern Ireland', *State Crime Journal* 2, no. 2 (Autumn 2013): 149–172.

Rooney, Eilish. 'Women in political conflict'. *Race and Class* 37, no. 1 (1995): 51–56.

Ross, F. Stuart. *Smashing H Block: The Rise and Fall of the Campaign Against Criminalization, 1976–1982*. Liverpool: Liverpool University Press, 2011.

Ruiz, Pollyanna. *Articulating Dissent: Protest and the Public Sphere*. London: Pluto Press, 2014.

Ryder, Chris. *Inside the Maze. The Untold Story of the Northern Ireland Prison Service*. London: Methuen, 2000.

Said, Edward. *Hufoumanism and Democratic Criticism*. Basingstoke: Palgrave Macmillan, 2004.

Saint, Andrew. *Towards a Social Architecture: The Role of School-building in Post-war England*. New Haven, CT: Yale University Press, 1987.

Sales, Rosemary. *Women Divided: Gender, Religion and Politics in Northern Ireland*. London: Routledge, 1997.

Sands, Bobby. *Writings from Prison*. Cork: Mercier Press, 1998.

Savage, Robert. *The BBC's Irish Troubles: Television, Conflict and Northern Ireland*. Manchester: Manchester University Press, 2015.

Seaton, A.V. 'Guided by the Dark: From Thanatopsis to Thanatourism'. *International Journal of Heritage Studies* 2, no. 4 (1996): 234–244.

Side, Katherine. 'Mairéad Farrell in Armagh Jail'. In *The Carceral Network in Ireland: History, Agency and Resistance*, ed. Fiona McCann, 155–177. London: Palgrave Macmillan, 2020.

Shirlow, Peter and Kieran McEvoy. *Beyond the Wire: Former Prisoners and Conflict Transformation in Northern Ireland*. London: Pluto, 2008.

Smith, Laurjane. *The Uses of Heritage*. Abingdon: Routledge, 2006.

Spencer, Graham. *From Armed Struggle to Political Struggle: Republican Tradition and Transformation in Northern Ireland*. London: Bloomsbury, 2015.

Taussig, Michael. 'I'm so Angry I Made a Sign'. *Critical Inquiry* 39, no. 1 (2012): 56–88.

Taylor, Peter. *Loyalists*. London: Bloomsbury, 2000.

Tonge, John. *Northern Ireland*. Cambridge: Polity, 2006.

Tyler, Imogen. *Revolting Subjects: Social Abjection and Resistance in Neoliberal Britain*. London: Zed Books, 2013.

Vandereycken, Walter and Ron van Deth. *From Fasting Saints to Anorexic Girls: The History of Self-Starvation*. London: Athlone Press, 1994.

Wahidin, Azrini. 'Menstruation as a Weapon of War: The Politics of the Bleeding Body of Women on Political Protest at Armagh Jail, Northern Ireland', *The Prison Journal* 99, no. 1 (2019): 121–131.

Walker, Lynda. *Living in an Armed Patriarchy*. Belfast: Unity Press, 2019.

Walters, Ian. 'Vietnam Zippos'. *Journal of Material Culture* 2, no. 1 (1997): 61–97.

Ward, Rachel. 'Invisible Women: The Political Roles of Loyalist and Unionist Women in Contemporary Northern Ireland'. *Parliamentary Affairs* 55 (2002): 167–178.

Watkins, Jonathan. 'Back to the Black Country'. In *Rita Donagh*, Rita Donagh, 7–19. Birmingham: Ikon Gallery, 2005.

Weiner, Annette. *Inalienable Possessions: The Paradox of Keeping-While-Giving*. Berkeley: University of California Press, 1992.

Weiner, Annette. 'Inalienable Wealth'. *American Ethnologist* 12, no. 2 (1985): 210–227.

Weiner, Annette and Jane Schneider, 'Introduction'. In *Cloth and the Human Experience*, ed. Annette Weiner and Jane Schneider, 1–29. Washington, DC: Smithsonian Institution Press, 1989.

Welch, Michael. 'Political Imprisonment and the Sanctity of Death: Performing Heritage in "Troubled" Ireland. *International Journal of Heritage Studies* 22, no. 9, (2016): 664–678.

Williams, Paul. *Memorial Museums: The Global Rush to Commemorate Atrocities*. Oxford: Berg, 2007.

Winter, George and A.H. Wilson, *Design of Concrete Structures*. New York: McGraw-Hill Book Company, 1972.

Wood, Ian S. *Crimes of Loyalty: A History of the UDA*. Edinburgh: Edinburgh University Press, 2006.

Wylie, Donovan. *The Maze*. London: Granta, 2004.

Index